CONTENTS

Accounting, 20e

Prepared by

Carl S. Warren
Professor of Accounting
University of Georgia, Athens

James M. Reeve
Professor of Accounting
University of Tennessee, Knoxville

Philip E. Fess
Professor Emeritus of Accountancy
University of Illinois, Champaign-Urbana

Verified by
Alice Sineath
Forsyth Technical Community College

SOUTH-WESTERN
———*———™
THOMSON LEARNING

Australia · Canada · Mexico · Singapore · Spain · United Kingdom · United States

Solutions Manual for Chapters 17 – 24 for ACCOUNTING, 20e
by Warren, Reeve, and Fess

Team Director: David L. Shaut
Senior Acquisitions Editor: Sharon Oblinger
Senior Developmental Editor: Ken Martin
Senior Marketing Manager: Dan Silverburg
Senior Production Editor: Deanna Quinn
Manufacturing Coordinator: Doug Wilke
Production House: Litten Editing and Production
Printer: Globus Printing

Printed in the United States of America
1 2 3 4 5 04 03 02 01

For more information contact South-Western, 5101 Madison Road, Cincinnati, Ohio, 45227 or
find us on the Internet at http://www.swcollege.com

For permission to use material from this text or product, contact us by
• **telephone: 1-800-730-2214**
• **fax: 1-800-730-2215**
• **web: http://www.thomsonrights.com**

ISBN: 0-324-05292-8

CHAPTER 17
INTRODUCTION TO MANAGERIAL ACCOUNTING AND JOB ORDER COST SYSTEMS

CLASS DISCUSSION QUESTIONS

1. Managerial accounting and financial accounting are different in several ways. Managerial accounting is concerned with the information needs of internal decision makers, rather than external decision makers. As such, managerial accounting is not subject to a defined set of reporting rules. Management accountants have reasonable latitude in providing information that is useful to managers. Managerial accounting has very few set rules to govern how it is done. The idea of different costs for different needs suggests that there isn't just one way to view business events. Like financial accounting, managerial accounting reports can be prepared periodically. In addition, managerial accounting reports can also be prepared at any time to support a decision. Like financial accounting, managerial accounting reports provide information about the business as a whole. Also, managerial accounting reports provide information about any level of the organization as required by management.

2. **a.** A line department is directly involved in the basic objectives of the organization, while a staff department provides service, assistance, or advice to line departments or other staff departments.
   b. (1) Sales Department
   (2) Personnel Department

3. **a.** The role of the controller is to provide financial and accounting advice and assistance to management.
   b. The controller has a staff responsibility.

4. Microcomputer chips would be considered a direct materials cost.

5. Direct materials cost, direct labor cost, and factory overhead cost

6. If the cost of wages paid to employees is not a significant portion of the total product cost, the wages cost would be classified as part of factory overhead cost.

7. The three inventory accounts for a manufacturing business are as follows:
   a. Finished goods, representing goods in the state in which they are to be sold.
   b. Work in process, representing goods in the process of manufacture.
   c. Materials, representing goods in the state in which they were acquired.

8. Cost of goods sold

9. Product cost information is used by managers to (1) establish product prices, (2) control operations, and (3) develop financial statements.

10. **a.** Job order cost system and process cost system.
    b. The job order cost system provides a separate record of each quantity of product that passes through the factory.
    c. Process cost systems accumulate costs for each department or process within a factory.

11. Job order costing is used by firms that sell custom goods and services to customers. The job order system is frequently associated with firms that will produce a product or service specifically to a customer's order.

12. No. A job order cost system is not appropriate because workers could not physically differentiate between the products in different orders that were being worked on.

13. Work in Process

14. Job cost sheets make up the subsidiary ledger for the work in process control account. The cost of materials, labor, and factory overhead are listed on the job cost sheet for each job. A job cost sheet is sometimes called a "traveler" because it may move with the job through the facility. A summary of all the job cost sheets during an accounting period is the basis for journal entries to the control accounts.

15. No materials should be issued by the storekeeper without a properly authorized materials requisition. Both the storekeeper and the recipient of the materials should initial the materials requisition when the materials are issued to indicate release of the proper amount of materials from the storeroom.

16. a. The clock card is a means of recording the hours spent by employees in the factory. The time ticket is a means of recording the time the employee spends on a specific job or, in cases of indirect labor (factory overhead), the department in which the time was spent.

    b. The total time reported on an employee's time tickets for a payroll period is compared with the time reported on the employee's clock cards as an internal check on the accuracy of payroll disbursements.

17. a. Materials requisition

    b. Time ticket or time summary

18. The sources of the debits to Work in Process are:

    a. Summary of the materials requisitions for direct materials.

    b. Summary of the time tickets for direct labor.

    c. Data obtained when applying the predetermined factory overhead rate for factory overhead.

19. The use of a predetermined factory overhead rate in job order cost accounting assists management in pricing jobs. By estimating the cost of direct materials and direct labor based on past experience and by applying the factory overhead rate, the cost of a job can be estimated. The predetermined rate also permits the determination of the cost of a job shortly after it is finished, which enables management to adjust future pricing policies to achieve the best combination of revenue and expense.

20. a. The predetermined factory overhead rate is determined by dividing the budgeted factory overhead for the forthcoming year by an estimated activity base, one that will equitably apply the factory overhead costs to the goods manufactured.

    b. Direct labor cost, direct labor hours, and machine hours.

21. a. (1) If the amount of factory overhead applied is greater than the actual factory overhead, factory overhead is overapplied.

       (2) If the amount of actual factory overhead is greater than the amount applied, factory overhead is underapplied.

    b. Underapplied

    c. Deferred credit

22. The simplest satisfactory procedure for disposing of a relatively minor balance in the factory overhead account is to transfer it to Cost of Goods Sold.

23. a. Materials

    b. Work in Process

    c. Finished Goods

24. Product costs are composed of three elements of manufacturing costs: direct materials cost, direct labor cost, and factory overhead cost. These costs are treated as assets until the product is sold. Product costs are sometimes referred to as inventoriable costs. Period costs are costs that are used in generating revenue during the current period. They are recognized as expenses on the current period's income statement.

25. Job cost information can be used to identify trends in unit costs over time for like products. Comparative job cost sheets for like products can be used to investigate possible reasons for cost changes. This information can help managers identify changes in efficiency, methods, procedures, and prices used in the manufacturing process.

26. Cost of Services

EXERCISES

Ex. 17–1

a. factory overhead
b. factory overhead
c. direct materials
d. direct labor

e. direct materials
f. direct labor
g. factory overhead
h. factory overhead

Ex. 17–2

a. factory overhead
b. factory overhead
c. direct materials
d. direct labor
e. direct materials

f. factory overhead
g. direct materials
h. factory overhead
i. direct labor
j. factory overhead

Ex. 17–3

a. Product   *Advertising*
b. Product
c. Period
d. Period
e. Period
f. Product
g. Product
h. Product   *or period mtn supp*

i. Product
j. Product
k. Period
l. Period
m. Period
n. Product
o. Product
p. Period

Ex. 17–4

a, b, d, h, j

Ex. 17–5

a. plant depreciation
b. direct materials
c. work in process inventory
d. period

e. costs
f. increases
g. conversion
h. product

Ex. 17–6

a. Materials requisitioned for use (both direct and indirect).

b. Factory labor used (both direct and indirect).

c. Application of factory overhead costs to jobs.

d. Jobs completed.

e. Cost of goods sold.

Ex. 17–7

a.

Cost of goods sold:

Sales	$710,000
Less gross profit	220,000
Cost of goods sold	$490,000

b.

Direct materials cost:

Materials purchased		$180,000
Less: Indirect materials	$25,000	
Materials inventory	20,000	45,000
Direct materials cost		$135,000

c.

Direct labor cost:

Total manufacturing costs for the period		$530,000
Less: Direct materials cost	$135,000	
Factory overhead	52,000	187,000
Direct labor cost		$343,000

Ex. 17–8

a.

RECEIVED			ISSUED			BALANCE			
Receiving Report Number	Quantity	Unit Price	Materials Requisition Number	Quantity	Amount	Date	Quantity	Amount	Unit Price
						May 1	150	$2,700	$18.00
23	210	$20.00				May 3	150	2,700	18.00
							210	4,200	20.00
			104	250	$4,700*	May 5	110	2,200	20.00
29	140	22.00				May 19	110	2,200	20.00
							140	3,080	22.00
			117	200	4,180**	May 25	50	1,100	22.00

*May 5 issuance	150 at $18.00	$2,700	
	100 at $20.00	2,000	$4,700
**May 25 issuance	110 at $20.00	$2,200	
	90 at $22.00	1,980	$4,180

b. Ending wire cable balance:

    50 at $22.00 .... $1,100

c. Work in Process ($4,700 + $4,180)   8,880

    Materials   8,880

d. Comparing quantities on hand as reported in the materials ledger with predetermined order points enables management to order materials before a lack of materials causes idle time. Also, the subsidiary ledger can include columns for recording quantities ordered, so that management can have easy access to information about materials on order.

Ex. 17–9

Work in Process	53,100	
Factory Overhead	150	
Materials		53,250

Ex. 17–10

a. Materials	1,595,300			
Accounts Payable.................................		1,595,300		
b. Work in Process....................................	1,555,200			
Factory Overhead	17,900			
Materials..		1,573,100		

c.

	Fabric	Polyester Filling	Lumber	Glue
Balance, June 1	$ 45,800	$ 9,200	$ 95,800	$ 2,200
June purchases	568,500	165,500	842,200	19,100
Less: June requisitions	516,700	164,000	874,500	17,900
Balance, June 30	$ 97,600	$ 10,700	$ 63,500	$ 3,400

Ex. 17–11

Work in Process	14,830	
Factory Overhead	10,100	
Wages Payable		24,930

Ex. 17–12

a. Work in Process..	4,032	
Factory Overhead	1,670	
Wages Payable		5,702
b. Work in Process..	6,336	
Factory Overhead		6,336

$4,032 ÷ $14 per hour = 288 hours
288 hours × $22 per hour = $6,336

Ex. 17–13

a. Factory 1: $18.00 per machine hour ($270,000 ÷ 15,000 machine hours)

b. Factory 2: $25.00 per direct labor hour ($235,000 ÷ 9,400 direct labor hours)

c. Factory 1:

Work in Process	22,680	
Factory Overhead...		22,680
($18.00 × 1,260)		

    Factory 2:

Work in Process	19,250	
Factory Overhead...		19,250
($25.00 × 770)		

d. Factory 1—$780 credit (overapplied) ($21,900 – $22,680)

    Factory 2—$150 debit (underapplied) ($19,400 – $19,250)

Ex. 17–14

The estimated shop overhead is determined as follows:

Shop and repair equipment depreciation..	$ 14,800
Shop and supervisor salaries	82,400
Shop property tax...	23,200
Shop supplies	12,400
Total shop overhead	$132,800

The auto parts and shop labor are direct to the jobs and are not included in the shop overhead rate. The advertising and administrative expenses are selling and administrative expenses that are not included in the shop overhead but are treated as period expenses.

The estimated activity base is determined by dividing the shop direct labor cost by the direct labor rate, as follows:

$$\frac{\$384,000}{\$12\,\text{per hour}} = 32,000 \text{ hours}$$

The predetermined shop overhead rate is:

$$\frac{\$132,800}{32,000} = \$4.15 \text{ per direct labor hour}$$

Ex. 17–15

a. Estimated annual operating room overhead: $367,500

Estimated operating room activity base, number of operating room hours:

Hours per day...	7
Days per week..	× 6
Weeks per year (net of maintenance weeks)....	× 50
Estimated annual operating room hours..........	2,100

Predetermined surgical overhead rate:

$$\frac{\$367,500}{2,100 \text{ hours}} = \$175 \text{ per hour}$$

b. LeVar Wilson's procedure:

Number of surgical room hours	3
Predetermined surgical room overhead rate....	× $175
Procedure overhead	$ 525

c.

Actual hours used in January..	190
Predetermined surgical room overhead rate...............	× $175
Surgical room overhead applied, January...................	$33,250
Actual surgical room overhead incurred, January	31,800
Overapplied surgical room overhead (credit bal.)	$ 1,450

Ex. 17–16

a.

Finished Goods...	240,200	
Work in Process		240,200

b. Cost of unfinished jobs at March 31:

Balance in Work in Process at March 1..................	$ 19,200	
Add: Direct materials...	121,400	
Direct labor..	52,500	
Factory overhead...	74,600	$267,700
Less: Jobs finished during March		240,200
Balance in Work in Process at March 31...............		$ 27,500

Ex. 17–17

a.	Work in Process..	23,600	
	Factory Overhead	960	
	Materials...		24,560
b.	Work in Process..	5,300	
	Factory Overhead	6,300	
	Wages Payable		11,600
c.	Work in Process..	6,360	
	Factory Overhead...		6,360

Predetermined overhead rate: $1,500 ÷ $1,250 = 120% or
$2,520 ÷ $2,100 = 120%

Direct labor cost × Predetermined factory overhead rate:
$5,300 × 120% = $6,360

| d. | Finished Goods.. | 22,570* | |
| | Work in Process .... | | 22,570 |

* $8,150 + $14,420

Ex. 17–18

a.

COMET SHOE COMPANY
Income Statement
For the Month Ended May 31, 2003

Revenues...		$450,000
Cost of goods sold		246,500
Gross profit...		$203,500
Selling expenses	$65,000	
Administrative expenses	41,400	106,400
Income from operations...		$ 97,100

b.   Materials inventory:

Purchased materials.......................................	$124,000
Less: Materials used in production......................	111,300
Materials inventory, May 31	$ 12,700

Work in process inventory:

Materials used in production	$111,300
Direct labor..	84,700
Factory overhead (80% × $84,700)	67,760
Additions to work in process...............................	$263,760
Less: Transferred to finished goods.....................	257,000
Work in process inventory, May 31.......................	$ 6,760

Ex. 17–18 Concluded

Finished goods inventory:

Transferred to finished goods	$257,000
Less: Cost of goods sold	246,500
Finished goods inventory, May 31	$ 10,500

Ex. 17–19

a.

Date	Job No.	Quantity	Product	Amount	Unit Cost
Jan. 1	1	400	XXY	$ 4,800	$12
Jan. 29	26	1,200	AAB	18,000	15
Feb. 15	43	600	AAB	9,600	16
Mar. 10	64	450	XXY	6,300	14
Mar. 31	75	900	MM	19,800	22
May 10	91	1,000	MM	21,000	21
June 20	104	400	XXY	6,800	17
Aug. 2	112	1,500	MM	25,500	17
Sept. 20	114	400	AAB	6,000	15
Nov. 1	126	600	XXY	10,800	18
Dec. 3	133	850	MM	12,750	15

Product MM Unit Costs

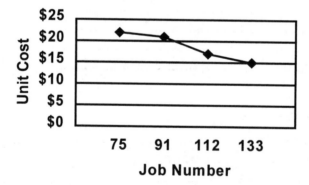

Product AAB Unit Costs

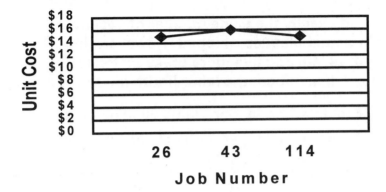

Job Number

Product XXY Unit Costs

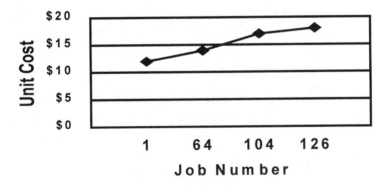

Job Number

As can be seen, the unit costs behave differently for each product. MM has decreasing unit costs during the year, AAB is steady, and XXY has increasing unit costs during the year.

b. Management should want to determine why XXY costs are increasing and why MM costs are decreasing. This information can be determined from the job cost sheets for each job. By comparing the cost sheets from job to job (for a particular product), management can isolate the cause of the cost changes. The cost sheets will show how materials, labor, and overhead are consumed across the production process for each job. This information can isolate the problem or opportunity areas.

Ex. 17–20

a. The first item to note is that the cost did not go up due to any increases in the cost of labor or materials. Rather, the cost of the plaques increased because Job 275 used more labor and materials per unit than did Job 223. Specifically, Job 223 required exactly the same number of backboards and brass plates as the number of actual plaques shipped. However, Job 275 required two more backboards (42 vs. 40) and five more brass plates (45 vs. 40) than the number actually shipped. In addition, the labor hours for Job 223 were as follows:

Engraving: (36 units × 10 min. per unit) / 60 min. = 6 hours

Assembly: (36 units × 5 min. per unit) / 60 min. = 3 hours

These are the labor hours to be expected for 36 plaques. However, the labor hours for Job 275 were:

Engraving: (45 units × 10 min. per unit) / 60 min. = 7.5 hours

Assembly: (42 units × 5 min. per unit) / 60 min. = 3.5 hours

Job 275's 11 labor hours is one more hour than should have been expected for a job of 40 plaques [(40 × 15 min.)/ 60 min. = 10 hrs.]. As a result, the additional hour of labor costs and applied factory overhead causes the unit cost of Job 275 to increase.

b. Apparently, the engraving and assembly work is becoming sloppy. Job 275 required 45 engraved brass plates in order to get 40 with acceptable quality. It is likely that the engraver is not being careful in correctly spelling the names. The names should be supplied to the engraver using large typewritten fonts so that it is easy to read the names. The engraver should be instructed to be careful in engraving the names. The assembly operation also needs some improvement. It took 42 assembly operations to properly assemble 40 plaques. It may be that the plates are assembled off-register (crooked) to the backboard. This could be improved by using a fixture to properly align the plate to the backboard.

Ex. 17–21

a.	Work in Process...	210,000	
	Salaries Payable		210,000
b.	Work in Process...	500,000	
	Accounts Payable...........................		500,000
c.	Work in Process (30% × $500,000)	150,000	
	Agency Overhead..........................		150,000
d.	Cost of Services................................	665,000	
	Work in Process		665,000

Cost of completed jobs, $665,000:

	Stone Bev.	Hampshire
March 1 balance	$120,000	$160,000
March costs:		
Direct labor...	48,000	25,000
Media..	150,000	90,000
Overhead	45,000	27,000
Total costs	$363,000	$302,000

Prob. 17–1A

Cost	Product Costs			Period Costs	
	Direct Materials Cost	Direct Labor Cost	Factory Overhead Cost	Selling Expense	Administrative Expense
a.	X				
b.				X	
c.	X				
d.			X		
e.			X		
f.		X			
g.					X
h.			X		
i.			X		
j.					X
k.			X		
l.			X		
m.	X				
n.	X				
o.					X
p.	X				
q.					X
r.				X	
s.	X				
t.			X		
u.					X
v.	X				
w.	X				
x.				X	
y.				X	
z.				X	

Prob. 17–2A

a.	Materials	107,600	
	Accounts Payable		107,600
b.	Work in Process	105,400	
	Factory Overhead	3,200	
	Materials		108,600
c.	Work in Process	115,900	
	Factory Overhead	18,300	
	Wages Payable		134,200
d.	Factory Overhead	66,600	
	Selling Expenses	39,600	
	Administrative Expenses	29,000	
	Accounts Payable		135,200
e.	Factory Overhead	2,400	
	Selling Expenses	800	
	Administrative Expenses	650	
	Prepaid Expenses		3,850
f.	Factory Overhead	11,200	
	Depreciation Expense—Office Equipment	8,400	
	Depreciation Expense—Store Equipment	1,500	
	Accumulated Depreciation—Fixed Assets		21,100
g.	Work in Process	102,500	
	Factory Overhead		102,500
h.	Finished Goods	320,600	
	Work in Process		320,600
i.	Cost of Goods Sold	316,400	
	Finished Goods		316,400

Prob. 17–3A

1. a. Materials... 150,500
        Accounts Payable   150,500

  b. Work in Process ....*126,200 + 86400*............ 212,600
       Factory Overhead.......*5300 + 32400*.......... 37,700
          Materials   131,500
          Wages Payable   118,800

  c. Factory Overhead.. 27,500
        Accounts Payable   27,500

  d. Factory Overhead... 5,100
        Accumulated Depreciation—Machinery and
        Equipment...   5,100

  e. Work in Process 69,000
        Factory Overhead (1,380 hours × $50)   69,000

  f. Finished Goods 193,900
       Work in Process   193,900

Computation of cost of jobs finished:

Job	Direct Materials	Direct Labor	Factory Overhead	Total
No. 601	$32,400	$19,300	$16,000	$ 67,700
No. 602	18,500	14,200	10,250	42,950
No. 603	21,300	15,200	11,250	47,750
No. 605	15,200	11,300	9,000	35,500
Total				$193,900

  g. Accounts Receivable 186,500
        Sales...   186,500

    Cost of Goods Sold 146,150
        Finished Goods   146,150

Computation of cost of jobs sold:

Job	
No. 601	$ 67,700
No. 602	42,950
No. 605	35,500
Total	$146,150

Prob. 17–3A   Continued

2.

Work in Process				Finished Goods			
(b)	212,600	(f)	193,900	(f)	193,900	(g)	146,150
(e)	69,000						
87,700	281,600			47,750			

3.   Schedule of unfinished jobs:

Job	Direct Materials	Direct Labor	Factory Overhead	Total
No. 604.................................	$10,400	$ 8,900	$ 7,500	$26,800
No. 606.................................	28,400	17,500	15,000	60,900
Balance of Work in Process, June 30..........				$87,700

4.   Schedule of completed jobs:

	Direct Materials	Direct Labor	Factory Overhead	Total
Finished Goods, June 30 (Job 603)	$21,300	$15,200	$11,250	$47,750

Prob. 17–3A   Concluded

This solution is applicable only if the GENERAL LEDGER SOFTWARE that accompanies the text is used.

INDUSTRIAL FITTINGS INC.
Trial Balance
June 30, 2003

Account Number	Account Title	Debit	Credit
120	Accounts Receivable	186,500	
130	Finished Goods	47,750	
140	Work in Process	87,700	
150	Materials	19,000	
171	Accum. Depr.—Mach. & Equipment		5,100
210	Accounts Payable		178,000
220	Wages Payable		118,800
410	Sales		186,500
510	Cost of Goods Sold	146,150	
610	Factory Overhead	1,300	
	Totals	488,400	488,400

Prob. 17–4A

1. and 2.

JOB ORDER COST SHEET

Customer	Kendra Brown	Date Sept. 1, 20—
Address	1244 Merchants Drive	Date wanted Oct. 13, 20—
	Columbus	Date completed Oct. 10, 20—
Item	Reupholster couch and chairs	Job. No. 00–10–23

ESTIMATE

Direct Materials	Amount	Direct Labor	Amount	Summary	Amount
14 meters at $18	252	20 hours at $16	320	Direct materials	252.00
meters at		hours at		Direct labor	320.00
meters at		hours at		Factory overhead	128.00
Total	252	Total	320	Total cost	700.00

ACTUAL

Mat. Req. No.	Description	Amount	Time Ticket No.	Description	Amount	Item	Amount
3480	9 meters at $18	162	H143	12 hours at $16	192	Direct materials	306.00
						Direct labor	352.00
3492	8 meters at $18	144	H151	10 hours at $16	160	Factory overhead	140.80
Total		306	Total		352	Total cost	798.80

Comments:
The direct materials cost exceeded the estimate by $54 because three meters of materials were spoiled. The direct labor cost exceeded the estimate by $32 because an additional two hours of labor was used by an inexperienced employee.

Prob. 17–5A

1. Supporting calculations:

Job No.	Quantity	Aug. 1 Work in Process	Direct Materials	Direct Labor	Factory Overhead	Total Cost	Unit Cost	Units Sold	Cost of Goods Sold
No. 111 DL-8	110	$18,000	$ 20,380	$15,600	$10,920	$ 64,900	$590	90	$ 53,100
No. 112 DL-18	120	35,000	25,450	19,500	13,650	93,600	780	105	81,900
No. 113 DL-11	50		14,120	11,400	7,980	33,500	670	40	26,800
No. 114 SL-101	150		9,400	4,200	2,940	16,540			0
No. 115 SL-110	70		27,500	24,300	17,010	68,810	983	55	54,065
No. 116 DL-14	75		4,000	3,000	2,100	9,100			0
Total	575	$53,000	$100,850	$78,000	$54,600	$286,450			$ 215,865

A. $103,350. Materials applied to production in August + indirect materials.
($100,850 + $2,500)

B. $53,000. From table above and problem.

C. $100,850. From table above.

D. $78,000. From table above.

E. $54,600. $78,000 × 0.7 and from table above.

F. $260,810. ($64,900 + $93,600 + $33,500 + $68,810)

G. $215,865. From table above.

H. $12,000. Wages incurred less direct labor applied to production in August.
($90,000 − $78,000)

2. August 31 balances:

Materials	$ 4,650	($8,000 + $100,000 − $103,350)
Work in Process	$25,640*	($16,540 + $9,100, Job 114 and Job 116)
Finished Goods	$44,945**	($260,810 − $215,865)
Factory Overhead	$ 3,100 Cr.	overapplied ($2,000 + $12,000 + $2,500 + $35,000 − $54,600)

* or ($53,000 + $100,850 + $78,000 + $54,600 − $260,810)

** Job 111:   20 units @ $590 = $11,800
   Job 112:   15 units @   780 =   11,700
   Job 113:   10 units @   670 =   6,700
   Job 115:   15 units @   983 =   14,745
                                     $44,945

Prob. 17–6A

1.

Sales		$5,200,000
Cost of goods sold		644,800
Gross profit		$4,555,200
Selling expenses:		
Advertising expenses	$1,500,000	
Salespersons commissions	520,000	
Salesperson training	750,000	
Advertising design	450,000	
Total selling expenses		3,220,000
Income from operations		$1,335,200

Supporting calculations:

Sales: 26,000 units × $200 = $5,200,000

Cost of goods sold: 26,000 units × $24.80 = $644,800

Manufacturing cost per unit:

Direct materials:		
Blank disk..	$ 8.00	
Packaging...	5.00	
Manual	10.00	
Total direct materials.....................................		$23.00
Direct labor		0.80
Factory overhead cost...		1.00[1]
Total manufacturing cost per disk		$24.80

[1]$1,000 ÷ 1,000 disks per hour

Salespersons commissions: $5,200,000 × 10% = $520,000

Training costs: 1,500 salespersons × $500 = $750,000

2. Finished Goods balance, December 31, 2003:
    (30,000 units – 26,000 units) × $24.80 = $99,200

Work in Process, December 31, 2003:
    500 units × ($23.00 + $1.00) = $12,000

The materials and copying have already been applied to the 500 units. Only the direct assembly labor has yet to be applied for these units.

Prob. 17–1B

Cost	Product Costs			Period Costs	
	Direct Materials Cost	Direct Labor Cost	Factory Overhead Cost	Selling Expense	Administrative Expense
a.			X		
b.			X		
c.					X
d.	X				
e.			X		
f.	X				
g.		X			
h.			X		
i.	X				
j.			X		
k.	X				
l.			X		
m.	X				
n.				X	
o.	X				
p.			X		
q.					X
r.	X				
s.	X				
t.				X	
u.			X		
v.			X		
w.			X		
x.				X	
y.		X			
z.			X		

Prob. 17–2B

a.	Materials	116,500	
	Accounts Payable..		116,500
b.	Work in Process...	106,600	
	Factory Overhead	2,600	
	Materials		109,200
c.	Work in Process...	180,500	
	Factory Overhead	24,500	
	Wages Payable		205,000
d.	Factory Overhead	95,800	
	Selling Expenses	57,800	
	Administrative Expenses	44,400	
	Accounts Payable..		198,000
e.	Factory Overhead	1,200	
	Selling Expenses	350	
	Administrative Expenses	300	
	Prepaid Expenses		1,850
f.	Factory Overhead	6,000	
	Depreciation Expense—Office Equipment	1,600	
	Depreciation Expense—Store Equipment	1,700	
	Accumulated Depreciation—Fixed Assets.............		9,300
g.	Work in Process...	130,000	
	Factory Overhead		130,000
h.	Finished Goods..	402,500	
	Work in Process		402,500
i.	Cost of Goods Sold	405,100	
	Finished Goods		405,100

Prob. 17–3B

1.   a. Materials..   8,200

         Accounts Payable   8,200

    b. Work in Process   12,705

       Factory Overhead...   2,690

         Materials   7,610

         Wages Payable...   7,785

    c. Factory Overhead..   4,100

       Accounts Payable   4,100

    d. Factory Overhead..   900

       Accumulated Depreciation—Machinery

        and Equipment   900

    e. Work in Process   7,860

       Factory Overhead (65.5 hours × $120)   7,860

    f. Finished Goods   14,845

       Work in Process...   14,845

Computation of cost of jobs finished:

Job	Direct Materials	Direct Labor	Factory Overhead	Total
No. 101	$1,340	$ 950	$1,320	$ 3,610
No. 102	950	740	1,140	2,830
No. 103	2,310	1,640	2,400	6,350
No. 105	690	525	840	2,055
				$14,845

    g. Accounts Receivable   19,400

       Sales...   19,400

    Cost of Goods Sold   12,790

       Finished Goods   12,790

Computation of cost of jobs sold:

Job	
No. 101	$ 3,610
No. 102	2,830
No. 103	6,350
Total	$12,790

Prob. 17–3B   Continued

2.

Work in Process				Finished Goods			
(b)	12,705	(f)	14,845	(f)	14,845	(g)	12,790
(e)	7,860			2,055			
5,720	20,565						

3.   Schedule of unfinished jobs:

Job	Direct Materials	Direct Labor	Factory Overhead	Total
No. 104...............................	$ 520	$ 540	$ 660	$1,720
No. 106...............................	1,420	1,080	1,500	4,000
Balance of Work in Process, April 30.............				$5,720

4.   Schedule of completed jobs:

	Direct Materials	Direct Labor	Factory Overhead	Total
Finished Goods, April 30 (Job 105)..........................	$690	$525	$840	$2,055

Prob. 17–3B   Concluded

This solution is applicable only if the GENERAL LEDGER SOFTWARE that accompanies the text is used.

CREATIVE GRAPHICS PRINTING COMPANY
Trial Balance
April 30, 2003

Account Number	Account Title	Debit	Credit
120	Accounts Receivable	19,400	
130	Finished Goods	2,055	
140	Work in Process	5,720	
150	Materials	590	
171	Accum. Depr.—Mach. & Equipment		900
210	Accounts Payable		12,300
220	Wages Payable		7,785
410	Sales		19,400
510	Cost of Goods Sold	12,790	
610	Factory Overhead		170
	Totals	40,555	40,555

Prob. 17–4B

1. and 2.

JOB ORDER COST SHEET

Customer	Jamal Price	Date	June 10, 20—
Address	1900 Peachtree	Date wanted	July 16, 20—
	Atlanta	Date completed	July 11, 20—
Item	Reupholster couch and chair	Job. No.	00–8–38

ESTIMATE

Direct Materials	Amount	Direct Labor	Amount	Summary	Amount
14 meters at $20	280.00	8 hours at $14	112.00	Direct materials	280.00
meters at		hours at		Direct labor	112.00
meters at		hours at		Factory overhead	44.80
Total	280.00	Total	112.00	Total cost	436.80

ACTUAL

Mat. Req. No.	Description	Amount	Time Ticket No.	Description	Amount	Item	Amount
U642	9 meters at $20	180.00	1519	5 hours at $14	70.00	Direct materials	320.00
						Direct labor	140.00
U651	7 meters at $20	140.00	1520	5 hours at $14	70.00	Factory overhead	56.00
Total		320.00	Total		140.00	Total cost	516.00

Comments:
The direct materials cost exceeded the estimate by $40 because two meters of materials were spoiled. The direct labor cost exceeded the estimate by $28 because an additional two hours of labor was used by an inexperienced employee.

Prob. 17–5B

1. Supporting calculations:

Job No.	Quantity	Jan. 1 Work in Process	Direct Materials	Direct Labor	Factory Overhead	Total Cost	Unit Cost	Units Sold	Cost of Goods Sold
No. 51 V-100	240	$ 4,000	$ 28,000	$ 14,800	$ 17,760	$ 64,560	$269	200	$ 53,800
No. 52 V-200	260	10,000	40,300	18,500	22,200	91,000	350	170	59,500
No. 53 V-500	200		19,000	11,500	13,800	44,300		0	0
No. 54 A-200	220		27,500	12,500	15,000	55,000	250	200	50,000
No. 55 V-400	280		42,300	28,500	34,200	105,000	375	240	90,000
No. 56 A-100	100		10,000	5,400	6,480	21,880		0	0
Total	1,300	$ 14,000	$ 167,100	$ 91,200	$ 109,440	$ 381,740			$253,300

A. $170,100. Materials applied to production in January + indirect materials. ($167,100 + $3,000)

B. $14,000. From table above and problem.

C. $167,100. From table above.

D. $91,200. From table above.

E. $109,440. $91,200 × 1.2 and from table above.

F. $315,560. ($64,560 + $91,000 + $55,000 + $105,000)

G. $253,300. From table above.

H. $8,800. Wages incurred less direct labor applied to production in January. ($100,000 – $91,200)

2. January 31 balances:

Materials	$29,900	($10,000 + $190,000 – $170,100)
Work in Process	$66,180*	($44,300 + $21,880, Job 53 and Job 56)
Finished Goods	$62,260**	($315,560 – $253,300)
Factory Overhead	$11,360 Dr.	underapplied ($4,000 + $8,800 + $3,000 + $105,000 – $109,440)

* or ($14,000 + $167,100 + $91,200 + $109,440 – $315,560)

** Job 51: 40 units @ $269 = $10,760
    Job 52: 90 units @ 350 = 31,500
    Job 54: 20 units @ 250 = 5,000
    Job 55: 40 units @ 375 = 15,000
                             $62,260

Prob. 17–6B

1.

Sales		$ 7,500,000
Cost of goods sold		4,837,500
Gross profit		$ 2,662,500
Selling expenses:		
Media campaign	$ 1,000,000	
Promotional materials...........................	400,000	
Shipping expenses..................................	187,500	
Total selling expenses	$1,587,500	
Administrative expenses:		
Legal expenses..	300,000	
Total operating expenses..		1,887,500
Income from operations		$ 775,000

Supporting calculations:

Sales: 750,000 units × $10 = $7,500,000

Cost of goods sold: 750,000 units × $6.45 = $4,837,500

Manufacturing cost per unit (CD):

Direct materials:		
Blank CD	$5.00	
Jewel case	0.50	
Song lyric insert..	0.25	
Total direct materials		$5.75
Direct labor		0.50
Factory overhead		0.20[1]
Total manufacturing cost per CD....................		$6.45

[1]$200 ÷ 1,000 CDs per hour

Promotional materials: 40,000 stores × $10 = $400,000

Shipping expenses: 750,000 units × $0.25 = $187,500

2. Finished Goods balance, December 31, 2003:

(800,000 units – 750,000 units) × $6.45 = $322,500

Work in Process, December 31, 2003:

10,000 units × ($5.75 + $0.20) = $59,500

The materials and copying have already been applied to the 10,000 units. Only the direct assembly labor has yet to be applied for these units.

SPECIAL ACTIVITIES

Activity 17–1

Although technically Cheryl complied with company policy, her computation of the cost of the lumber is unethical. The *Statement of Ethical Conduct for Management Accountants* requires that Cheryl avoid all actual or apparent conflict-of-interest situations. Thus, although it is appropriate for Cheryl to take advantage of Oak's policy of allowing employees to purchase materials at cost, she should have had someone else (such as her supervisor) determine the amount that she owed for the lumber. Clearly, selecting the lowest price has opened the door for criticism.

Activity 17–2

The objectives of managerial accounting and financial accounting are different; therefore, the vice-president's statement is very incomplete. In one sense, the statement may be true at only very high levels in the organization. For example, the division manager may be evaluated on the basis of financial accounting profit. Thus, the divisional manager would be evaluated by central management in nearly the same way that central management is evaluated by shareholders.

Lower in the organization, the financial concerns of the stockholder begin to diverge significantly from the day-to-day operating decision needs of the manager. As such, the statement becomes very inaccurate the closer one gets to the actual operations. Internal measures of performance closer to operations will focus on cost, quality, delivery time, equipment availability, inventory levels, scrap, waste, and efficiency. This list is much broader and more detailed than the financial statement numbers provided to the stockholders.

The stockholders' interest in profit is related to increasing shareholder value. Managers must increase long-term shareholder value by engaging in strategies that enhance people, product, and processes in the delivery of value to customers. These strategies can be measured by both financial and nonfinancial means. Therefore, it is not surprising to see a much broader set of objective and subjective measures used internally in the organization to guide strategy and operations.

Activity 17–3

1. Gail's bill has a number of points that should be considered. Some of the points, with the appropriate argument, are identified below.

    a. The trip back to the shop caused a $35 labor charge. Gail should argue that the whole hour should not be billed. The hour is the result of stocking out of a circuit board on the truck. The circuit board should have been with the repair person. There was a board for the previous customer. However, since only one was stocked, the repair person had to go back to the shop. The trip back to the shop was nonproductive time that should not have been directly charged to Gail but should be part of Reliable's overhead cost to all customers. In other words, Gail should not be responsible for this mistake.

    b. The overtime premium should not have been charged to Gail. What if Gail was the first appointment in the morning? If so, then there would be no overtime premium. It's only random misfortune that Gail was the last client of the day and therefore received the overtime premium. Add to this the fact that the overtime would not have been necessary without the trip back to the shop, and the conclusion is that Gail should not be directly charged for overtime. The overtime premium should be part of Reliable's overhead charged to all clients equally. Gail should be charged the overtime only if the decision for overtime was caused by or required by Gail.

    Thus, the labor portion of the bill should only be $30 + $25 + $25 = $80.

    There are other parts of the bill that should not be in dispute.

    *   The materials storage and handling charge is a normal charge of maintaining a parts inventory for the benefit of clients that need parts.

    *   The fringe benefits and overhead added to the hourly rate are both reasonable. The fringe benefit attaches directly to the direct labor. Fringe benefits are just another form of compensation. The overhead must be covered by all customers. Therefore, including overhead in the hourly rate is the most logical method of covering these costs.

    *   The additional charge for the first hour is also reasonable. The first hour charge covers the costs of transit, which are directly attributable to making a home visit. Gail requires a home visit, so Gail should be responsible for the costs of making the visit. If Gail brought the TV to the shop, this cost would not be incurred.

Activity 17–3   Concluded

2.

Cost	Direct Materials	Direct Labor	Overhead
Circuit board	X		
Storage and handling			X
Straight-time labor		X	
Fringe benefits*		X	
Overhead			X
Vehicle depreciation and fuel			X
Overtime premium			X

*Could be considered overhead in a nonunion shop.

Activity 17–4

There appear to be two or three trends. Starting with the most obvious:

a. There appears to be a strong "Friday effect." The unit cost on Friday increases dramatically, then falls on Monday. Apparently the workforce is preparing early for the weekend.

b. There also appears to be a general increasing trend in the unit cost. Every Friday effect is larger than the previous Friday. Much the same can be said about the other days of the week.

c. It's hard to tell, but there may also be a "within week" trend. The unit cost appears to increase gradually from Monday through Thursday, before jumping on Friday. At the very least, Mondays are the best operating days, while Fridays are the worst.

There are a number of further pieces of information that should be requested.

a. First, it would be good to verify these trends with some other products. This trend is probably not product-related but related generally to the day of the week. This would mean that the trend should be apparent in the other products.

b. The data should be sorted by shift and by employee. It's possible that the effect is stronger on one shift than on another or that just a few employees are responsible for the effect. It may not be prevalent in the general population of workers.

Activity 17–4   Concluded

c. The Friday–Monday phenomenon is likely related to the workforce, but the same cannot be said about the larger increasing trend over the four weeks. It could be caused by any number of factors. A good first look would be to isolate materials costs to see if these are contributors. How much of the effect is labor and how much is material should be verified. It's possible that the general increase in cost over time is the result of loss of machine tolerances. Thus, more and more material is being required to produce a unit of product.

d. Has there been any significant change in supervisors or crucial employees that may explain this effect?

e. Have prices increased gradually for the raw materials?

Activity 17–5

1. The engineer is concerned that direct labor is not related to overhead consumption because direct labor is a small part of the cost structure. Apparently, the company has replaced labor with expensive machine technology and support. This, of course, represents more factory overhead. Just because the direct labor is "designed out" of the product will not mean that this overhead will magically disappear. More likely, the direct labor hours will be replaced by machine-related factory overhead. Thus, the factory overhead goes up while the activity base (direct labor) goes down. Hence, the factory overhead rate will go up.

2. Since each direct labor hour now has $1,000 of factory overhead, small mistakes in the direct labor time estimates can have a large impact on the estimated cost of a product. This is very critical. If the company underestimates the direct labor content by a small amount, it will underbid and win the job. Unfortunately, the job will turn out to have less profitability than expected because the price is smaller than it should be. If the company overestimates the labor time, it will overbid the job. Thus, it will lose out to competitors who bid more accurately. This puts the company into a lose-lose situation when such small labor time errors have such large dollar impacts on the final cost estimate.

3. The engineer's concern is valid. The company should consider replacing its direct labor time activity base with one that more accurately reflects its present resources. If the company is now highly automated, then machine hours may be a much more reasonable activity base.

Activity 17–6

1. Jeff should record the debits for factory wages as a debit to Work in Process. The factory wages are product costs that must be accumulated in the cost of producing the product. Eventually, these wage costs will become part of finished goods inventory and cost of goods sold when the gift items are sold. Likewise, the depreciation should be recorded as a debit to Factory Overhead. The overhead is then applied to production work in process. Like the wages, the depreciation will also eventually become part of the finished goods inventory and cost of goods sold when the gift items are sold. Thus, both the wages and depreciation will end up on the income statement as cost of goods sold, not as individual expenses. The reason is because the accountant wants to match revenues and costs. Costs that are accumulated in the manufacture of products do not become expenses until the items are sold. Until that time, the costs are capitalized as inventory. If these costs were expensed immediately, the income for the firm would be understated for the period to the extent that there were any increases in the work in process or finished goods inventories.

2. Hanna would not be concerned about immediately expensing administrative wages and depreciation because the benefits received from these costs are not product costs. Instead, these costs benefit a period of time. Thus, these costs should be expensed for the period.

Activity 17–7

Note to Instructors: Consider having the teams compete for the most examples. Have half the class do the pizza restaurant and the other the copy shop, and compare results.

Some examples that may be offered by the students are the following:

Graphic and Copy Shop

Cost	Direct Materials	Direct Labor	Overhead	Selling Expenses
Paper	X			
Graphic designer wages		X		
Manager salary			X	
Lease cost of copy machine			X	
Coupon costs				X
Advertising				X
Packaging (bags and boxes)	X			
Ink			X	
Repair costs			X	
Property taxes			X	
Store depreciation			X	
Cashier salary			X	
Building heat and A/C			X	
Copy machine operator wages		X		
Covers	X			
Computer depreciation			X	
Brochures			X	

Activity 17–7 Concluded

Pizza Restaurant

Cost	Direct Materials	Direct Labor	Overhead	Selling Expenses
Ingredients	X			
Cook wages................................		X		
Manager salary			X	
Depreciation on equipment and fixtures.............................			X	
Coupon costs.............................				X
Advertising.................................				X
To-go boxes	X			
Disposable plates, utensils, cups...	X			
Nondisposable plates, utensils, cups...			X	
Repair costs			X	
Property taxes............................			X	
Store depreciation			X	
Cashier salary			X	
Beverage	X			
Building heat and A/C			X	
Salad ingredients.......................	X			
Handbills				X
Delivery person wages..............		X		
Power costs for ovens			X	

In service businesses, such as those above, the distinction between direct labor and overhead will not always be clear.

CHAPTER 18
PROCESS COST SYSTEMS

CLASS DISCUSSION QUESTIONS

1. **a.** A job order cost system is best suited for a custom jewelry manufacturer because most of the production consists of job orders, and costs can be reasonably identified with each job.

   b. A process cost system would be best suited for a paper manufacturer because the processes are continuous and the products are homogeneous.

   c. A job order cost system is best suited for an automobile repair shop because costs can be reasonably identified with each job.

   d. A job order cost system would be used by a building contractor to accumulate the costs for each individual building because the costs can be identified with each job without great difficulty.

   e. An assembly-type industry using mass production methods, such as TV assembly, would use the process cost system because the products are somewhat standard and lose their identities as individual items. In such industries, it is neither practical nor necessary to identify output by jobs.

2. **a.** Yes

   b. Yes

3. Since all goods produced in a process cost system are identical units, it is not necessary to classify production costs into job orders.

4. In a process cost system, the direct labor and factory overhead applied are debited to the work in process accounts of the individual production departments in which they occur. The reason is that all products produced by the department are similar. Thus, there is no need to charge these costs to individual jobs. For the process manufacturer, the direct materials and the conversion costs may be charged to the department and divided by the completed production of the department to determine a cost per unit.

5. Direct labor and factory overhead.

6. Transferred-out materials are materials that are completed in one department and transferred to another department or to finished goods.

7. Work in Process for that department

8. (1) Determine the units to be costed.
   (2) Calculate the equivalent units of production.
   (3) Determine the cost per equivalent unit.
   (4) Allocate costs to completed and partially completed units.

9. *Equivalent units* is the term used to represent the total number of units that would have been completed within a processing department as a result of the productive efforts during a period had there been no work in process at the beginning or end of the period. Equivalent units may be said to measure the productive activity for a given period.

10. The cost per equivalent unit is frequently determined separately for direct materials and conversion costs because these two costs are frequently incurred at different rates in the production process. For example, materials may be incurred at the beginning of the process and conversion costs incurred evenly throughout the process.

11. The cost per equivalent unit is used to allocate direct materials and conversion costs between completed and partially completed units.

12. The transferred-in cost from Department A to Department B includes the materials costs, direct labor, and applied factory overhead incurred to complete units in Department A.

13. Actual factory overhead incurred is debited to departmental factory overhead accounts.

14. The two sections of the cost of production report are for summarizing (a) the units for which the department is accountable and the disposition of these units and (b) the costs charged to the department and the allocation of these costs.

15. The most important purpose of the cost of production report is to assist in the control of costs. This is accomplished by holding each department head responsible for the costs incurred in the department.

16. Cost of production reports can provide detailed data about the process. The reports can provide information on the department by individual cost elements. This can enable management to investigate problems and opportunities.

17. Yield is a measure of the materials usage efficiency of a process manufacturer. It is determined by dividing the output volume of product by the input volume of product. For example, if 950 tons of aluminum were rolled from 1,000 tons of ingot, then the yield would be said to be 95%. Five percent of the ingot was scrapped during the rolling process.

18. Just-in-time processing is a business philosophy that focuses on reducing time and cost and eliminating poor quality within processes.

19. Just-in-time processing emphasizes combining process functions into manufacturing cells, involving employees in process improvement efforts, eliminating wasteful activities, and reducing the amount of work in process inventory required to fulfill production targets.

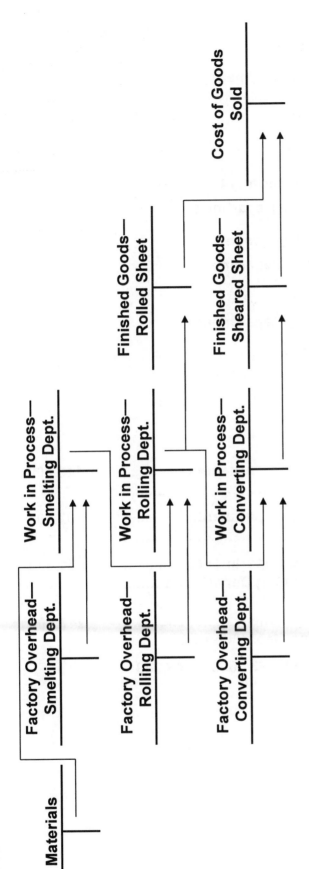

EXERCISES

Ex. 18–1

Ex. 18–2

a. Work in Process—Blending Department
     Materials—Cocoa beans
     Materials—Sugar
     Materials—Dehydrated milk

b. Work in Process—Molding Department
     Work in Process—Blending Department

c. Work in Process—Packing Department
     Work in Process—Molding Department

d. Finished Goods
     Work in Process—Packing Department

e. Cost of Goods Sold
     Finished Goods

Ex. 18–3

a. 1. Work in Process—Refining Department 145,000
     Materials 145,000

   2. Work in Process—Refining Department 102,000
     Wages Payable 102,000

   3. Work in Process—Refining Department 31,600
     Factory Overhead—Refining Department 31,600

b. Work in Process—Sifting Department 247,600*
     Work in Process—Refining Department 247,600

*$14,000 + $145,000 + $102,000 + $31,600 − $45,000

Ex. 18–4

a. Factory overhead rate:

   $520,000 \div \$400,000 = 130\%$

b. Work in Process—Blending Department....................... 44,850

   Factory Overhead—Blending Department.............   44,850

   $34,500 \times 130\% = \$44,850$

c. $850 credit

d. Overapplied factory overhead

Ex. 18–5

		Equivalent Units	
	Whole Units	Direct Materials	Conversion
Inventory in process, beginning (60% completed).......................	1,200	0	480
Started and completed...................	9,300*	9,300	9,300
Transferred to Packing Dept.........	10,500	9,300	9,780
Inventory in process, ending (30% complete)........................	600	600	180
Total...	11,100	9,900	9,960

*10,500 – 1,200

Ex. 18–6

a. Drawing Department

	Whole Units	Equivalent Units Direct Materials	Equivalent Units Conversion
Inventory in process, October 1 (65% completed)............................	2,000	0	700
Started and completed in October...	72,000*	72,000	72,000
Transferred to Winding Department in October.......................................	74,000	72,000	72,700
Inventory in process, October 31 (75% complete).............................	3,600	3,600	2,700
Total...	77,600	75,600	75,400

*74,000 – 2,000

b. Winding Department

	Whole Units	Equivalent Units Direct Materials	Equivalent Units Conversion
Inventory in process, October 1 (30% completed)............................	1,400	0	980
Started and completed in October	71,600*	71,600	71,600
Transferred to finished goods in October.......................................	73,000	71,600	72,580
Inventory in process, October 31 (20% complete).............................	2,400	2,400	480
Total...	75,400	74,000	73,060

*73,000 – 1,400

Note: Of the 74,000 units transferred in, 71,600 units were started and completed and 2,400 units are in ending work in process.

Ex. 18–7

a.

Units in process, March 1	14,000
Units placed into production for March	103,000
Less units finished during March	(89,500)
Units in process, March 31	27,500

b.

	Whole Units	Equivalent Units Direct Materials	Equivalent Units Conversion
Inventory in process, March 1 (2/5 completed)	14,000	0	8,400
Started and completed in March	75,500*	75,500	75,500
Transferred to finished goods in March	89,500	75,500	83,900
Inventory in process, March 31 (3/5 complete)	27,500	27,500	16,500
Total	117,000	103,000	100,400

*89,500 – 14,000

Ex. 18–8

Equivalent units of production:

	Cereal (in pounds)	Boxes (in boxes)	Conversion Cost (in boxes)
Inventory in process, February 1	—	—	800
Started and completed in February	21,300	14,200	14,200
Transferred to finished goods in February..	21,300	14,200	15,000
Inventory in process, February 28	300	200	—
Total..	21,600	14,400	15,000

Supporting explanation:

The inventory in process on February 1 includes both the cereal in the hopper and the boxes in the carousel, and thus, includes no equivalent units for the material during the current period. The reason is because the costs for the cereal and boxes were introduced to the Packing Department in January. Since conversion costs are incurred only when the cereal is filled into boxes, all 800 boxes of the February 1 inventory in process will have conversion costs incurred in February.

The product started and completed in February includes 14,200 boxes (15,000 boxes completed less the 800 in the carousel on February 1). These boxes represent 21,300 pounds of cereal (14,200 × 24 oz./16 oz.), since there are 16 ounces to a pound. Alternatively, there were a total of 22,500 pounds of cereal boxed during February (15,000 boxes × 24 oz./16 oz.); however, 1,200 of these pounds were already introduced in January and accounted for in the February 1 inventory in process.

The inventory in process on February 28 includes the remaining pounds of cereal in the hopper and boxes in the carousel that are properly included in the equivalent unit computation for February (since the costs were incurred in the department in February). No conversion costs have been applied to these boxes since they remain unfilled.

Instructor's note: An actual cereal-filling line begins with the empty box carousel. The box carousel holds flattened boxes that are fed into a high-speed line that opens the box up and places it on a conveyor. The conveyor brings the opened box under a filler head. The cereal pours from the hopper through the filler head into the open box (actually into the inner sealer bag). The box then moves down the line to be boxed into a large shipping carton, which is then moved to the warehouse.

Ex. 18–9

a.
Direct labor	$30,000
Factory overhead applied	18,900
Total conversion cost	$48,900

b. Equivalent units of production for conversion costs:

Beginning inventory	0
Started and completed	32,000
Ending inventory (2/3 × 900)	600
Total equivalent units for conversion costs	32,600

Conversion cost per equivalent unit:

$$\frac{\$48,900}{32,600} = \$1.50 \text{ conversion cost per equivalent unit}$$

c. Equivalent units of production for direct materials costs:

Beginning inventory	0
Started and completed	32,000
Ending inventory (all units completed as to direct materials)...	900
Total equivalent units for direct materials costs	32,900

Direct materials cost per equivalent unit:

$$\frac{\$180,950}{32,900} = \$5.50 \text{ direct materials cost per equivalent unit}$$

Ex. 18–10

a.

	Whole Units	Equivalent Units Direct Materials	Conversion
Inventory in process, beginning (70% completed)...............................	8,000	0	2,400
Started and completed..................	67,400	67,400	67,400
Transferred to finished goods..........	75,400	67,400	69,800
Inventory in process, ending........	0	0	0
Total units	75,400	67,400	69,800

b.

	Costs Direct Materials	Conversion
Total costs for period in Baking Department..	$148,280	$ 73,290
Total equivalent units (from above)...	÷ 67,400	÷ 69,800
Cost per equivalent unit...	$ 2.20	$ 1.05

Ex. 18–11

1. In computing the equivalent units for conversion costs applicable to the June 1 inventory, the 3,000 units are multiplied by 3/5 rather than 2/5, which is the portion of the work completed in June. Therefore, the equivalent units should be 1,800.

2. In computing the equivalent units for conversion costs for units started and completed in June, the June 1 inventory of 3,000 units, rather than the June 30 inventory of 3,900 units, was subtracted from 16,500 units started in the department during June. Therefore, the equivalent units started and completed should be 12,600.

3. The correct equivalent units for conversion costs should be 15,700, determined as follows:

To process units in inventory on June 1:	
$3,000 \times 3/5$	1,800
To process units started and completed in June:	
$16,500 - 3,900$	12,600
To process units in inventory on June 30:	
$3,900 \times 1/3$	1,300
Equivalent units of production	15,700

:

Ex. 18–12

| | Whole Units | Equivalent Units | |
		Direct Materials	Conversion
Inventory in process, September 1 (40% completed)..............................	5,500	0	3,300
Started and completed in September	32,800*	32,800	32,800
Transferred to finished goods in September	38,300	32,800	36,100
Inventory in process, September 30 (30% complete)..............................	3,200	3,200	960
Total units	41,500	36,000	37,060

*36,000 – 3,200

| | Costs | |
	Direct Materials	Conversion
Total costs for September in Forging Department	$284,400	$166,770
Total equivalent units (from above)...	÷ 36,000	÷ 37,060
Cost per equivalent unit...	$ 7.90	$ 4.50

Ex. 18–13

BETTER BEANS COMPANY
Cost of Production Report—Cooking Department
For the Month Ended January 31, 2003

| | | Equivalent Units | |
Units	Whole Units	Direct Materials (a)	Conversion (a)
Units charged to production:			
Inventory in process, January 1 .	800		
Received from materials storeroom................................	48,600		
Total units accounted for by the Cooking Department...............	49,400		
Units to be assigned cost:			
Inventory in process, January 1 (30% completed)	800	0	560
Started and completed in January......................................	48,100*	48,100	48,100
Transferred to finished goods in January................................	48,900	48,100	48,660
Inventory in process, January 31 (60% complete)	500	500	300
Total units to be assigned cost...	49,400	48,600	48,960

*48,600 – 500

Continued

49

Ex. 18–13   Concluded

Costs	Direct Materials	Conversion	Total Costs
Unit costs:			
Total costs for January in Cooking Department...............	$ 58,320	$ 24,480	
Total equivalent units	÷ 48,600	÷ 48,960	
Cost per equivalent unit (b).........	$ 1.20	$ 0.50	
Costs charged to production:			
Inventory in process, January 1...............................			$ 1,050
Costs incurred in January...........			82,800
Total costs accounted for by the Cooking Department........			$83,850
Costs allocated to completed and partially completed units:			
Inventory in process, January 1 balance...................			$ 1,050
To complete inventory in process, January 1	$ 0	$ 280[1]	280
Started and completed in January...............................	57,720[2]	24,050[3]	81,770
Transferred to finished goods in January (c)...............			$83,100
Inventory in process, January 31 (d)	600[4]	150[5]	750
Total costs assigned by the Cooking Department........			$83,850

[1] 560 units × $0.50
[2] 48,100 units × $1.20
[3] 48,100 units × $0.50
[4] 500 units × $1.20
[5] 300 units × $0.50

Ex. 18–14

ARIZONA CARPET COMPANY
Cost of Production Report—Cutting Department
For the Month Ended July 31, 2003

Units	Whole Units	Equivalent Units Direct Materials (a)	Equivalent Units Conversion (a)
Units charged to production:			
Inventory in process, July 1	10,000		
Received from Weaving			
Department.............................	182,000		
Total units accounted for by the			
Cutting Department	192,000		
Units to be assigned cost:			
Inventory in process, July 1			
(70% completed)	10,000	0	3,000
Started and completed in July	168,000*	168,000	168,000
Transferred to finished goods			
in July	178,000	168,000	171,000
Inventory in process, July 31			
(20% complete)	14,000	14,000	2,800
Total units to be assigned cost...	192,000	182,000	173,800

*182,000 – 14,000

Continued

Ex. 18–14   **Concluded**

Costs	Direct Materials	Costs Conversion	Total Costs
Unit costs:			
Total costs for July in Cutting Department	$ 837,200	$ 121,660	
Total equivalent units	÷ 182,000	÷ 173,800	
Cost per equivalent unit	$ 4.60	$ 0.70	
Costs charged to production:			
Inventory in process, July 1			$ 50,000
Costs incurred in July			958,860
Total costs accounted for by the Cutting Department			$ 1,008,860
Costs allocated to completed and partially completed units:			
Inventory in process, July 1 balance			$ 50,000
To complete inventory in process, July 1	$ 0	$ 2,100[1]	2,100
Started and completed in July	772,800[2]	117,600[3]	890,400
Transferred to finished goods in July			$ 942,500
Inventory in process, July 31	64,400[4]	1,960[5]	66,360
Total costs assigned by the Cutting Department			$ 1,008,860

[1] 3,000 units × $0.70
[2] 168,000 units × $4.60
[3] 168,000 units × $0.70
[4] 14,000 units × $4.60
[5] 2,800 units × $0.70

Ex. 18–15

a. Work in Process—Casting Department 420,000
     Materials—Alloy..   420,000

b. Work in Process—Casting Department 266,000
     Wages Payable   140,000
     Factory Overhead..   126,000*

   *$140,000 × 90%

c. Work in Process—Machining Department.................... 667,020*
     Work in Process—Casting Department..................   667,020

   *Supporting calculations:

   Cost of 11,500 transferred-out pounds:

Inventory in Process, March 1	$ 20,000
Cost to complete March 1 inventory:	
140 pounds × $23/lb. (see calculations below)	3,220
Pounds started and completed in March (11,100 lbs. × $58/lb.)	643,800
Transferred to Machining Department...	$667,020

Supporting equivalent unit and cost per equivalent unit calculations:

	Equivalent Units		
	Whole Units	Materials	Conversion
Inventory in process, March 1			
(65% completed)	400	—	140
Started and completed in March..............	11,100	11,100	11,100
Transferred to finished goods in March .	11,500	11,100	11,240
Inventory in process, March 31			
(36% complete)	900	900	324
Total	12,400	12,000	11,564

Cost per equivalent unit of materials: $\dfrac{\$420,000}{12,000}$ = $35 per pound

Cost per equivalent unit of conversion: $\dfrac{\$266,000}{11,564}$ = $23 per pound (rounded)

Ex. 18–16

Memo

To: Production Manager

The cost of production report was used to identify the cost per case for each of the four flavors as shown below.

	Orange	Cola	Lemon-Lime	Root Beer
Total cost..............................	$ 15,800	$ 99,300	$ 65,200	$ 9,400
Number of cases..................	÷ 2,000	÷ 15,000	÷ 10,000	÷ 1,000
Cost per case.......................	$ 7.90	$ 6.62	$ 6.52	$ 9.40

As can be seen, the cost per case of Root Beer is significantly above the cost per case of the other three flavors. A more detailed analysis is necessary. The individual cost elements that determine the total cost can be divided by the number of cases. This analysis is provided below.

	Cost per Case by Cost Element			
	Orange	Cola	Lemon-Lime	Root Beer
Concentrate................................	$1.80	$2.20	$2.10	$1.80
Water..	0.60	0.60	0.60	0.60
Sugar	1.00	1.00	1.00	1.00
Bottles	2.20	2.20	2.20	2.20
Flavor changeover......................	1.50	0.12	0.12	3.00
Conversion cost	0.80	0.50	0.50	0.80
Total cost per case....................	$7.90	$6.62	$6.52	$9.40

The table above indicates that the concentrate per case is actually less for Orange and Root Beer than for Cola and Lemon-Lime. This is because the concentrate supplier charges a higher price for the more popular flavors. The costs per case for water, sugar, and bottles are the same for each flavor. However, the costs per case for changeover are much greater for Orange and Root Beer than for the other two flavors. In addition, the conversion costs per unit for Orange and Root Beer are $0.30 higher than for Cola and Lemon-Lime. These last two cost elements are sufficient to cause the cost per case of Orange and Root Beer to be greater than Cola and Lemon Lime.

Although further analysis is necessary, it appears that Orange and Root Beer are either bottled in short production runs, meaning more frequent changeovers, or that each Orange and Root Beer changeover is very difficult and expensive. The conversion cost per case is larger because the bottling line rate appears slower for Orange and Root Beer, compared to Cola and Lemon-Lime. It's possible that shorter run sizes are related to the slower line rate because it takes some run time to work the line rate up to a fast speed after a changeover. Root Beer costs more per case than Orange because it has the shortest run length.

Ex. 18–17

The solution to this exercise is to determine if cost per pound trends in materials, conversion, and coating costs are remaining stable over time. The following table can be developed from the data:

	January	February	March	April	May	June
Transferred-in materials ($ ÷ pounds output).......	$0.70	$0.70	$0.70	$0.70	$0.70	$0.70
Coating cost ($ ÷ pounds output).......	0.20	0.22	0.25	0.28	0.29	0.32
Conversion cost ($ ÷ pounds output).......	0.50	0.50	0.50	0.50	0.50	0.50
Yield (pounds transferred out ÷ pounds input).......	0.96	0.96	0.96	0.96	0.96	0.96

The cost per pound information is determined by dividing the costs by the pounds transferred out. The yield is determined by dividing the pounds transferred out by the pounds input.

Operator 1 believes that energy consumption is becoming less efficient. The energy cost is part of the conversion cost. The conversion cost per output pound has remained constant for the six months. If the energy efficiency were declining, it would take more energy per pound of output over time. Thus, we would expect to see the conversion rate per pound increasing if Operator 1 were correct.

Operator 2 believes that there are increasing materials losses from increasing startup and shutdown activity. Yield data would help determine if this were true. If materials losses were growing, then there would be less materials transferred out per pound of inputs over time. The yield has remained constant over the six-month period. Thus, Operator 2's hypothesis is not validated. This is also supported by the constant materials rate per output pound.

Operator 3 is concerned about coating costs. The coating cost per output pound is increasing over time. Thus, we can conclude that the coating efficiency is declining over time. Apparently, more coating material was being spread per pound of output in June than in January. The coating operation may need to be repaired or recalibrated. Too much coating is being spread on the film.

Ex. 18–18

The Manning Machining managers are displaying typical fears to a just-in-time processing system. Just-in-time removes the safety provided by materials, in-process, and finished goods inventory balances. Indeed, these types of comments reflect conventional manufacturing philosophy, which views inventory as a necessary buffer against surprises and other unwelcome events. The just-in-time philosophy focuses on removing the causes that require a need for inventory.

In the case of materials inventories, a just-in-time philosophy requires all suppliers to provide high-quality materials on a daily basis in just the right quantities needed for a day's production. If the supplier has unreliable production schedules or quality, then the sources of unreliability would need to be fixed before moving to just-in-time delivery. Only when suppliers are reliable can Manning Machining move to a just-in-time strategy without exposing the company to significant risk.

The in-process inventories can be reduced significantly if the underlying manufacturing processes are made reliable. The Director of Manufacturing is correct in his observation, but his solution is wrong. The solution is not to increase inventory but to improve the reliability of the machines so that they do not experience emergency breakdowns. Thus, the manufacturing operation must be improved to produce the right product, in the right quantities, at the right quality, and at the right time. Only with this level of reliability can a plant responsibly remove in-process inventories from the system.

The finished goods inventory can also be reduced if the manufacturing system can be made responsive to customer demands. A company will no longer have to stock warehouses with product based on guesses at what the customer will want many weeks ahead of demand. Rather, goods are produced at the time the customer orders them. This is what Dell Computer Corporation does. It builds a computer to order, rather than stocking the computer and selling it from inventory.

In other words, inventory covers a "multitude of sins." When the "sins" are removed, the inventory can be removed.

PROBLEMS

Prob. 18–1A

1.
a. Materials 732,400
   Accounts Payable   732,400

b. Work in Process—Spinning Department 489,300
   Work in Process—Tufting Department 192,300
   Factory Overhead—Spinning Department 34,000
   Factory Overhead—Tufting Department 9,500
   Materials   725,100

c. Work in Process—Spinning Department 234,200
   Work in Process—Tufting Department 165,700
   Factory Overhead—Spinning Department 92,300
   Factory Overhead—Tufting Department 54,200
   Wages Payable   546,400

d. Factory Overhead—Spinning Department 63,200
   Factory Overhead—Tufting Department 31,200
   Accumulated Depreciation   94,400

e. Factory Overhead—Spinning Department 14,000
   Factory Overhead—Tufting Department 12,000
   Prepaid Insurance   26,000

f. Work in Process—Spinning Department 205,000
   Work in Process—Tufting Department 105,000
   Factory Overhead—Spinning Department   205,000
   Factory Overhead—Tufting Department   105,000

g. Work in Process—Tufting Department 914,300
   Work in Process—Spinning Department   914,300

h. Finished Goods 1,380,100
   Work in Process—Tufting Department   1,380,100

i. Cost of Goods Sold 1,393,000
   Finished Goods   1,393,000

Prob. 18–1A   Concluded

2.

	Materials	Work in Process— Spinning Dept.	Work in Process— Tufting Dept.	Finished Goods
Balance, March 1	$ 18,600	$ 5,800	$ 24,300	$ 32,600
Debits..............................	732,400	928,500	1,377,300	1,380,100
Credits	(725,100)	(914,300)	(1,380,100)	(1,393,000)
Balance, March 31	$ 25,900	$ 20,000	$ 21,500	$ 19,700

3.

	Factory Overhead— Spinning Dept.	Factory Overhead— Tufting Dept.
Balance, March 1	$ 0	$ 0
Debits..	203,500	106,900
Credits	(205,000)	(105,000)
Balance, March 31	$ (1,500) Cr.	$ 1,900

Prob. 18–2A

a.	Materials	280,000	
	Accounts Payable...		280,000
b.	Work in Process—Baking Department	215,000	
	Work in Process—Packing Department.......................	45,000	
	Factory Overhead—Baking Department......................	7,000	
	Factory Overhead—Packing Department	5,000	
	Materials		272,000
c.	Work in Process—Baking Department	91,000	
	Work in Process—Packing Department.......................	70,000	
	Factory Overhead—Baking Department......................	6,500	
	Factory Overhead—Packing Department	3,200	
	Wages Payable		170,700
d.	Factory Overhead—Baking Department......................	10,300	
	Factory Overhead—Packing Department	4,300	
	Accounts Payable...		14,600
e.	Factory Overhead—Baking Department......................	15,500	
	Factory Overhead—Packing Department	7,300	
	Accumulated Depreciation—Fixed Assets.............		22,800
f.	Factory Overhead—Baking Department......................	2,400	
	Factory Overhead—Packing Department	1,100	
	Prepaid Expenses		3,500
g.	Work in Process—Baking Department	42,000	
	Work in Process—Packing Department.......................	21,000	
	Factory Overhead—Baking Department.................		42,000
	Factory Overhead—Packing Department...............		21,000
h.	Work in Process—Packing Department.......................	348,000	
	Work in Process—Baking Department...................		348,000*

*$215,000 + $91,000 + $42,000

i.	Finished Goods..	484,000	
	Work in Process—Packing Department		484,000*

*$348,000 + $45,000 + $70,000 + $21,000

j.	Accounts Receivable..	784,000	
	Sales		784,000
	Cost of Goods Sold	493,300	
	Finished Goods		493,300

Summary of cost of goods sold:

500 units at $45.00..	$ 22,500	
10,700 units at $44.00*	470,800	
Total	$ 493,300	

*$484,000 ÷ 11,000 cases = $44.00

Prob. 18–2A   Continued

This solution is applicable only if the GENERAL LEDGER SOFTWARE that accompanies the text is used.

TASTY BAKERY CO.
Income Statement
For the Period Ended March 31, 2003

Operating revenue:		
Sales...		$1,189,800
Cost:		
Cost of goods sold..		673,700
Gross profit..		$ 516,100
Operating expenses:		
Selling expenses..	$ 89,900	
Administrative expenses...	81,000	
Total operating expenses...................................		170,900
Net income before income tax..		$ 345,200
Income tax:		
Income tax		20,000
Net income after income tax...		$ 325,200

TASTY BAKERY CO.
Retained Earnings Statement
For the Period Ended March 31, 2003

Retained earnings (beginning of period)...	$ 164,255
Net income	325,200
Retained earnings (end of period)	$ 489,455

TASTY BAKERY CO.
Balance Sheet
March 31, 2003

Assets

Cash	$ 83,000	
Marketable securities	36,000	
Accounts receivable	917,200	
Allowance for doubtful accounts	(38,000)	
Finished goods	13,200	
Materials	90,850	
Prepaid expenses	15,600	
Total current assets		$ 1,117,850
Fixed assets	$ 999,500	
Accumulated depreciation—Fixed assets	(579,800)	
Total fixed assets		419,700
Patents		37,180
Total assets		$ 1,574,730

Liabilities

Accounts payable	$ 482,700	
Wages payable	212,800	
Total current liabilities		$ 695,500
Mortgage note payable		106,000
Factory overhead—Baking	$ 475	
Factory overhead—Packing	200	
Total deferred debits		(675)
Total liabilities		$ 800,825

Stockholders' Equity

Common stock	$ 284,450	
Retained earnings	489,455	
Total stockholders' equity		773,905
Total liabilities and stockholders' equity		$ 1,574,730

VALDEZ COFFEE COMPANY
Cost of Production Report—Roasting Department
For the Month Ended March 31, 2003

Units	Whole Units	Equivalent Units	
		Direct Materials	Conversion
Units charged to production:			
Inventory in process, March 1.....	13,800		
Received from materials			
storeroom	258,000		
Total units accounted for by the			
Roasting Department..............	271,800		
Units to be assigned cost:			
Inventory in process, March 1			
(4/5 completed)	13,800	0	2,760
Started and completed in March.	246,700*	246,700	246,700
Transferred to packing			
in March...................................	260,500	246,700	249,460
Inventory in process, March 31			
(1/5 complete).........................	11,300	11,300	2,260
Total units to be assigned cost...	271,800	258,000	251,720

*260,500 – 13,800

Continued

Prob. 18–3A   Concluded

Costs	Costs Direct Materials	Conversion	Total Costs
Unit costs:			
Total costs for March in			
Roasting Department..............	$1,444,800	$ 906,192	
Total equivalent units	÷ 258,000	÷ 251,720	
Cost per equivalent unit	$ 5.60	$ 3.60	
Costs charged to production:			
Inventory in process,			
March 1			$ 114,600
Costs incurred in March			2,350,992
Total costs accounted for by			
the Roasting Department			$ 2,465,592
Costs allocated to completed and			
partially completed units:			
Inventory in process,			
March 1 balance......................			$ 114,600
To complete inventory in			
process, March 1	$ 0	$ 9,936[1]	9,936
Started and completed			
in March..................................	1,381,520[2]	888,120[3]	2,269,640
Transferred to Packing			
Dept. in March..........................			$ 2,394,176
Inventory in process,			
March 31	63,280[4]	8,136[5]	71,416
Total costs assigned by			
the Roasting Department			$ 2,465,592

Costs transferred to Packing Department: $2,394,176
Work in Process, March 31: 11,300 units at a cost of $71,416

[1]   2,760 units × $3.60
[2]   246,700 units × $5.60
[3]   246,700 units × $3.60
[4]   11,300 units × $5.60
[5]   2,260 units × $3.60

Prob. 18–4A

1.

BAKER'S CHOICE FLOUR COMPANY
Cost of Production Report—Sifting Department
For the Month Ended July 31, 2003

Units	Whole Units	Equivalent Units Direct Materials	Conversion
Units charged to production:			
Inventory in process, July 1........	25,800		
Received from Milling			
Department..............................	640,000		
Total units accounted for by the			
Sifting Department..................	665,800		
Units to be assigned cost:			
Inventory in process, July 1			
(3/4 completed)	25,800	0	6,450
Started and completed in July	624,200*	624,200	624,200
Transferred to Packaging Dept.			
in July	650,000	624,200	630,650
Inventory in process, July 31			
(1/4 complete)..........................	15,800	15,800	3,950
Total units to be assigned cost...	665,800	640,000	634,600

*640,000 – 15,800

Continued

Prob. 18–4A   Concluded

Costs	Direct Materials	Costs Conversion	Total Costs
Unit costs:			
Total costs for July in			
Sifting Department..................	$ 736,000	$ 241,148	
Total equivalent units	÷ 640,000	÷ 634,600	
Cost per equivalent unit	$ 1.15	$ 0.38	
Costs charged to production:			
Inventory in process, July 1........			$ 38,700
Costs incurred in July			977,148
Total costs accounted for by			
the Sifting Department			$1,015,848
Costs allocated to completed and partially completed units:			
Inventory in process,			
July 1 balance			$ 38,700
To complete inventory in			
process, July 1........................	$0	$2,451[1]	2,451
Started and completed in July	717,830[2]	237,196[3]	955,026
Transferred to Packaging Dept.			
in July			$ 996,177
Inventory in process, July 31......	18,170[4]	1,501[5]	19,671
Total costs assigned by the			
Sifting Department..................			$1,015,848

[1] 6,450 units × $0.38
[2] 624,200 units × $1.15
[3] 624,200 units × $0.38
[4] 15,800 units × $1.15
[5] 3,950 units × $0.38

2. Work in Process—Sifting Department 736,000
      Work in Process—Milling Department.................... 736,000

    Work in Process—Packaging 996,177
      Work in Process—Sifting Department.................... 996,177

3. The cost of production report may be used as the basis for allocating product costs between Work in Process and Transferred-Out (or Finished) Goods. The report can also be used to control costs by holding each department head responsible for the units entering production and the costs incurred in the department. Any differences in unit product costs from one month to another can be studied carefully and any significant differences investigated.

Prob. 18–5A

1. and 2.   Work in Process—Filling Department

Date		Item	Dr.	Cr.	Balance Dr.	Balance Cr.
July	1	Bal., 1,500 units, 35% completed	....	....	9,225	....
	31	Cooking Dept., 90,000 units at $5.40	486,000	....	495,225	....
	31	Direct labor	100,346	....	595,571	....
	31	Factory overhead	61,393	....	656,964	....
	31	Finished goods	....	648,900*	8,064	....
	31	Bal., 1,400 units, 20% completed	....	....	8,064	....
Aug.	31	Cooking Dept., 85,000 units at $5.50	467,500	....	475,564	....
	31	Direct labor	101,199	....	576,763	....
	31	Factory overhead	61,916	....	638,679	....
	31	Finished goods	....	629,202*	9,477	....
	31	Bal., 1,350 units, 80% completed	....	....	9,477	....

*The credits are determined from the supporting cost of production reports.

CAMDEN SOUP CO.
Cost of Production Report—Filling Department
For the Month Ended July 31, 2003

Units	Whole Units	Direct Materials (a)	Conversion (a)
Units charged to production:			
Inventory in process, July 1...............	1,500		
Received from Cooking Department .	90,000		
Total units accounted for by the			
Filling Department...........................	91,500		
Units to be assigned cost:			
Inventory in process, July 1			
(35% completed)..............................	1,500	0	975
Started and completed in July	88,600*	88,600	88,600
Transferred to finished goods			
in July..	90,100	88,600	89,575
Inventory in process, July 31			
(20% complete)...............................	1,400	1,400	280
Total units to be assigned cost..........	91,500	90,000	89,855

*90,000 – 1,400

Continued

Prob. 18–5A   Continued

Costs	Costs Direct Materials	Costs Conversion	Total Costs
Unit costs:			
Total costs for July in			
Filling Department	$486,000	$161,739	
Total equivalent units	÷ 90,000	÷ 89,855	
Cost per equivalent unit (b).........	$ 5.40	$ 1.80	
Costs charged to production:			
Inventory in process, July 1........			$ 9,225
Costs incurred in July			647,739
Total costs accounted for by			
the Filling Department............			$ 656,964
Costs allocated to completed and			
partially completed units:			
Inventory in process,			
July 1 balance (c)...................			$ 9,225
To complete inventory in			
process, July 1 (c)	$ 0	$ 1,755[1]	1,755
Started and completed			
in July (c)................................	478,440[2]	159,480[3]	637,920
Transferred to finished			
goods in July (c)			$ 648,900
Inventory in process,			
July 31 (d)...............................	7,560[4]	504[5]	8,064
Total costs assigned by			
the Filling Department............			$ 656,964

[1] 975 units × $1.80
[2] 88,600 units × $5.40
[3] 88,600 units × $1.80
[4] 1,400 units × $5.40
[5] 280 units × $1.80

Prob. 18–5A   Continued

2.

CAMDEN SOUP CO.
Cost of Production Report—Filling Department
For the Month Ended August 31, 2003

| | | Equivalent Units | |
| | | Direct Materials | Conversion |
Units	Whole Units	(a)	(a)
Units charged to production:			
Inventory in process, August 1..........	1,400		
Received from Cooking Department .	85,000		
Total units accounted for by the			
Filling Department............................	86,400		
Units to be assigned cost:			
Inventory in process, August 1			
(20% completed)...............................	1,400	0	1,120
Started and completed in August......	83,650*	83,650	83,650
Transferred to finished goods			
in August..	85,050	83,650	84,770
Inventory in process, August 31			
(80% complete)...............................	1,350	1,350	1,080
Total units to be assigned cost..........	86,400	85,000	85,850

*85,000 – 1,350

Continued

Prob. 18–5A   Concluded

Costs	Costs Direct Materials	Conversion	Total Costs
Unit costs:			
Total costs for August in			
Filling Department	$ 467,500	$ 163,115	
Total equivalent units	÷ 85,000	÷ 85,850	
Cost per equivalent unit (b).........	$ 5.50	$ 1.90	
Costs charged to production:			
Inventory in process,			
August 1			$ 8,064
Costs incurred in August			630,615
Total costs accounted for by			
the Filling Department............			$ 638,679
Costs allocated to completed and			
partially completed units:			
Inventory in process,			
August 1 balance (c)...............			$ 8,064
To complete inventory in			
process, August 1 (c)	$ 0	$ 2,128[1]	2,128
Started and completed in			
August (c)................................	460,075[2]	158,935[3]	619,010
Transferred to finished goods			
in August (c)............................			$ 629,202
Inventory in process,			
August 31 (d)...........................	7,425[4]	2,052[5]	9,477
Total costs assigned by the			
Filling Department			$ 638,679

[1] 1,120 units × $1.90
[2] 83,650 units × $5.50
[3] 83,650 units × $1.90
[4] 1,350 units × $5.50
[5] 1,080 units × $1.90

Prob. 18–1B

1. a. Materials.. 158,900
        Accounts Payable   158,900

    b. Work in Process—Making Department................... 112,400
        Work in Process—Packing Department 36,700
        Factory Overhead—Making Department 3,200
        Factory Overhead—Packing Department............... 1,470
        Materials   153,770

    c. Work in Process—Making Department................... 67,900
        Work in Process—Packing Department 42,700
        Factory Overhead—Making Department 14,300
        Factory Overhead—Packing Department............... 23,700
        Wages Payable   148,600

    d. Factory Overhead—Making Department 12,500
        Factory Overhead—Packing Department............... 9,400
        Accumulated Depreciation   21,900

    e. Factory Overhead—Making Department 2,600
        Factory Overhead—Packing Department............... 1,000
        Prepaid Insurance   3,600

    f. Work in Process—Making Department................... 32,000
        Work in Process—Packing Department 36,000
        Factory Overhead—Making Department...........   32,000
        Factory Overhead—Packing Department   36,000

    g. Work in Process—Packing Department 210,470
        Work in Process—Making Department   210,470

    h. Finished Goods 324,700
        Work in Process—Packing Department...........   324,700

    i. Cost of Goods Sold................................... 330,500
        Finished Goods   330,500

Prob. 18–1B   Concluded

2.

	Materials	Work in Process—Making Dept.	Work in Process—Packing Dept.	Finished Goods
Balance, October 1.........	$ 2,400	$ 3,580	$ 6,450	$ 15,800
Debits...............................	158,900	212,300	325,870	324,700
Credits	(153,770)	(210,470)	(324,700)	(330,500)
Balance, October 31.......	$ 7,530	$ 5,410	$ 7,620	$ 10,000

3.

	Factory Overhead—Making Dept.	Factory Overhead—Packing Dept.
Balance, October 1..........................	$ 0	$ 0
Debits..	32,600	35,570
Credits	(32,000)	(36,000)
Balance, October 31.......................	$ 600	$ (430) Cr.

Prob. 18–2B

a.	Materials	485,200	
	Accounts Payable...		485,200
b.	Work in Process—Refining Department......................	412,300	
	Work in Process—Blending Department.....................	54,200	
	Factory Overhead—Refining Department....................	5,200	
	Factory Overhead—Blending Department...................	3,400	
	Materials...		475,100
c.	Work in Process—Refining Department......................	83,200	
	Work in Process—Blending Department.....................	31,400	
	Factory Overhead—Refining Department....................	23,100	
	Factory Overhead—Blending Department...................	13,200	
	Wages Payable		150,900
d.	Factory Overhead—Refining Department....................	13,200	
	Factory Overhead—Blending Department...................	4,300	
	Accounts Payable...		17,500
e.	Factory Overhead—Refining Department....................	4,000	
	Factory Overhead—Blending Department...................	1,500	
	Prepaid Expenses		5,500
f.	Factory Overhead—Refining Department....................	35,400	
	Factory Overhead—Blending Department...................	12,300	
	Accumulated Depreciation—Fixed Assets.............		47,700
g.	Work in Process—Refining Department......................	82,000	
	Work in Process—Blending Department.....................	34,275	
	Factory Overhead—Refining Department		82,000
	Factory Overhead—Blending Department		34,275
h.	Work in Process—Blending Department.....................	577,500*	
	Work in Process—Refining Department.................		577,500
	*$412,300 + $83,200 + $82,000		
i.	Finished Goods—Gasoline	697,375	
	Work in Process—Blending Department...............		697,375*
	*$577,500 + $54,200 + $31,400 + $34,275		
j.	Accounts Receivable..	900,000	
	Sales		900,000
	Cost of Goods Sold	797,750	
	Finished Goods—Gasoline................................		797,750

Summary of cost of goods sold:

5,000 barrels at $40.00	$200,000
15,000 barrels at $39.85*	597,750
Total	$797,750

*$697,375 ÷ 17,500 barrels = $39.85

Prob. 18–2B   **Continued**

This solution is applicable only if the GENERAL LEDGER SOFTWARE that accompanies the text is used.

BLACK GOLD REFINING CO.
Income Statement
For the Period Ended July 31, 2003

Operating revenue:		
Sales		$ 3,222,800
Cost:		
Cost of goods sold		976,350
Gross profit		$ 2,246,450
Operating expenses:		
Selling expenses	$ 150,900	
Administrative expenses	113,400	
Total operating expenses		264,300
Net income before income tax		$ 1,982,150
Income tax:		
Income tax		306,400
Net income after income tax		$ 1,675,750

BLACK GOLD REFINING CO.
Retained Earnings Statement
For the Period Ended July 31, 2003

Retained earnings (beginning of period)	$ 355,000
Net income	1,675,750
Retained earnings (end of period)	$ 2,030,750

BLACK GOLD REFINING CO.
Balance Sheet
July 31, 2003

Assets

Cash	$ 574,989	
Marketable securities	134,000	
Accounts receivable	1,215,400	
Allowance for doubtful accounts	(36,000)	
Finished goods—Gasoline	99,625	
Materials	10,100	
Prepaid expenses	6,400	
Total current assets		$ 2,004,514
Fixed assets	$ 1,829,711	
Accumulated depreciation—Fixed assets	(484,700)	
Total fixed assets		1,345,011
Patents		245,100
Total assets		$ 3,594,625

Liabilities

Accounts payable	$ 612,000	
Wages payable	170,300	
Total current liabilities		$ 782,300
Mortgage note payable		94,000
Factory overhead—net deferred credits		675
Total liabilities		$ 876,975

Stockholders' Equity

Common stock	$ 686,900	
Retained earnings	2,030,750	
Total stockholders' equity		2,717,650
Total liabilities and stockholders' equity		$3,594,625

Prob. 18–3B

WONDER CHOCOLATE COMPANY
Cost of Production Report—Blending Department
For the Month Ended December 31, 2003

Units	Whole Units	Equivalent Units Direct Materials	Conversion
Units charged to production:			
Inventory in process, December 1	3,500		
Received from materials storeroom	145,000		
Total units accounted for by the Blending Department	148,500		
Units to be assigned cost:			
Inventory in process, December 1 (40% completed)	3,500	0	2,100
Started and completed in December	140,300*	140,300	140,300
Transferred to Molding in December	143,800	140,300	142,400
Inventory in process, December 31 (30% complete)	4,700	4,700	1,410
Total units to be assigned cost	148,500	145,000	143,810

*143,800 – 3,500

Continued

76

Costs	Direct Materials	Costs Conversion	Total Costs
Unit costs:			
Total costs for December in Blending Department...............	$ 638,000	$ 244,477	
Total equivalent units	÷ 145,000	÷ 143,810	
Cost per equivalent unit	$ 4.40	$ 1.70	
Costs charged to production:			
Inventory in process, December 1			$ 17,000
Costs incurred in December			882,477
Total costs accounted for by the Blending Department			$ 899,477
Costs allocated to completed and partially completed units:			
Inventory in process, December 1 balance			$ 17,000
To complete inventory in process, December 1...............	$ 0	$ 3,570[1]	3,570
Started and completed in December	617,320[2]	238,510[3]	855,830
Transferred to Molding in December			$ 876,400
Inventory in process, December 31	20,680[4]	2,397[5]	23,077
Total costs assigned by the Blending Department			$ 899,477

Costs transferred to Molding Department: $876,400

Work in Process, December 31: 4,700 units at a cost of $23,077

[1] 2,100 units × $1.70
[2] 140,300 units × $4.40
[3] 140,300 units × $1.70
[4] 4,700 units × $4.40
[5] 1,410 units × $1.70

Prob. 18–4B

1.

COASTAL CHEMICAL COMPANY
Cost of Production Report—Filling Department
For the Month Ended October 31, 2003

Units	Whole Units	Equivalent Units Direct Materials	Equivalent Units Conversion
Units charged to production:			
Inventory in process, October 1 .	800		
Received from Reaction			
Department............................	24,500		
Total units accounted for by			
the Filling Department............	25,300		
Units to be assigned cost:			
Inventory in process, October 1			
(60% completed)	800	0	320
Started and completed in			
October.....................................	23,300*	23,300	23,300
Transferred to finished goods			
in October................................	24,100	23,300	23,620
Inventory in process, October 31			
(60% complete)	1,200	1,200	720
Total units to be assigned cost...	25,300	24,500	24,340

*24,500 – 1,200

Prob. 18–4B   Concluded

Costs	Direct Materials	Conversion	Total Costs
		Costs	
Unit costs:			
Total costs for October in			
Filling Department	$ 352,800	$ 221,494	
Total equivalent units	÷ 24,500	÷ 24,340	
Cost per equivalent unit	$ 14.40	$ 9.10	
Costs charged to production:			
Inventory in process,			
October 1			$ 15,520
Costs incurred in October			574,294
Total costs accounted for by			
the Filling Department			$ 589,814
Costs allocated to completed			
and partially completed units:			
Inventory in process,			
October 1 balance...................			$ 15,520
To complete inventory in			
process, October 1	$ 0	$ 2,912[1]	2,912
Started and completed			
in October...............................	335,520[2]	212,030[3]	547,550
Transferred to finished			
goods in October			$ 565,982
Inventory in process,			
October 31	17,280[4]	6,552[5]	23,832
Total costs assigned by			
the Filling Department			$ 589,814

(handwritten annotation: 18,432)

[1] 320 units × $9.10   [4] 1,200 units × $14.40
[2] 23,300 units × $14.40   [5] 720 units × $9.10
[3] 23,300 units × $9.10

2. Work in Process—Filling Department..........................		352,800	
Work in Process—Reaction Department................			352,800
Finished Goods...		565,982	
Work in Process—Filling Department			565,982

3. The cost of production report may be used as the basis for allocating product costs between Work in Process and Finished Goods. The report can also be used to control costs by holding each department head responsible for the units entering production and the costs incurred in the department. Any differences in unit product costs from one month to another can be studied carefully and any significant differences investigated.

Prob. 18–5B

1. and 2. Work in Process—Rolling Department

Date	Item	Dr.	Cr.	Balance Dr.	Balance Cr.
Sept. 1	Bal., 3,700 units, 10% completed	....	....	183,150	....
30	Smelting Dept., 114,500 units at $45.00	5,152,500	....	5,335,650	....
30	Direct labor	459,123	....	5,794,773	....
30	Factory overhead	1,348,642	....	7,143,415	....
30	Finished goods...............	....	6,920,015*	223,400	....
30	Bal., 4,000 units, 70% completed	....	....	223,400	....
Oct. 31	Smelting Dept., 120,200 units at $46.50	5,589,300	....	5,812,700	....
31	Direct labor	458,373	....	6,271,073	....
31	Factory overhead	1,346,427	....	7,617,500	....
31	Finished goods...............	....	7,301,600*	315,900	....
31	Bal., 5,400 units, 80% completed	....	....	315,900	....

*The credits are determined from the supporting cost of production reports.

Prob. 18–5B   Continued

INTERNATIONAL ALUMINUM COMPANY
Cost of Production Report—Rolling Department
For the Month Ended September 30, 2003

| | | Equivalent Units | |
| | | Direct Materials | Conversion |
Units	Whole Units	(a)	(a)
Units charged to production:			
Inventory in process, September 1....	3,700		
Received from Smelting Department	114,500		
Total units accounted for by the			
Rolling Department..........................	118,200		
Units to be assigned cost:			
Inventory in process, September 1			
(10% completed).............................	3,700	0	3,330
Started and completed in September	110,500*	110,500	110,500
Transferred to finished goods			
in September	114,200	110,500	113,830
Inventory in process, September 30			
(70% complete)................................	4,000	4,000	2,800
Total units to be assigned cost..........	118,200	114,500	116,630

*114,500 – 4,000

Continued

Prob. 18–5B   Continued

Costs	Direct Materials	Costs Conversion	Total Costs
Unit costs:			
Total costs for September in			
Rolling Department.................	$5,152,500	$1,807,765	
Total equivalent units	÷ 114,500	÷ 116,630	
Cost per equivalent unit (b).........	$ 45.00	$ 15.50	
Costs charged to production:			
Inventory in process,			
September 1			$ 183,150
Costs incurred in September			6,960,265
Total costs accounted for by			
the Rolling Department			$ 7,143,415
Costs allocated to completed and			
partially completed units:			
Inventory in process,			
September 1 balance (c).........			$ 183,150
To complete inventory in			
process, September 1 (c)	$ 0	$ 51,615[1]	51,615
Started and completed			
in September (c)......................	4,972,500[2]	1,712,750[3]	6,685,250
Transferred to finished goods			
in September (c)......................			$ 6,920,015
Inventory in process,			
September 30 (d).....................	180,000[4]	43,400[5]	223,400
Total costs assigned by			
the Rolling Department			$7,143,415

[1] 3,330 units × $15.50
[2] 110,500 units × $45.00
[3] 110,500 units × $15.50
[4] 4,000 units × $45.00
[5] 2,800 units × $15.50

Prob. 18–5B   Continued

2.

INTERNATIONAL ALUMINUM COMPANY
Cost of Production Report—Rolling Department
For the Month Ended October 31, 2003

Units	Whole Units	Equivalent Units Direct Materials (a)	Conversion (a)
Units charged to production:			
Inventory in process, October 1	4,000		
Received from Smelting			
Department	120,200		
Total units accounted for by the			
Rolling Department	124,200		
Units to be assigned cost:			
Inventory in process, October 1			
(70% completed).............................	4,000	0	1,200
Started and completed in October.....	114,800*	114,800	114,800
Transferred to finished goods			
in October	118,800	114,800	116,000
Inventory in process, October 31			
(80% complete)...............................	5,400	5,400	4,320
Total units to be assigned cost..........	124,200	120,200	120,320

*120,200 – 5,400

Continued

Costs	Costs Direct Materials	Costs Conversion	Total Costs
Unit costs:			
Total costs for October in			
Rolling Department.................	$5,589,300	$1,804,800	
Total equivalent units	÷ 120,200	÷ 120,320	
Cost per equivalent unit (b).........	$ 46.50	$ 15.00	
Costs charged to production:			
Inventory in process,			
October 1			$ 223,400
Costs incurred in October...........			7,394,100
Total costs accounted for by			
the Rolling Department			$ 7,617,500
Costs allocated to completed and partially completed units:			
Inventory in process,			
October 1 balance (c)			$ 223,400
To complete inventory in			
process, October 1 (c)............	$ 0	$ 18,000[1]	18,000
Started and completed			
in October (c)	5,338,200[2]	1,722,000[3]	7,060,200
Transferred to finished goods			
in October (c)			$ 7,301,600
Inventory in process,			
October 31 (d)	251,100[4]	64,800[5]	315,900
Total costs assigned by			
the Rolling Department			$ 7,617,500

[1] **1,200 units × $15.00**
[2] **114,800 units × $46.50**
[3] **114,800 units × $15.00**
[4] **5,400 units × $46.50**
[5] **4,320 units × $15.00**

SPECIAL ACTIVITIES

Activity 18–1

This case comes from a real story. In the real story, the first reduction in chips had no impact on the marketplace. The manager was promoted, and the next manager attempted the same strategy—reduce chips by 5%. Again, it worked. The next manager did the same thing. All of a sudden, the market demand dropped for the cookie. A threshold was reached, and the cookie was in trouble in the marketplace. The current cookie was nothing like the original recipe. The cookie's integrity was slowly eroded until it wasn't "Chock Full of Chips." The company had no idea this was happening, since it occurred slowly over a period of many years. Now, with respect to the controller, there are a number of options.

a. Do nothing. This is a safe strategy. It would be highly unlikely that failing to reveal this information to anybody would ever by discovered or "pinned" on you. Unfortunately, this is one of those situations where silence has very little penalty, yet speaking up entails some risk. Yet, silence may not be the best option.

b. Talk to Davis. You can have a conversation with Davis. This is also a reasonably safe strategy and probably the best start. For example, you may discover that the reduction in chips was okayed by the vice-president or that there was a market study that revealed that the market thought the cookie had too many chips. This kind of information could be discovered very easily and without any risk with a personal conversation with Davis.

c. Talk to the vice-president. You could also go right over Davis's head to the vice-president. This strategy might label you as "not a team player," so some care is in order here. You might get Davis in hot water, or you may get yourself in some hot water. This is probably not the best first move. It is within Davis's authority to make the chip decision, so you are, in a sense, second-guessing Davis when you go to the vice-president. You could be accused of being out of your expertise. After all, what do you know about chips and the marketplace?

Probably the best move is to talk to Davis. If you discover that Davis is acting on his own, with the primary motivation being to improve the "bottom line," then you may need to talk to the vice-president. This is a tricky situation. You would need to make your case that the reduction in chips strikes you as a short-term decision that may have transitory benefits but may be a poor long-term decision. Again, Davis has the prerogative to make the chip decision; so in a sense, you are second-guessing Davis. This must be done with care.

Activity 18–2

a. This accounting procedure has the effect of rewarding the production of broke. In essence, the procedure communicates to operating personnel that broke is a normal part of doing business. In fact, not only is broke a normal part of business, but its production is actually attractive because of the favorable impact on direct materials costs of the papermaking operation. Recording broke as acceptable and favorable is inconsistent with a total quality perspective, which is based on the concept of producing the product right the first time, every time. Recycling is considered nonvalue-added in the context of a total quality perspective.

b. The accounting for broke that is typical in the industry fails to account for the total impact of broke. It is true that the use of recycled materials may reduce the direct materials cost to the operation. However, such a view is very limited. For example, the production of broke has a cost. Machine capacity was used to produce the broke in the first place. Therefore, broke has an original materials cost and a machine cost. Both of these together are likely to be greater than the cost of virgin material. One mill manager once commented, "There is a free paper machine out there." What he was implying is that if all the machine capacity used to produce broke could be harnessed for good production, it would have been equal to a "free" paper machine. The cost of misused capacity is not captured by most accounting systems in the accounting for broke.

There are other hidden costs. Broke production makes the total amount produced difficult to predict. As a result of this source of variation (broke), production schedules are difficult to maintain. For example, if a particular production run has a high amount of broke, then the scheduled run will need to be longer. The longer run, however, has ripple effects throughout the mill, since all the following production runs will be delayed, as will downstream operations. Also, the complete recycle operation has a cost associated with it (flow control, piping, maintenance, etc.). Typical accounting systems aggregate the cost of the recycle operation with papermaking. Therefore, it is not made visible as a source of wasted resources.

Activity 18–3

This case is abstracted from a real situation, where higher raw materials costs due to tin content were more than offset by lower energy costs. The cost system used in the real situation was a sophisticated "real-time" expense tracking system. The subtlety of this trade-off analysis is impressive. Few firms would be able to conduct this type of an analysis.

The first step is to translate the weekly materials and energy costs into their respective costs per unit of weekly production. In this way, the costs can be compared across the weeks.

Energy cost per unit..........	$0.13	$0.120	$0.11	$0.100	$0.09	$0.075
Materials cost per unit	0.12	0.125	0.13	0.135	0.14	0.145
	$0.25	$0.245	$0.24	$0.235	$0.23	$0.220

The graph below shows the total unit cost data for each week.

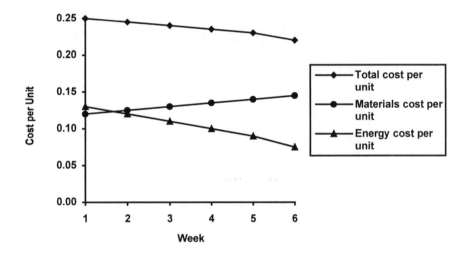

The graph reveals that the tin content and energy costs are inversely related. In other words, as the materials cost increased due to higher tin content, the energy costs dropped by more. In fact, the total cost line shows that the energy savings exceeds the additional materials cost, due to higher tin content. Thus, the recommendation should be to purchase raw can stock with the tin content at the $0.145-per-unit level (week 6 level). This is the material that optimizes the total production cost.

Activity 18–4

To: Fred Greenbar

From: Sally Kramer

Re: Analysis of November Increase in Unit Costs for Papermaking Department

The increase in the unit costs from October to November occurred for both the conversion and materials (pulp and chemicals) costs in the Papermaking Department, as indicated in the table below.

	October	November
Materials cost per ton	$480.00	$533.91
Conversion cost per ton	240.00	266.09
Total	$720.00	$800.00

An analysis was done to isolate the cause of the increased cost per ton. My interviews indicated that there were two possible causes. First, we changed the specification of the red paper in early November. This may have altered the way the paper machines process the red paper. Thus, it is possible that the paper machines have improper settings for the new specification and are overapplying materials. Secondly, there is some question as to whether paper machine 1 is in need of some repairs. It is possible that our problem is due to lack of repairs on this machine.

Fortunately, we run both colors on paper machine 1. Thus, we can separate the analysis between these two possible explanations. I have provided the following cost per ton data for the two paper machines and the two product colors:

Paper machine analysis:

	Materials Cost per Ton	Conversion Cost per Ton
Paper Machine 1	$596.98	$298.87
Paper Machine 2	480.00	238.06

Product color analysis:

	Materials Cost per Ton	Conversion Cost per Ton
Red	$532.07	$264.83
Blue	535.79	267.37

Activity 18–4   Concluded

The results are clear. Paper machine 1 has a much higher materials and conversion cost per ton in November. Apparently, the paper machine is overapplying pulp. This is resulting in an increase in both the materials and conversion cost per ton. Paper machine 2 is running at or near our historical cost per ton. There is no evidence of a color problem. Both color papers are running at or near the same materials and conversion cost per ton. Thus, the specification change for red has not appeared to cause a problem in the papermaking operation. I predict that if we improve the operation of paper machine 1, we will be able to run the department near the historical average cost per ton.

Note to Instructors: The paper machine and product line analysis are determined by summarizing the data from the computer run provided in the problem. Students must divide costs by ton-volume for each paper machine and then do the same thing for each product color. The tables in the memo show the results of the following analysis:

Average materials cost per ton for Paper Machine 1:
   ($35,800 + $41,700 + $44,600 + $36,100) ÷ (60 + 70 + 75 + 60) = $596.98

Average conversion cost per ton for Paper Machine 1:
   ($17,400 + $21,200 + $22,500 + $18,100) ÷ (60 + 70 + 75 + 60) = $298.87

Average materials cost per ton for Paper Machine 2:
   ($38,300 + $41,300 + $35,600 + $33,600) ÷ (80 + 85 + 75 + 70) = $480.00

Average conversion cost per ton for Paper Machine 2:
   ($18,800 + $19,900 + $18,100 + $17,000) ÷ (80 + 85 + 75 + 70) = $238.06

Average materials cost per ton for red paper:
   ($35,800 + $44,600 + $38,300 + $35,600) ÷ (60 + 75 + 80 + 75) = $532.07

Average conversion cost per ton for red paper:
   ($17,400 + $22,500 + $18,800 + $18,100) ÷ (60 + 75 + 80 + 75) = $264.83

Average materials cost per ton for blue paper:
   ($41,700 + $36,100 + $41,300 + $33,600) ÷ (70 + 60 + 85 + 70) = $535.79

Average conversion cost per ton for blue paper:
   ($21,200 + $18,100 + $19,900 + $17,000) ÷ (70 + 60 + 85 + 70) = $267.37

Activity 18–5

This activity can be accomplished with multiple groups assigned to one or more of the industry categories. Assign at least one group to each industry category (some are easier than others, so some groups may be assigned multiple categories). Have the groups report their research back to the class. The class's final product should be a table identifying a company, products, materials, and processes used by these industries. The most difficult information to obtain is the processes and the materials used in the processes. However, Internet and annual report information provide good information for answers. The text problems also provide examples of processes used in these industries. Use this case to familiarize students with process industries. Note that a set of example companies is provided for these industry categories early in the chapter. The instructor may require that the groups select different companies than those already listed in the text. A suggested solution following this approach is provided on the next page.

Activity 18–5   Concluded

Industry Category	Example Company	Products	Materials	Processes
Beverages	PepsiCo	Pepsi, Diet Pepsi	Sugar, carbonated water, concentrate	Mixing, bottling
Chemicals	E.I. DuPont	Stainmaster®, Kevlar®, Lycra®, Teflon®, refrigerants, electronic materials	Petroleum and petroleum-based intermediates (esters and olefins)	Reaction, blending, distilling, extruding
Food	H.J. Heinz	Ketchup	Tomato, sugar, salt, spices	Cooking, blending, packaging
Forest & paper products	International Paper	Paper, paperboard, cardboard	Wood, wood chips, water, sulfuric acid	Chipping, pulping, papermaking, pressing, cutting
Metals	Bethlehem Steel	Steel	Iron ore, coke	Melting, casting, rolling
Petroleum refining	BP Amoco	Gasoline, diesel, kerosene	Oil	Catalytic converting, distilling
Pharmaceuticals	Eli Lilly	Prozac®, Humulin®	Hydrochloride	Blending, distilling, packing, pelletizing
Soap and cosmetics	Unilever	Lever 2000® soap	Fatty acids, water, fragrances	Making, column blowing, packing

CHAPTER 19
COST BEHAVIOR AND
COST-VOLUME-PROFIT ANALYSIS

CLASS DISCUSSION QUESTIONS

1. Variable costs, fixed costs, and mixed costs.
2. Total variable costs vary in direct proportion to changes in the level of activity. Unit variable costs remain the same with changes in the level of activity.
3. **a.** Variable costs
   b. Variable costs
   c. Variable costs
4. **a.** Total fixed costs remain the same as the level of activity increases.
   b. Unit fixed costs decrease as the level of activity increases.
5. **a.** Fixed costs
   b. Fixed costs
   c. Fixed costs
6. Mixed costs are separated into their fixed and variable cost components.
7. (a)
8. (b)
9. (a)
10. The total variable cost (variable cost per unit times total units produced) at either the highest or lowest level of production is determined, and this amount is subtracted from the total cost at that level to determine the total fixed cost.
11. Contribution margin is sales revenues minus variable costs and expenses.
12. **a.** No impact on the contribution margin.
    b. Income from operations would decline.
13. A high contribution margin ratio, coupled with idle capacity, indicates a potential for increased income from operations if additional sales can be made. A large percentage of each additional sales dollar would be available, after providing for variable costs, to cover promotion efforts and to increase income from operations. Thus, a substantial sales promotion campaign should be considered in order to expand sales to maximum capacity and to take advantage of the low ratio of variable costs to sales.

14. Break-even sales (units) =

$$\frac{\text{Fixed costs}}{\text{Unit contribution margin}}$$

15. Decreases in unit variable costs, such as a decrease in the unit cost of direct materials, will decrease the break-even point.
16. Increases in total fixed costs will increase the break-even point.
17. Simmons Company had lower fixed costs and a higher percentage of variable costs to sales than did Pate Company. Such a situation resulted in a lower break-even point for Simmons Company.
18. The individual products are treated as components of one overall enterprise product. These components are weighted by the sales mix percentages.
19. The margin of safety is total sales minus sales at the break-even point, if it is expressed in dollars. If it is expressed as a percentage of sales, it is computed as follows:

Margin of safety =

$$\frac{\text{Sales} - \text{Sales at break-even point}}{\text{Sales}}$$

20. **a.** Operating leverage is computed as follows:

Operating leverage =

$$\frac{\text{Contribution margin}}{\text{Income from operations}}$$

   b. Operating leverage measures the relative mix of a business's variable costs and fixed costs.

EXERCISES

Ex. 19–1

1.	Variable	9.	Variable
2.	Fixed	10.	Variable
3.	Variable	11.	Fixed
4.	Variable	12.	Mixed
5.	Mixed	13.	Variable
6.	Fixed	14.	Fixed
7.	Variable	15.	Variable
8.	Variable		

Ex. 19–2

a. Cost Graph One
b. Cost Graph Three
c. Cost Graph Four
d. Cost Graph Three
e. Cost Graph Two

Ex. 19–3

1. b
2. c
3. c
4. e
5. d
6. a

Ex. 19–4

1. d
2. h
3. b

Ex. 19–5

a.	Fixed	g.	Variable
b.	Variable	h.	Variable
c.	Fixed	i.	Variable
d.	Variable	j.	Fixed
e.	Variable	k.	Fixed*
f.	Fixed	l.	Variable

*The developer salaries are fixed because they are more variable to the number of titles or releases, rather than the number of units sold. For example, a title could sell one copy or a million copies, and the salaries of the developers would not be affected.

Ex. 19–6

Cassettes produced		200,000		300,000		400,000
Total costs:						
Total variable costs...		$ 1,400,000	(d)	$ 2,100,000	(j)	$ 2,800,000
Total fixed costs........		600,000	(e)	600,000	(k)	600,000
Total costs		$ 2,000,000	(f)	$ 2,700,000	(l)	$ 3,400,000
Cost per unit:						
Variable cost per unit	(a) $	7.00	(g) $	7.00	(m) $	7.00
Fixed cost per unit	(b)	3.00	(h)	2.00	(n)	1.50
Total cost per unit	(c) $	10.00	(i) $	9.00	(o) $	8.50

Supporting calculations:

a. $7.00 ($1,400,000 ÷ 200,000 units)

b. $3.00 ($600,000 ÷ 200,000 units)

d. $2,100,000 ($7.00 × 300,000)

e. $600,000 (fixed costs do not change with volume)

g. $7.00 ($2,100,000 ÷ 300,000 units; variable costs per unit do not change with changes in volume)

h. $2.00 ($600,000 ÷ 300,000 units)

j. $2,800,000 ($7.00 × 400,000 units)

k. $600,000 (fixed costs do not change with volume)

m. $7.00 ($2,800,000 ÷ 400,000 units, variable costs per unit do not change with changes in volume)

n. $1.50 ($600,000 ÷ 400,000 units)

Ex. 19–7

a. Variable cost per unit = $\dfrac{\text{Difference in total costs}}{\text{Difference in production}}$

Variable cost per unit = $\dfrac{\$557,500 - \$292,500}{15,000\ \text{units} - 5,000\ \text{units}}$

Variable cost per unit = $\dfrac{\$265,000}{10,000\ \text{units}}$ = $26.50 per unit

The fixed cost can be determined by subtracting the estimated total variable cost from the total cost at either the highest or lowest level of production, as follows:

Total cost = (Variable cost per unit × Units of production) + Fixed cost

Highest level:

$557,500 = ($26.50 × 15,000 units) + Fixed cost

$557,500 = $397,500 + Fixed cost

$160,000 = Fixed cost

Lowest level:

$292,500 = ($26.50 × 5,000 units) + Fixed cost

$292,500 = $132,500 + Fixed cost

$160,000 = Fixed cost

b. Total cost = (Variable cost per unit × Units of production) + Fixed cost

Total cost for 12,000 units:

Variable cost:

Units	12,000	
Variable cost per unit...............	× $26.50	
Total variable cost.....................		$318,000
Fixed cost....................................		160,000
Total cost		$478,000

97

Ex. 19–8

$$\text{Variable cost per gross-ton mile} = \frac{\text{Difference in total costs}}{\text{Difference in gross-ton miles}}$$

$$\text{Variable cost per gross-ton mile} = \frac{\$2,145,000 - \$1,632,500}{610,000 \text{ gross-ton miles} - 405,000 \text{ gross-ton miles}}$$

$$\text{Variable cost per gross-ton mile} = \frac{\$512,500}{205,000 \text{ gross-ton miles}} = \$2.50 \text{ per gross-ton mile}$$

The fixed cost can be determined by subtracting the estimated total variable cost from the total cost at either the highest or lowest level of gross-ton miles, as follows:

Total cost = (Variable cost per gross-ton mile × Gross-ton miles) + Fixed cost

Highest level:
    $2,145,000 = ($2.50 × 610,000 gross-ton miles) + Fixed cost
    $2,145,000 = $1,525,000 + Fixed cost
    $620,000 = Fixed cost

Lowest level:
    $1,632,500 = ($2.50 × 405,000 gross-ton miles) + Fixed cost
    $1,632,500 = $1,012,500 + Fixed cost
    $620,000 = Fixed cost

Ex. 19–9

a.

Sales	$480,000
Variable costs	360,000
Contribution margin	$120,000

$$\text{Contribution margin ratio} = \frac{\text{Sales} - \text{Variable costs}}{\text{Sales}}$$

$$\text{Contribution margin ratio} = \frac{\$120,000}{\$480,000} = 25\%$$

b.

Sales	$850,000
Contribution margin ratio...	× 32%
Contribution margin	$272,000
Less fixed costs..................	190,000
Income from operations	$ 82,000

Ex. 19–10

a.

Sales	$12,421
Variable costs:	
Food..	$ 2,997
Payroll	2,220
General, selling, and administrative expenses (40% × $1,720).	688
Total variable costs...	$ 5,905
Contribution margin	$ 6,516

b.

$$\text{Contribution margin ratio} = \frac{\text{Sales} - \text{Variable costs}}{\text{Sales}}$$

$$\text{Contribution margin ratio} = \frac{\$6,516}{\$12,421} = 52.46\%$$

c.

Same-store sales increase...	$280,000,000
Contribution margin ratio (from b)	× 52.46%
Increase in income from operations	$146,888,000

Note: Part (c) emphasizes "same-store sales" because of the assumption of no change in fixed costs. McDonald's will also increase sales from opening new stores. However, the impact on income from operations for these additional sales would need to include an increase in fixed costs into the calculation.

Ex. 19–11

a. Break-even sales (units) $= \dfrac{\text{Fixed costs}}{\text{Unit contribution margin}}$

Break-even sales (units) $= \dfrac{\$437,600}{\$80 - \$48} = 13,675$ units

b. Sales (units) $= \dfrac{\text{Fixed costs} + \text{Target profit}}{\text{Unit contribution margin}}$

Sales (units) $= \dfrac{\$437,600 + \$67,200}{\$80 - \$48} = 15,775$ units

Ex. 19–12

a. Break-even sales (units) $= \dfrac{\text{Fixed costs}}{\text{Unit contribution margin}}$

Break-even sales (units) $= \dfrac{\$3,225,500,000^{1}}{\$101.32^{2} - \$45.17^{3} - \$7.94^{4}} = 66,905,206$ barrels

The variable costs per unit are determined by multiplying the total amount of each cost by the variable cost percentage (70% for production costs and 45% for marketing and distribution costs), then dividing by the number of barrels.

[1] ($7,162,000,000 × 30%) + ($1,958,000,000 × 55%)

[2] $11,246,000,000 ÷ 111,000,000

[3] ($7,162,000,000 × 70%) ÷ 111,000,000

[4] ($1,958,000,000 × 45%) ÷ 111,000,000

b. Break-even sales (units) $= \dfrac{\$3,225,500,000 + \$40,000,000}{\$101.32 - \$45.17 - \$7.94} = 67,734,910$ barrels

Ex. 19–13

a. Break-even sales (units) = $\dfrac{\text{Fixed costs}}{\text{Unit contribution margin}}$

Break-even sales (units) = $\dfrac{\$675,000}{\$165 - \$105}$ = 11,250 units

b. Break-even sales (units) = $\dfrac{\text{Fixed costs}}{\text{Unit contribution margin}}$

Break-even sales (units) = $\dfrac{\$675,000}{\$180 - \$105}$ = 9,000 units

Ex. 19–14

The cost of the promotion campaign is a fixed cost in this analysis, since we're trying to determine the break-even adoption rate of the campaign (not break-even for AOL as a whole):

500,000 people × $2.50 = $1,250,000

The revenue earned per new customer is essentially the contribution margin per unit, since the variable costs per account per month would be insignificant. Thus, the contribution margin value of each new customer is:

(36 mos. − 3 free mos.) × $20/mo. = $660 per new account

The break-even number of new accounts necessary to cover the fixed cost of the promotion would be:

Break-even = $\dfrac{\text{Fixed cost}}{\text{Contribution margin per unit}}$

Break-even = $\dfrac{\$1,250,000}{\$660 \text{ per account}}$ = 1,894 accounts

Therefore, if AOL yielded more than 1,894 new accounts out of 500,000 mailings (0.38%), the costs of the campaign would be covered. However, AOL would need to yield much more than this in order to be successful as a company, since its corporate fixed costs must also be covered.

Ex. 19–15

a. Break-even = $\dfrac{\text{Fixed cost}}{\text{Revenue per subscriber} - \text{Variable cost per subscriber}}$

Break-even = $\dfrac{\$2,175,607,200^{3}}{\$513^{1} - \$201^{2}}$

Break-even = 6,973,100 subscribers

[1]Revenue per subscriber:

$1,846,758,000 ÷ 3,600,000 subscribers = $513 (rounded)

[2]Variable cost per subscriber:

Cost of revenue......................................	$ 516,393,000 ×	20% =	$ 103,278,600
Selling, general, and administrative expenses	1,550,323,000 ×	40%	620,129,200
Total variable cost			$ 723,407,800
Divided by number of subscribers....			÷ 3,600,000
Variable cost per subscriber (rounded)			$ 201

[3]Fixed costs:

Cost of revenue......................................	$ 516,393,000 ×	80%	$ 413,114,400
Selling, general, and administrative expenses	1,550,323,000 ×	60%	930,193,800
Depreciation	832,299,000 ×	100%	832,299,000
Total fixed costs.................................			$2,175,607,200

b. Break-even = $\dfrac{\text{Fixed cost}}{\text{Revenue per subscriber} - \text{Variable cost per subscriber}}$

$3,600,000 \text{ subscribers} = \dfrac{\$2,175,607,200}{X - \$201}$

$3,600,000X - \$723,600,000 = \$2,175,607,200$

$3,600,000X = \$2,899,207,200$

$X = \$805 \text{ (rounded)}$

The rate charged per minute and the number of average minutes of digital service influence the revenue per subscriber.

Note to Instructors: An interesting question is whether the costs are variable to the number of minutes or number of subscribers. If we assume that the costs are variable to the number of minutes, then the break-even analysis revolves around the number of minutes. More likely, the costs are more variable to the number of subscribers for this business (mostly customer acquisition and service costs), while the variable cost per minute is likely to be small.

Ex. 19–16

a.

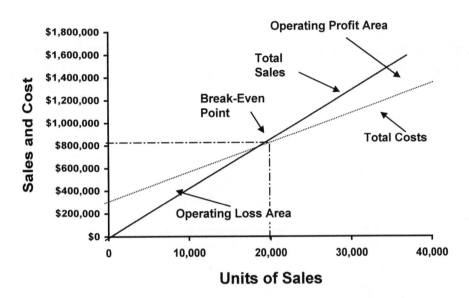

b. $800,000 (the intersection of the total sales line and the total costs line)

c. The graphic format permits the user (management) to visually determine the break-even point and the operating profit or loss for any given level of sales.

Ex. 19–17

a. $300,000 (total fixed costs)

b.
Sales (40,000 units × $40)		$1,600,000
Fixed costs	$ 300,000	
Variable costs (40,000 units × $25).........................	1,000,000	1,300,000
Income from operations		$ 300,000

c.

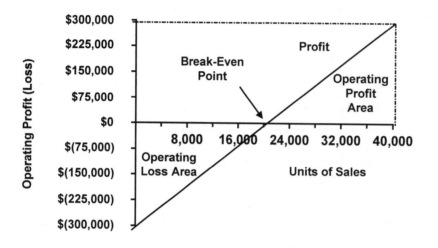

d. 20,000 units (the intersection of the profit line and the horizontal axis)

Ex. 19–18

Cost-volume-profit chart

a. fixed costs

b. operating loss area

c. operating profit area

d. break-even point

e. total costs

f. sales

Ex. 19–19

Profit-volume chart

a.   break-even point

b.   fixed costs

c.   operating loss area

d.   operating profit area

e.   profit line

f.   maximum income from operations

Ex. 19–20

a.   Unit selling price of E = ($2.20 × 0.70) + ($1.70 × 0.30)
     Unit selling price of E = $1.54 + $0.51 = $2.05
     Unit variable cost of E = ($1.50 × 0.70) + ($1.10 × 0.30)
     Unit variable cost of E = $1.05 + $0.33 = $1.38
     Unit contribution margin of E = $2.05 – $1.38 = $0.67

$$\text{Break-even sales (units)} = \frac{\text{Fixed costs}}{\text{Unit contribution margin}}$$

$$\text{Break-even sales (units)} = \frac{\$167,500}{\$0.67} = 250,000 \text{ units}$$

b.   175,000 units of potato chips (250,000 units × 0.70)
     75,000 units of pretzels (250,000 units × 0.30)

Ex. 19–21

a. Unit contribution margin of overall product (E):

Unit selling price of E [(25% × $400) + (75% × $240)]....................... $280
Unit variable cost of E [(25% × $58) + (75% × $34)]......................... 40
Unit contribution margin of E $240

Fixed costs of the New York to Miami round trip flight:

Fuel	$ 6,520
Flight crew salaries.............	3,400
Depreciation	1,600
Total fixed costs...................	$11,520

Break-even in sales (units) of overall product:

$$\text{Break-even sales (units)} = \frac{\text{Fixed costs}}{\text{Unit contribution margin}}$$

$$\text{Break-even sales (units)} = \frac{\$11,520}{\$240 \text{ per seat}} = 48 \text{ seats (tickets)}$$

b. Business class break-even (48 seats × 25%) .... 12 seats
Tourist class break-even (48 seats × 75%) .... 36 seats
Total break-even .... 48 seats

Ex. 19–22

a. (1) $50,000 ($400,000 – $350,000)
(2) 12.5% ($50,000 ÷ $400,000)

b. The break-even point (S) is determined as follows:

Sales = $600,000 + 60% Sales
Sales – 60% Sales = $600,000
40% Sales = $600,000
Sales = $1,500,000

If the margin of safety is 25%, the sales are determined as follows:

Sales = $1,500,000 + 25% Sales
Sales – 25% Sales = $1,500,000
75% Sales = $1,500,000
Sales = $2,000,000

Ex. 19–23

If 20,000 units are sold and sales at the break-even point are 23,000 units, there is no margin of safety.

Ex. 19–24

a. Duncan Inc.:

$$\text{Operating leverage} = \frac{\text{Contribution margin}}{\text{Income from operations}}$$

$$\text{Operating leverage} = \frac{\$150,000}{\$100,000} = 1.50$$

Chow Inc.:

$$\text{Operating leverage} = \frac{\text{Contribution margin}}{\text{Income from operations}}$$

$$\text{Operating leverage} = \frac{\$275,000}{\$50,000} = 5.50$$

b. Duncan Inc.'s income from operations would increase by 30% (1.50 × 20%), or $30,000 (30% × $100,000), and Chow Inc.'s income from operations would increase by 110% (5.5 × 20%), or $55,000 (110% × $50,000).

c. The difference in the increases of income from operations is due to the difference in the operating leverages. Chow Inc.'s higher operating leverage means that its fixed costs are a larger percentage of contribution margin than are Duncan Inc.'s. Thus, increases in sales increase operating profit at a faster rate for Chow than for Duncan.

Appendix Ex. 19–25

a. Variable cost of goods sold

b. Variable selling and administrative expenses

c. Fixed costs and expenses

Appendix Ex. 19–26

INDIGO INK COMPANY
Income Statement—Variable Costing
For the Month Ended July 31, 2002

Sales		$408,000
Variable cost of goods sold:		
Variable cost of goods manufactured	$265,600	
Less ending inventory (400 units × $41.50)	16,600	
Variable cost of goods sold		249,000
Manufacturing margin		$159,000
Variable selling and administrative expenses		84,000
Contribution margin		$ 75,000
Fixed costs:		
Fixed manufacturing costs	$ 19,200	
Fixed selling and administrative expenses	32,400	51,600
Income from operations		$ 23,400

Computations:

   Variable cost of goods manufactured: $284,800 – $19,200 = $265,600

   Unit cost of ending inventory:

      Variable cost of goods manufactured per unit:

         $265,600 ÷ 6,400 units manufactured = $41.50

      Thus, variable cost of goods sold could alternatively be calculated:

         $249,000 = 6,000 units × $41.50/unit

   Fixed selling and administrative expenses: $116,400 – $84,000 = $32,400

Appendix Ex. 19–27

EXCEL ELECTRONICS COMPANY
Income Statement—Absorption Costing
For the Month Ended June 30, 2002

Sales		$360,000
Cost of goods sold:		
Cost of goods manufactured (1,350 units × $185)...	$249,750	
Less ending inventory (150 units × $185)	27,750	
Cost of goods sold		222,000
Gross profit..		$138,000
Selling and administrative expenses ($21,600 + $68,500)		90,100
Income from operations...		$ 47,900

Computations:

    Cost of goods manufactured: $216,000 + $33,750 = $249,750

    Unit cost of ending inventory:

        Total cost of goods manufactured: $249,750 ÷ 1,350 units
            manufactured = $185

PROBLEMS

Prob. 19–1A

Cost	Fixed Cost	Variable Cost	Mixed Cost
a.			X
b.		X	
c.	X		
d.		X	
e.		X	
f.	X		
g.			X
h.	X		
i.		X	
j.		X	
k.	X		
l.		X	
m.	X		
n.		X	
o.		X	
p.		X	
q.	X		
r.		X	
s.	X		
t.			X

Prob. 19–2A

1.

	Fixed Costs	Variable Costs
Cost of goods sold	$2,000,000	$ 6,000,000
Selling expenses	600,000	900,000
Administrative expenses	1,600,000	400,000
Total	$4,200,000	$ 7,300,000

2. a. $25 ($7,300,000 ÷ 292,000 units)
   b. $20 ($45 – $25)

3. Break-even sales (units) = $\dfrac{\text{Fixed costs}}{\text{Unit contribution margin}}$

   Break-even sales (units) = $\dfrac{\$4,200,000}{\$20}$ = 210,000 units

4. Break-even sales (units) = $\dfrac{\text{Fixed costs}}{\text{Unit contribution margin}}$

   Break-even sales (units) = $\dfrac{\$4,200,000 \ + \ \$600,000}{\$20}$ = 240,000 units

5. Sales (units) = $\dfrac{\text{Fixed costs} \ + \ \text{Target profit}}{\text{Unit contribution margin}}$

   Sales (units) = $\dfrac{\$4,800,000 \ + \ \$1,640,000}{\$20}$ = $\dfrac{\$6,440,000}{\$20}$ = 322,000 units

6.

Sales (342,000* units × $45)		$15,390,000
Less: Fixed costs	$4,800,000	
Variable costs (342,000* units × $25)	8,550,000	13,350,000
Income from operations		$ 2,040,000

   *342,000 units = ($13,140,000 + $2,250,000) ÷ $45 per unit

7.

Present operating income	$ 1,640,000
Less additional fixed costs	600,000
Income from operations	$ 1,040,000

Prob. 19–2A   Concluded

8. In favor of the proposal is the possibility of increasing income from operations from $1,640,000 to $2,040,000. However, there are many points against the proposal, including:

   a. The break-even point increases by 30,000 units (from 210,000 to 240,000).

   b. The sales necessary to maintain the current income from operations of $1,640,000 would be 322,000 units, or $1,350,000 (30,000 units × $45) in excess of 2003 sales.

   c. If future sales remain at the 2003 level, the income from operations of $1,640,000 will decline to $1,040,000.

The company should determine the sales potential if the additional product is produced and then evaluate the advantages and the disadvantages enumerated above, in light of these sales possibilities. Unless market research strongly indicates that $1,350,000 to $2,250,000 of additional sales can be made, the proposal should not be accepted.

Prob. 19–3A

1. Break-even sales (units) = $\dfrac{\text{Fixed costs}}{\text{Unit contribution margin}}$

    Break-even sales (units) = $\dfrac{\$540,000}{\$30}$ = 18,000 units

2. Sales (units) = $\dfrac{\text{Fixed costs + Target profit}}{\text{Unit contribution margin}}$

    Sales (units) = $\dfrac{\$540,000\ +\ \$84,000}{\$30}$

    Sales (units) = $\dfrac{\$624,000}{\$30}$ = 20,800 units

3.

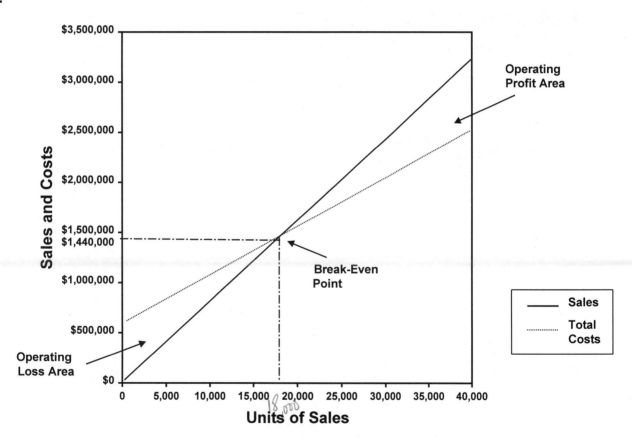

4. $150,000 [23,000 units × ($80 – $50) – $540,000]

Prob. 19–4A

1.

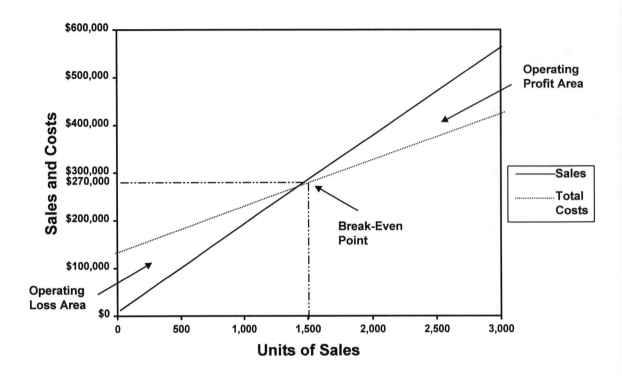

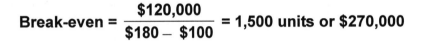

Break-even = $\dfrac{\$120,000}{\$180 - \$100}$ = **1,500 units or $270,000**

Prob. 19–4A   Continued

2. a. ($20,000) = ($225,000 – $245,000), as indicated in the chart below.

    b. $120,000 ($540,000 – $420,000), as indicated in the chart below.

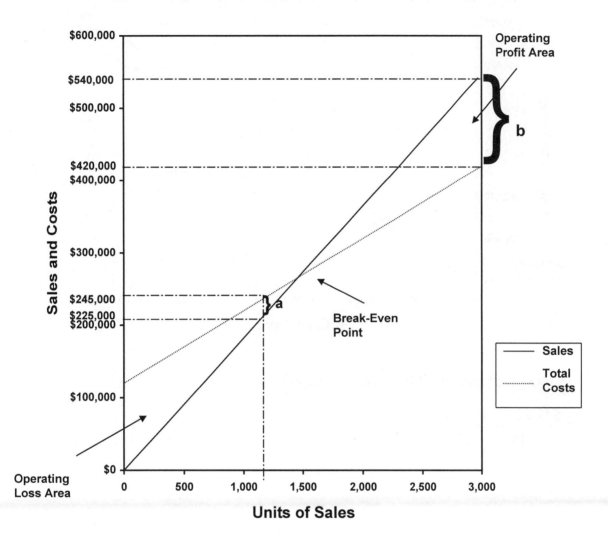

Prob. 19–4A   Continued

3.

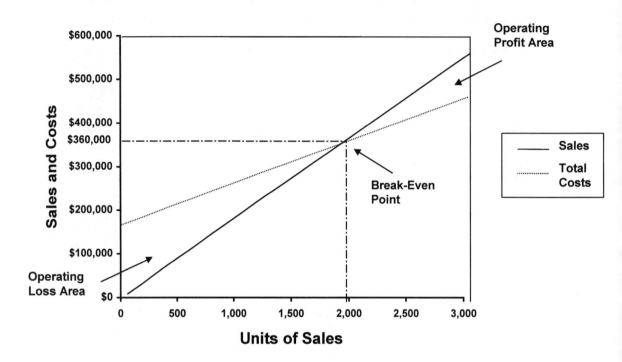

Break-even point: 2,000* units or $360,000

$$\ast \frac{\$120,000 \ + \ \$40,000}{\$180 \ - \ \$100}$$

Prob. 19–4A   Concluded

4.   a.   **$40,000 ($450,000 – $410,000), as indicated in the chart below.**
     b.   **$80,000 ($540,000 – $460,000), as indicated in the chart below.**

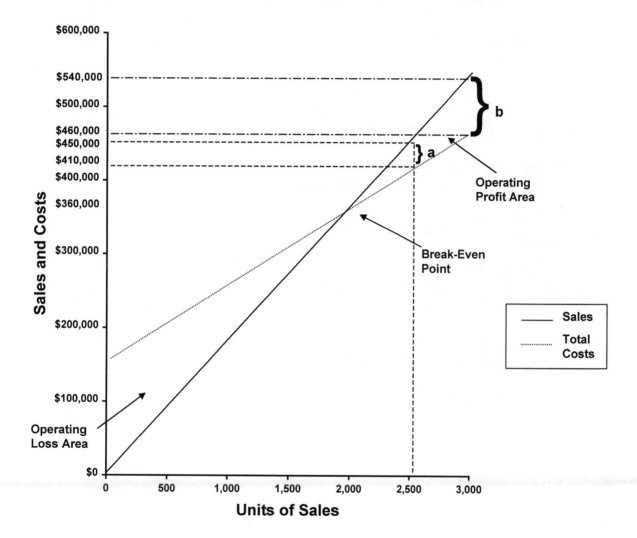

Prob. 19–5A

(Overall product is labeled E.)

1. Unit selling price of E [($18 × 75%) + ($12 × 25%)]................. $16.50
    Unit variable cost of E [($11 × 75%) + ($7 × 25%)].................. 10.00
    Unit contribution margin .... $ 6.50

    $$\text{Break-even sales (units)} = \frac{\text{Fixed costs}}{\text{Unit contribution margin}}$$

    $$\text{Break-even sales (units)} = \frac{\$357,500}{\$6.50} = 55,000 \text{ units}$$

2. 55,000 units of E × 75% = 41,250 units of CDs
    55,000 units of E × 25% = 13,750 units of cassette tapes

3. $\dfrac{\$357,500}{\$5.50^*} = 65,000$ units

    *Units selling price of E [($18 × 25%) + ($12 × 75%)]............. $13.50
    Unit variable cost of E [($11 × 25%) + ($7 × 75%)]................ 8.00
    Unit contribution margin .... $ 5.50

    The break-even point increases because the mix is weighted toward the low contribution margin per unit product.

Prob. 19–6A

1.

JARVIS INC.
Estimated Income Statement
For the Year Ending December 31, 2003

Sales		$600,000
Cost of goods sold:		
Direct materials	$136,000	
Direct labor	64,000	
Factory overhead	111,500	
Cost of goods sold		311,500
Gross profit...		$288,500
Operating expenses:		
Selling expenses:		
Sales salaries and commissions...... $53,300		
Advertising 12,500		
Travel 3,200		
Miscellaneous selling expense......... 14,200		
Total selling expenses	$ 83,200	
Administrative expenses:		
Office and officers salaries............... $75,400		
Supplies... 9,000		
Miscellaneous administrative expense 45,900		
Total administrative expenses	130,300	
Total operating expenses......................		213,500
Income from operations.............................		$ 75,000

2. Contribution margin ratio = $\dfrac{\text{Sales } - \text{ Variable costs}}{\text{Sales}}$

Contribution margin ratio = $\dfrac{\$600,000 - (20,000 \times \$15)}{\$600,000} = \dfrac{\$300,000}{\$600,000} = 50\%$

3. Break-even sales (units) = $\dfrac{\text{Fixed costs}}{\text{Unit contribution margin}}$

Break-even sales (units) = $\dfrac{\$225,000}{\$30 - \$15} = 15,000$ units

Prob. 19–6A   Concluded

4.

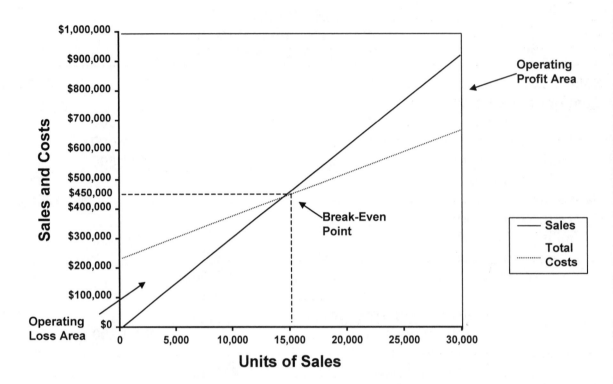

5. **Margin of safety:**
    Expected sales (20,000 units × $30)....................................... $600,000
    Break-even point (15,000 units × $30)...................................   450,000
    Margin of safety $150,000

or

$$\text{Margin of safety} = \frac{\text{Sales} - \text{Sales at break-even point}}{\text{Sales}}$$

$$\text{Margin of safety} = \frac{\$150,000}{\$600,000} = 25\%$$

6. $$\text{Operating leverage} = \frac{\text{Contribution margin}}{\text{Income from operations}}$$

$$\text{Operating leverage} = \frac{(20,000 \text{ units} \times \$15)}{\$75,000} = \frac{\$300,000}{\$75,000} = 4$$

Prob. 19–1B

Cost	Fixed Cost	Variable Cost	Mixed Cost
a.			X
b.		X	
c.		X	
d.	X		
e.		X	
f.		X	
g	X		
h.		X	
i.	X		
j.	X		
k.	X		
l.		X	
m.		X	
n.		X	
o.			X
p.	X		
q.		X	
r.			X
s.			X
t.	X		

Prob. 19–2B

1.

	Fixed Costs	Variable Costs
Cost of goods sold	$1,600,000	$2,400,000
Selling expenses	600,000	1,800,000
Administrative expenses	300,000	300,000
Total	$2,500,000	$4,500,000

2. a. $75 ($4,500,000 ÷ 60,000 units)

   b. $50 ($125 – $75)

3. $$\text{Break-even sales (units)} = \frac{\text{Fixed costs}}{\text{Unit contribution margin}}$$

   $$\text{Break-even sales (units)} = \frac{\$2,500,000}{\$50} = 50,000 \text{ units}$$

4. $$\text{Break-even sales (units)} = \frac{\text{Fixed costs}}{\text{Unit contribution margin}}$$

   $$\text{Break-even sales (units)} = \frac{\$2,500,000 + \$300,000}{\$50} = 56,000 \text{ units}$$

5. $$\text{Sales (units)} = \frac{\text{Fixed costs} + \text{Target profit}}{\text{Unit contribution margin}}$$

   $$\text{Sales (units)} = \frac{\$2,800,000 + \$500,000}{\$50} = \frac{\$3,300,000}{\$50} = 66,000 \text{ units}$$

6.

Sales (69,600* units × $125)		$ 8,700,000
Less: Fixed costs	$2,800,000	
Variable costs (69,600* units × $75)	5,220,000	8,020,000
Income from operations		$ 680,000

   *69,600 units = ($7,500,000 + $1,200,000) ÷ $125 per unit

7.

Present operating income	$ 500,000
Less additional fixed costs	300,000
Income from operations	$ 200,000

Prob. 19–2B   Concluded

8. In favor of the proposal is the possibility of increasing income from operations from $500,000 to $680,000. However, there are many points against the proposal, including:

   a.   The break-even point increases by 6,000 units (from 50,000 to 56,000).

   b.   The sales necessary to maintain the current income from operations of $500,000 would be 66,000 units, or $750,000 (6,000 units × $125), in excess of 2003 sales.

   c.   If future sales remain at the 2003 level, the income from operations of $500,000 will decline to $200,000.

The company should determine the sales potential if the additional product is produced and then evaluate the advantages and the disadvantages enumerated above, in light of these sales possibilities. Unless market research strongly indicates that $750,000 to $1,200,000 of additional sales can be made, the proposal should not be accepted.

Prob. 19–3B

1. Break-even sales (units) = $\dfrac{\text{Fixed costs}}{\text{Unit contribution margin}}$

   Break-even sales (units) = $\dfrac{\$1,200,000}{\$120}$ = 10,000 units

2. Sales (units) = $\dfrac{\text{Fixed costs + Target profit}}{\text{Unit contribution margin}}$

   Sales (units) = $\dfrac{\$1,200,000 + \$120,000}{\$120} = \dfrac{\$1,320,000}{\$120}$ = 11,000 units

3.

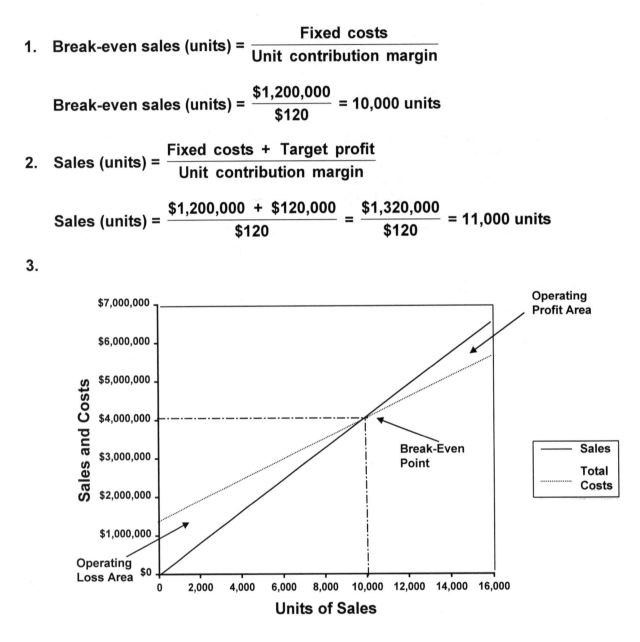

4. $180,000 [11,500 × ($400 – $280) – $1,200,000]

Prob. 19–4B

1.

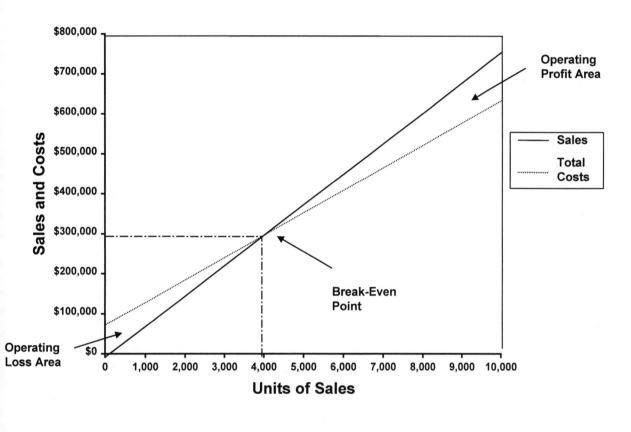

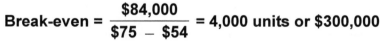

Break-even = $\dfrac{\$84,000}{\$75 - \$54}$ = **4,000 units or $300,000**

Prob. 19–4B   Continued

2.   a. $21,000 = ($375,000 – $354,000), as indicated in the chart below.

   b. $126,000 ($750,000 – $624,000), as indicated in the chart below.

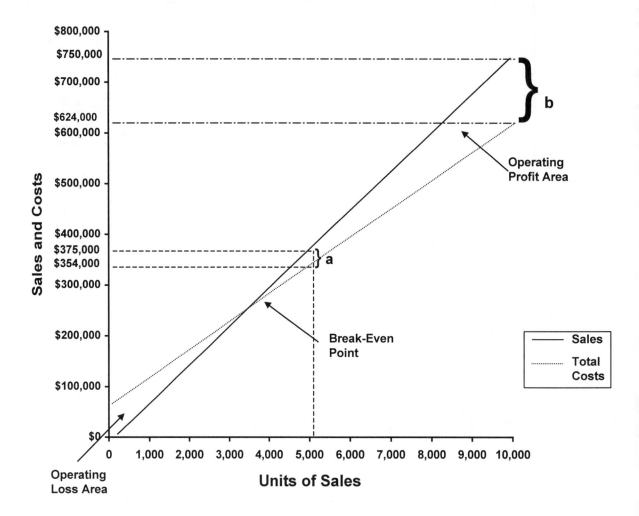

Units sold: $375,000 ÷ $75 per unit = 5,000 units

3.

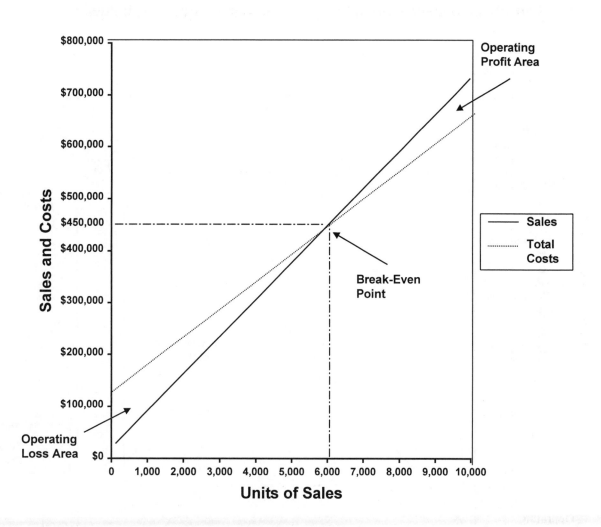

Break-even point: 6,000* units or $450,000

$$* \frac{\$84,000 \ + \ \$42,000}{\$75 \ - \ \$54}$$

Prob. 19–4B   Concluded

4.   a. $63,000 ($675,000 – $612,000), as indicated in the chart below.

     b. $84,000 ($750,000 – $666,000), as indicated in the chart below.

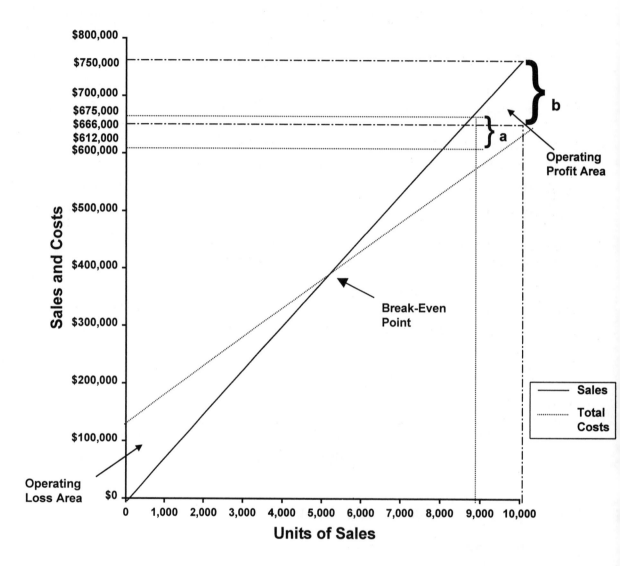

Prob. 19–5B

(Overall product is labeled E.)

1. Unit selling price of E [($24.00 × 36%) + ($6.50 × 64%)]............... $12.80
    Unit variable cost of E [($15.50 × 36%) + ($3.00 × 64%)]............. <u>7.50</u>
    Unit contribution margin .... <u>$ 5.30</u>

$$\text{Break-even sales (units)} = \frac{\text{Fixed costs}}{\text{Unit contribution margin}}$$

$$\text{Break-even sales (units)} = \frac{\$111,300}{\$5.30} = 21,000 \text{ units}$$

2. 21,000 units of E × 36% = 7,560 units of golf balls
    21,000 units of E × 64% = 13,440 units of tennis balls

3. $\dfrac{\$111,300}{\$7.00^*} = 15,900$ units

    * Units selling price of E [($24.00 × 70%) + ($6.50 × 30%)]......... $18.75
      Unit variable cost of E [($15.50 × 70%) + ($3.00 × 30%)].......... <u>11.75</u>
      Unit contribution margin .... <u>$ 7.00</u>

    The break-even point decreased because the sales mix is weighted toward
    the product with the higher contribution margin per unit of product.

Prob. 19–6B

1.

UNIVERSAL PRODUCTS INC.
Estimated Income Statement
For the Year Ending December 31, 2003

Sales		$ 2,812,500
Cost of goods sold:		
Direct materials	$764,375	
Direct labor	659,375	
Factory overhead	390,875	
Cost of goods sold		1,814,625
Gross profit...		$ 997,875
Operating expenses:		
Selling expenses:		
Sales salaries and commissions...........	$311,875	
Advertising	75,000	
Travel	39,500	
Miscellaneous selling expense..............	66,375	
Total selling expenses	$492,750	
Administrative expenses:		
Office and officers' salaries..................	$220,000	
Supplies...	29,375	
Miscellaneous administrative expense.	30,750	
Total administrative expenses	280,125	
Total operating expenses............................		772,875
Income from operations.................................		$ 225,000

2. Contribution margin ratio $= \dfrac{\text{Sales} - \text{Variable costs}}{\text{Sales}}$

    Contribution margin ratio $= \dfrac{\$2,812,500 - (6,250 \times \$270)}{\$2,812,500} = \dfrac{\$1,125,000}{\$2,812,500} = 40\%$

3. Break-even sales (units) $= \dfrac{\text{Fixed costs}}{\text{Unit contribution margin}}$

    Break-even sales (units) $= \dfrac{\$900,000}{\$450 - \$270} = 5,000 \text{ units}$

Prob. 19–6B   Concluded

4.

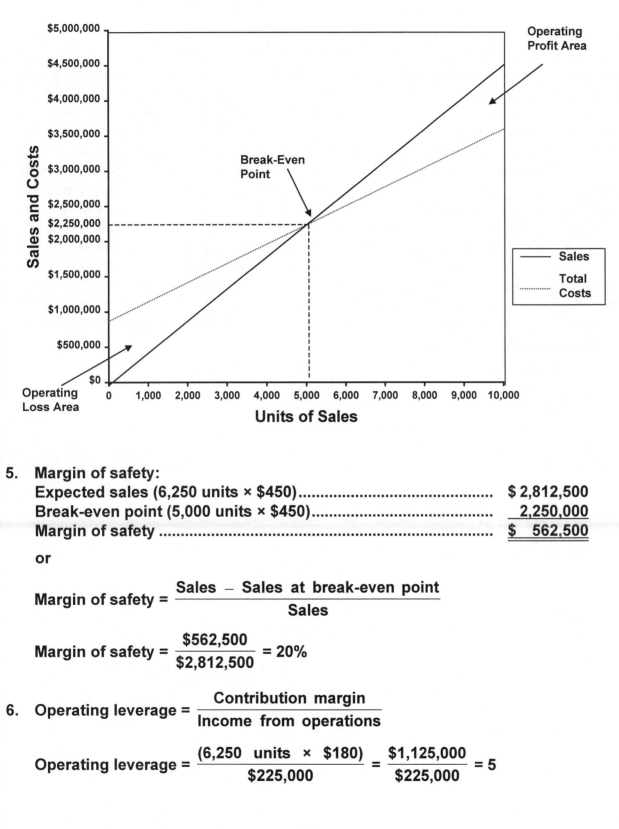

5.   Margin of safety:

Expected sales (6,250 units × $450)..	$ 2,812,500
Break-even point (5,000 units × $450).......................................	2,250,000
Margin of safety	$ 562,500

or

$$\text{Margin of safety} = \frac{\text{Sales} - \text{Sales at break-even point}}{\text{Sales}}$$

$$\text{Margin of safety} = \frac{\$562,500}{\$2,812,500} = 20\%$$

6.   Operating leverage $= \dfrac{\text{Contribution margin}}{\text{Income from operations}}$

$$\text{Operating leverage} = \frac{(6,250 \text{ units} \times \$180)}{\$225,000} = \frac{\$1,125,000}{\$225,000} = 5$$

SPECIAL ACTIVITIES

Activity 19–1

In an absolute sense, Howard's actions are devious. He is clearly attempting to use the first four-year scenario, which is favorable, as a way to market the partnerships. They are really longer-term investments. After the first four years, the risk increases dramatically. The break-even occupancy becomes much more difficult to achieve at 85% than it does at 60%. Focusing on the 60% and remaining silent about the increase to 85% is deceptive. One might argue "let the buyer beware." After all, the information is in the fine print. A little spadework would reveal the longer-term reality of these partnerships. This is not a compelling argument. Clearly, Howard is putting some favorable spin on this offering. It's likely that this will come back to haunt him in a court of law. Some investors may claim they were defrauded by less than complete disclosure. Howard has a responsibility to provide objective information. The integrity standard requires that Howard communicate constraints that would preclude the successful performance of an activity. Also, Howard must communicate unfavorable as well as favorable information. Clearly, the increase in the mortgage rate and its impact on the break-even point is unfavorable information that should be given as much visibility as the favorable 60% break-even information.

Activity 19–2

The airline industry has a high operating leverage. This means that fixed costs are a large part of the cost structure. The break-even volume is apparently around 65% of capacity. When the volume falls below 65%, the industry loses money. As the percentage increases above 65%, the industry becomes very profitable. There is a difference between profitability and cash flow. Since a large part of the cost structure in airlines is fixed costs, this means that depreciation makes up a large part of the expense base. Depreciation is a noncash expense. Therefore, it is likely that the industry is not profitable but has positive cash flow at capacity use that is below break-even. There is a point, however, where the industry will not generate sufficient cash to maintain operations.

The airline strategy of raising ticket prices and consolidating routes may be a successful strategy; however, there are a number of considerations. First, the higher ticket prices would increase the revenue per passenger-mile and reduce the break-even occupancy percentage only if it is assumed that there is no change in passenger volume. However, this is unlikely. The revenue from price increases would need to increase faster than the lost revenue from lower traffic volume for a price increase to lower break-even. To raise ticket prices, the airline would have to minimize the impact on lost volume. This might be possible for fare increases targeted to business travelers that need to fly anyway. The airline can minimize volume losses by keeping fares lower for nonbusiness travelers. Restrictions such as allowing reduced fares only on round-trip fares that go over a Saturday night achieve this objective, since business travelers do not wish to be out of town over the weekend. Likewise, requiring higher fares for seats reserved with little advance notice would also achieve this objective, since much business travel cannot be planned weeks in advance.

The strategy of consolidating routes attacks a major cost of airlines. The number of flights and terminals served drives fuel and airport ground- and terminal-related costs. Therefore, consolidating routes by either reducing the number of terminals served and/or the number of flights is a method of achieving some economies of scale. For example, an airline could consolidate three flights departing in the morning from Tulsa to Dallas into just two flights departing in the morning. This would reduce the airline's costs but would increase the airline passengers' inconvenience. This strategy works only if there is little loss in revenue by going to two flights, meaning that the people bumped from the third flight go to the other two, rather than a competitor. Alternatively, an airline flying into LaGuardia and Newark airports in the New York metropolitan area might decide to fly into only one of the terminals in order to reduce ground-related costs. Again, this strategy would only be successful if there was little loss in revenue relative to the cost savings.

Activity 19–3

Do-Nothing Strategy:

Revenue – Variable costs – Fixed costs	= Profit
($25 × 750,000) – ($5 × 750,000) – $15,000,000	= Profit
$18,750,000 – $3,750,000 – $15,000,000	= $0

Thus, 750,000 units is the break-even volume.

Julie's Strategy:

Revenue – Variable costs – Fixed costs	= Profit
($25 × 1,500,000) – ($5 × 1,500,000) – $18,000,000	= Profit
$37,500,000 – $7,500,000 – $18,000,000	= $12,000,000

Steve's Strategy:

Revenue – Variable costs – Fixed costs	= Profit
($20 × 1,600,000) – ($5 × 1,600,000) – $15,000,000	= Profit
$32,000,000 – $8,000,000 – $15,000,000	= $9,000,000

Julie's strategy, which is to maintain the price but increase advertising, appears superior.

Activity 19–4

The direct labor costs are not variable to the increase in unit volume. The unit volume is the wrong activity base for direct labor costs. The "number of impressions" is a more accurate reflection of the direct labor cost. An impression is a separate silk screen color application on the T-shirt. Thus, the analysis should be done as follows:

	One Color	Two Color	Three Color	Four Color	Total
Number of T-shirts	300	800	900	1,000	3,000
Number of impressions	300	1,600	2,700	4,000	8,600

Last year's impressions: 4,600 (300 + 1,600 + 2,700)

Total increase: $\dfrac{8,600 - 4,600}{4,600} = 87\%$

Thus, a 50% assumed increase from the unit volume information will understate the potential increase in direct labor cost.

Activity 19–5

The Shipping Department manager should respond by pointing out that the activities performed by his department are not related to sales volume but to sales orders. The orders require inventory pulling and sorting activities as well as paperwork activities. Thus, even though the sales volume is decreasing, the number of sales orders processed has increased from 500 to 640 (28%) over the last eight months. The reason for this increase in sales orders is that customers are ordering lower quantities per order than in the past. Thus, it is no wonder that the Shipping Department manager is experiencing financial pressure. The amount of work performed by the department is increasing, even though sales volume is down.

Activity 19–6

There are many possible applications of break-even in a school environment. Below are just a few possible ideas.

	Break-Even Analysis	Revenue	Fixed Costs	Variable Costs
1.	Break-even number of students in a class	Student tuition for a class	Faculty salary, space costs	Supplies, copying
2.	Break-even sales in the bookstore	Book sales	Manager's salary, space costs	Cashier salaries, cost of books
3.	Break-even daily meal revenues	Meal revenue	Salaries, space	Food costs
4.	Break-even students in a dorm	Room revenue	Space, staff salaries, utilities	Janitorial costs
5.	Break-even number of tickets sold for a basketball game	Ticket and concession revenue	Space, staff salaries, utilities	Clean-up costs, concession costs
6.	Break-even number of users on a computer network	Network user fees	Network depreciation, network maintenance, trunk line lease costs	User support, electricity

Activity 19–7

a. The following solution projects 2000 income. Your students will have different numbers.

Microsoft Corporation Project Template
(In millions, except earnings per share)

	Year Ended June 30			Projected Growth June 30	
	1997	1998	1999	2000	Change
Revenue....................................	$11,936	$15,262	$19,747	$22,117	12%
Operating expenses:					
Cost of revenue	2,170	2,460	2,814	3,096	10%
Research and development.........	1,863	2,601	2,970	3,297	11%
Acquired in-process technology.	—	296	—	—	—
Sales and marketing	2,411	2,828	3,231	3,554	10%
General and administrative	362	433	689	744	8%
Other expenses	259	230	115	100	(13)%
Total operating expenses........	7,065	8,848	9,819	10,791	10%
Operating income	4,871	6,414	9,928	11,325	14%
Investment income	443	703	1,803	2,000	11%
Gains on sales	—	—	160	156	
Income before income taxes............	5,314	7,117	11,891	13,481	13%
Provision for income taxes..............	1,860	2,627	4,106	4,044	(1)%
Net income	$ 3,454	$ 4,490	$ 7,785	$ 9,437	21%
Diluted earnings per share*	$0.66	$0.84	$1.42	$1.72	21%
Weighted average shares outstanding...................................	5,244	5,362	5,482	5,500	

*Restated to reflect a two-for-one stock split in March 1999

b. Using the data above, all of the major expenses changed less than did the sales. The sales grew by 12% from the prior year, while the cost of sales, research and development, sales and marketing, and general and administrative expenses all grew less than this amount. These costs may be behaving this way because they are mixed costs. Specifically, a portion of these costs may be fixed, while only a portion are variable to sales. Thus, the total costs don't change as much as the revenue. The taxes are expressed as a percentage of income before taxes and have obviously improved some since the previous year (according to the analysis above). The other items are related to investment assets (interest revenue) and outstanding debt (other expense, such as interest), so they are variable to balances that may not be related to sales. The net result is that the net income is projected, under these assumptions, to grow by 21% on a 12% increase in sales.

CHAPTER 20
BUDGETING

CLASS DISCUSSION QUESTIONS

1. The three major objectives of budgeting are (1) to establish specific goals for future operations, (2) to direct and coordinate plans to achieve the goals, and (3) to periodically compare actual results with the goals.

2. Managers are given authority and responsibility for responsibility center performance. They are then accountable for the performance of the responsibility center.

3. If goals set by the budgets are viewed as unrealistic or unachievable, management may become discouraged and may not be committed to the achievement of the goals, resulting in the budget becoming less effective as a planning and control tool.

4. Involving all levels of management and all departments in preparing and submitting budget estimates heightens awareness of each department's importance to company goals and to the control of operations. It also encourages cooperation both within and among departments.

5. Budgeting more resources for travel than requested by department personnel is an example of budgetary slack.

6. A budget that is set too loosely may fail to motivate managers and other employees to perform efficiently. In addition, a loose budget may cause a "spend it or lose it" mentality, where excess budget resources are spent in order to protect the budget from future reductions.

7. Conflicting goals can cause employees to act in their own self-interests to the detriment of the organization's objectives.

8. Zero-based budgeting is used when an organization wishes to take a "clean slate" view of operations. It is often used when the organization wants to cut costs by reevaluating the need for and usefulness of all operations.

9. A static budget is most appropriate in situations where costs are not variable to an underlying activity level. As a result, it is reasonable to plan spending on the basis of a fixed quantity of resources for the year. This will occur in some administrative functions, such as human resources, accounting, or public relations.

10. Computers not only speed up the budgeting process, but they also reduce the cost of budget preparation when large quantities of data need to be processed. In addition, by using computerized simulation models, management can determine the impact of various operating alternatives on the master budget.

11. The first step in preparing a master budget is estimating the sales levels of each product by regions or territories.

12. The production requirements must be carefully coordinated with the sales budget to ensure that production and sales are kept in balance during the period. Ideally, manufacturing operations should be maintained at 100% of capacity, with no idle time or overtime, and there should be neither excessive inventories nor inventories insufficient to fill sales orders.

13. Purchases of direct materials should be closely coordinated with the production budget so that inventory levels can be maintained within reasonable limits.

14. Direct materials purchases budget, direct labor cost budget, and factory overhead cost budget.

15. a. The cash budget contributes to effective cash planning. This involves advance planning so that a cash shortage does not arise and excess cash is not permitted to remain "idle."

    b. The excess cash can be invested in readily marketable income-producing securities or used to reduce loans.

16. The schedule of collections from sales is used to determine the amount of cash collected from current and prior period sales, based on collection history. The schedule is used to help determine the estimated cash receipts portion of the cash budget.

17. The plans for financing the capital expenditures budget may affect the cash budget.

EXERCISES

Ex. 20–1

a.

JENNIFER BELL
Cash Budget
For the Four Months Ending December 31, 2003

	September	October	November	December
Estimated cash receipts from:				
Part-time job	$ 900	$ 900	$ 900	$ 900
Deposit..................................				500
Total cash receipts	$ 900	$ 900	$ 900	$ 1,400
Estimated cash payments for:				
Season football tickets	$ 180			
Additional entertainment.....	250	$ 250	$ 250	$ 250
Tuition	4,000			
Rent.......................................	480	480	480	480
Food	320	320	320	320
Deposit..................................	500			
Total cash payments	$ 5,730	$1,050	$1,050	$ 1,050
Cash increase (decrease)	$(4,830)	$ (150)	$ (150)	$ 350
Cash balance at beginning				
of month..............................	5,000	170	20	(130)
Cash balance at end of month..	$ 170	$ 20	$ (130)	$ 220

b. The four-month budgets do not change with any identified activity level; thus, they are static budgets.

c. Jennifer Bell will run out of money in November because her checking account balance becomes negative. During a normal month, Bell pays $150 more in cash than she receives. The balance turns positive at the end of December, only because the deposit is returned in December. Thus, Bell will likely need to adjust the plan, especially considering the remaining months of the academic year. Some possibilities would be to rent a lower-cost apartment. At $330 rent per month, Bell would be able to maintain her end-of-September cash position through November. Other possibilities include lowering monthly entertainment expenses, increasing part-time hours worked to earn more per month, getting a roommate to share living expenses, or forgoing season tickets for football.

Ex. 20–2

MEDICO MEDICAL SUPPLY
Flexible Selling and Administrative Expenses Budget
For the Month Ending May 31, 2003

Total sales	$120,000	$160,000	$200,000
Variable cost:			
Sales commissions	$ 6,000	$ 8,000	$ 10,000
Advertising expense	14,400	19,200	24,000
Miscellaneous selling expense	3,600	4,800	6,000
Office supplies expense	2,400	3,200	4,000
Miscellaneous administrative expense	1,200	1,600	2,000
Total variable cost	$ 27,600	$ 36,800	$ 46,000
Fixed cost:			
Miscellaneous selling expense	$ 2,000	$ 2,000	$ 2,000
Office salaries expense	8,000	8,000	8,000
Miscellaneous administrative expense	500	500	500
Total fixed cost	$ 10,500	$ 10,500	$ 10,500
Total selling and administrative expenses	$ 38,100	$ 47,300	$ 56,500

Ex. 20–3

a.

NUNLY COMPANY—WELDING DEPARTMENT
Flexible Production Budget
For the Three Months Ending March 31, 2003

	January	February	March
Units of production.........................	45,000	40,000	35,000
Wages.................................	$405,000	$360,000	$315,000
Utilities..............................	90,000	80,000	70,000
Depreciation.............................	50,000	50,000	50,000
Total.....................................	$545,000	$490,000	$435,000

Supporting calculations:

	January	February	March
Units of production.........................	45,000	40,000	35,000
Hours per unit..............................	× 0.50	× 0.50	× 0.50
Total hours of production..............	22,500	20,000	17,500
Wages per hour	× $18.00	× $18.00	× $18.00
Total wages..................................	$405,000	$360,000	$315,000
Total hours of production..............	22,500	20,000	17,500
Utility cost per hour.......................	× $4.00	× $4.00	× $4.00
Total utilities	$ 90,000	$ 80,000	$ 70,000

Depreciation is a fixed cost, so it does not "flex" with changes in production. Since it is the only fixed cost, the variable and fixed costs are not classified in the budget.

b.

	January	February	March
Total flexible budget......................	$545,000	$490,000	$435,000
Actual cost....................................	560,000	520,000	500,000
Excess of actual cost over budget	$ (15,000)	$ (30,000)	$ (65,000)

The excess of actual cost over the flexible budget suggests that the Welding Department has not performed as well as originally thought. Indeed, the department is spending more than would be expected, and it's getting worse, given the level of production for the first three months.

Ex. 20–3   **Continued**

This solution is applicable only if the GENERAL LEDGER SOFTWARE that accompanies the text is used.

NUNLY COMPANY
Budget Report
For the Period Ended January 31, 2003

	Budget	Actual	Difference from Budget	%
Operating revenue:				
Operating revenue	675,000	652,000	(23,000)	(3.41)
Operating expenses:				
January wages	405,000	415,000	10,000	2.47
January utilities.....................	90,000	95,000	5,000	5.56
January depreciation	50,000	50,000		
February wages				
February utilities				
February depreciation				
March wages				
March utilities				
March depreciation				
Total operating expenses	545,000	560,000	15,000	2.75
Net income	130,000	92,000	(38,000)	(29.23)

Ex. 20–3   **Concluded**

NUNLY COMPANY
Budget Report
For the Period Ended February 28, 2003

	Budget	Actual	Difference from Budget	%
Operating revenue:				
Operating revenue	650,000	610,000	(40,000)	(6.15)
Operating expenses:				
January wages				
January utilities				
January depreciation				
February wages....................	360,000	389,000	29,000	8.06
February utilities	80,000	81,000	1,000	1.25
February depreciation	50,000	50,000		
March wages				
March utilities				
March depreciation				
Total operating expenses	490,000	520,000	30,000	6.12
Net income	160,000	90,000	(70,000)	(43.75)

NUNLY COMPANY
Budget Report
For the Period Ended March 31, 2003

	Budget	Actual	Difference from Budget	%
Operating revenue:				
Operating revenue	625,000	582,000	(43,000)	(6.88)
Operating expenses:				
January wages				
January utilities				
January depreciation				
February wages				
February utilities				
February depreciation				
March wages..........................	315,000	395,000	80,000	25.40
March utilities	70,000	55,000	(15,000)	(21.43)
March depreciation	50,000	50,000		
Total operating expenses	435,000	500,000	65,000	14.94
Net income	190,000	82,000	(108,000)	(56.84)

Ex. 20–4

STEELCASE CORPORATION
Fabrication Department
May 2003
(assumed data)

Units of production	10,000	11,000	12,000
Variable cost:			
Direct labor	$ 84,000[1]	$ 92,400[2]	$100,800[3]
Direct materials	490,000[4]	539,000[5]	588,000[6]
Total variable cost	$574,000	$631,400	$688,800
Fixed cost:			
Supervisor salaries	$ 12,000	$ 12,000	$ 12,000
Depreciation	2,500	2,500	2,500
Total fixed cost	$ 14,500	$ 14,500	$ 14,500
Total department cost	$588,500	$645,900	$703,300

[1] 10,000 × 36/60 × $14
[2] 11,000 × 36/60 × $14
[3] 12,000 × 36/60 × $14
[4] 10,000 × 35 × $1.40
[5] 11,000 × 35 × $1.40
[6] 12,000 × 35 × $1.40

Ex. 20–5

a.

GRAND ELECTRONICS COMPANY
Sales Budget
For the Month Ending September 30, 2004

Product and Area	Unit Sales Volume	Unit Selling Price	Total Sales
Model CR1:			
East Region	4,700	$65	$305,500
West Region	3,400	65	221,000
Total	8,100		$526,500
Model CR2:			
East Region	3,200	$80	$256,000
West Region	2,400	80	192,000
Total	5,600		$448,000
Total revenue from sales			$974,500

b.

GRAND ELECTRONICS COMPANY
Production Budget
For the Month Ending September 30, 2004

	Units	
	Model CR1	Model CR2
Expected units to be sold	8,100	5,600
Plus desired inventory, September 30, 2004......................	410	100
Total..	8,510	5,700
Less estimated inventory, September 1, 2004...................	350	120
Total units to be produced..	8,160	5,580

Ex. 20–6

GARCIA AND BERRY, CPAs
Professional Fees Budget
For the Year Ending December 31, 2003

	Billable Hours	Hourly Rate	Total Revenue
Audit Department:			
Staff	36,000	$ 90	$ 3,240,000
Partners...................................	5,200	$225	1,170,000
Total	41,200		$ 4,410,000
Tax Department:			
Staff	30,600	$ 90	$ 2,754,000
Partners...................................	4,100	$225	922,500
Total	34,700		$ 3,676,500
Computer Consulting Department:			
Staff	40,200	$ 90	$ 3,618,000
Partners...................................	15,800	$225	3,555,000
Total	56,000		$ 7,173,000
Total professional fees			$ 15,259,500

Ex. 20–7

GARCIA AND BERRY, CPAs
Professional Labor Cost Budget
For the Year Ending December 31, 2003

	Billable Hours Required	
	Staff	Partners
Audit Department	36,000	5,200
Tax Department	30,600	4,100
Computer Consulting Department	40,200	15,800
Total..	106,800	25,100
Average compensation per hour............................	× $40.00	× $120.00
Total labor cost...	$4,272,000	$3,012,000

Ex. 20–8

MAMA LEONA'S FROZEN PIZZA INC.
Direct Materials Purchases Budget
For the Month Ending August 31, 2003

	Dough	Tomato	Cheese	Total
Units required for production:				
12" pizza...............................	28,500[1]	14,250[2]	19,950[3]	
16" pizza...............................	62,700[4]	33,440[5]	45,980[6]	
Plus desired inventory,				
August 31, 2003....................	450	240	350	
Total...	91,650	47,930	66,280	
Less estimated inventory,				
August 1, 2003......................	500	200	450	
Total units to be purchased......	91,150	47,730	65,830	
Unit price....................................	× $1.30	× $2.10	× $2.40	
Total direct materials to be				
purchased............................	$118,495	$100,233	$157,992	$376,720

[1] 28,500 × 1 lb.
[2] 28,500 × 0.50 lb.
[3] 28,500 × 0.70 lb.
[4] 41,800 × 1.50 lbs.
[5] 41,800 × 0.80 lb.
[6] 41,800 × 1.10 lbs.

Ex. 20–9

COCA-COLA ENTERPRISES—CHATTANOOGA PLANT
Direct Materials Purchases Budget
For the Month Ending September 30, 2003
(assumed data)

	Concentrate	2-Liter Bottles	Carbonated Water
Materials required for production:			
Coke	620* pounds	155,000 bottles	310,000 liters
Sprite	378*	126,000	252,000
Total materials	998 pounds	281,000 bottles	562,000 liters
Direct material unit price	× $90	× $0.09	× $0.04
Total direct materials to be purchased	$89,820	$25,290	$22,480

	Coke	Sprite
*Production in liters (bottles × 2)	310,000	252,000
Divide by 100	÷ 100	÷ 100
	3,100	2,520
Multiple by concentrate pounds per 100 liters	× 0.20	× 0.15
Concentrate pounds required for production........	620	378

Ex. 20–10

SUREGRIP TIRE COMPANY
Direct Materials Purchases Budget
For the Year Ending December 31, 2003

	Rubber	Steel Belts	Total
Pounds required for production:			
Passenger tires[1]	800,000 lbs.	96,000 lbs.	
Truck tires[2]...	720,000	96,000	
Plus desired inventory, Dec. 31, 2003 ...	40,000	6,000	
Total...	1,560,000 lbs.	198,000 lbs.	
Less estimated inventory, Jan. 1, 2003 .	70,000	5,000	
Total units purchased	1,490,000 lbs.	193,000 lbs.	
Unit price..	× $2.00	× $3.20	
Total direct materials to be purchased..	$2,980,000	$617,600	$3,597,600

[1] Rubber: 32,000 units × 25 lbs. per unit = 800,000 lbs.
Steel belts: 32,000 units × 3 lbs. per unit = 96,000 lbs.

[2] Rubber: 12,000 units × 60 lbs. per unit = 720,000 lbs.
Steel belts: 12,000 units × 8 lbs. per unit = 96,000 lbs.

Errors:

1. The sales should be adjusted by the desired ending inventory in the finished goods in order to determine the number of units to be produced (32,000 for passenger tires and 12,000 for truck tires). The desired ending inventory should be added to the sales figures to determine the current period production requirements.

2. The materials used to satisfy current period production should be adjusted by the estimated beginning materials inventory and desired ending materials inventory to determine materials to be purchased.

ACE RACKET COMPANY
Direct Labor Cost Budget
For the Month Ending August 31, 2003

	Molding Department	Finishing Department
ours required for production:		
Junior[1]	860	1,290
Pro-Striker[2]	4,380	7,300
Total	5,240	8,590
ourly rate	× $15.00	× $18.00
otal direct labor cost	$ 78,600	$ 154,620

Junior: 0.20 hour × 4,300 = 860 hours
0.30 hour × 4,300 = 1,290 hours

Pro-Striker: 0.30 hour × 14,600 = 4,380 hours
0.50 hour × 14,600 = 7,300 hours

Ex. 20–12

a.

Levi Strauss & Co.
Production Budget
March 2003
(assumed data)

	Dockers®	501 Jeans®
Expected units to be sold	25,400	49,600
Plus: March 31 desired inventory	250	100
Less: March 1 estimated inventory................	300	140
Total units to be produced............................	25,350	49,560

b.

Levi Strauss & Co.
Direct Labor Cost Budget
March 2003
(assumed data)

	Inseam	Outerseam	Pockets	Zipper
Dockers®...........................	38,025*	50,700*	12,675*	15,210*
501 Jeans®........................	59,472**	69,384**	39,648**	29,736**
Total minutes	97,497	120,084	52,323	44,946
Total direct labor hours (÷ 60 minutes)	1,624.95	2,001.40	872.05	749.10
× Direct labor rate..............	× $9.00	× $9.00	× $10.00	× $10.00
Total direct labor cost.......	$ 14,624.55	$ 18,012.60	$ 8,720.50	$7,491.00

* (25,350/10 pairs) × 15 min. = 38,025 minutes
 (25,350/10 pairs) × 20 min. = 50,700 minutes
 (25,350/10 pairs) × 5 min. = 12,675 minutes
 (25,350/10 pairs) × 6 min. = 15,210 minutes

** (49,560/10 pairs) × 12 min. = 59,472 minutes
 (49,560/10 pairs) × 14 min. = 69,384 minutes
 (49,560/10 pairs) × 8 min. = 39,648 minutes
 (49,560/10 pairs) × 6 min. = 29,736 minutes

Ex. 20–13

HANS WATCH COMPANY
Factory Overhead Cost Budget
For the Month Ending January 31, 2003

Variable factory overhead costs:		
Manufacturing supplies	$ 12,000	
Power and light..	45,000	
Supervisor wages...	123,000	
Production control salaries	32,000	
Materials management salaries	25,000	
Total variable factory overhead costs		$237,000
Fixed factory overhead costs:		
Factory insurance...	$ 20,000	
Factory depreciation	19,000	
Total fixed factory overhead costs........................		39,000
Total factory overhead costs...		$276,000

Note: Advertising expenses, sales commissions, and executive officer salaries are selling and administrative expenses.

Ex. 20–14

MODEL CERAMIC COMPANY
Cost of Goods Sold Budget
For the Month Ending June 30, 2003

Finished goods inventory, June 1, 2003.............			$ 10,030
Work in process inventory, June 1, 2003		$ 2,900	
Direct materials:			
Direct materials inventory, June 1, 2003.......	$ 8,190		
Direct materials purchases	130,320		
Cost of direct materials available for use	$138,510		
Less direct materials inventory,			
June 30, 2003	9,150		
Cost of direct materials placed in			
production	$129,360		
Direct labor..	142,300		
Factory overhead..	69,100		
Total manufacturing costs.....................................		340,760	
Total work in process during the period		$343,660	
Less work in process inventory, June 30, 2003.		1,350	
Cost of goods manufactured................................			342,310
Cost of finished goods available for sale...........			$352,340
Less finished goods inventory, June 30, 2003 ..			10,290
Cost of goods sold			$342,050

TREVOR COMPANY
Schedule of Collections from Sales
For the Three Months Ending May 31, 2003

	March	April	May
Receipts from cash sales:			
Cash sales (10% × current month's sales)	$ 48,000	$ 59,000	$ 50,500
March sales on account:			
Collected in March ($432,000[1] × 60%).......	259,200		
Collected in April ($432,000 × 30%)		129,600	
Collected in May ($432,000 × 10%)			43,200
April sales on account:			
Collected in April ($531,000[2] × 60%).........		318,600	
Collected in May ($531,000 × 30%)			159,300
May sales on account:			
Collected in May ($454,500[3] × 60%)			272,700
Total cash collected	**$307,200**	**$507,200**	**$525,700**

[1] $480,000 × 90% = $432,000
[2] $590,000 × 90% = $531,000
[3] $505,000 × 90% = $454,500

Ex. 20–16

TUTOR.COM INC.
Schedule of Cash Payments for Selling and Administrative Expenses
For the Three Months Ending August 31, 2003

	June	July	August
June expenses:			
Paid in June ($83,400[1] × 75%)	$62,550		
Paid in July ($83,400 × 25%)......................		$ 20,850	
July expenses:			
Paid in July ($114,800[2] × 75%)		86,100	
Paid in August ($114,800 × 25%)			$ 28,700
August expenses:			
Paid in August ($144,300[3] × 75%)			108,225
Total cash payments	$62,550	$106,950	$136,925

[1] $95,400 – $12,000
[2] $126,800 – $12,000
[3] $156,300 – $12,000

Note: Insurance, property taxes, and depreciation are expenses that do not result in cash payments in June, July, or August.

Ex. 20–17

THE SEA BREEZE HOTEL
Schedule of Cash Payments for Operations
For the Three Months Ending December 31, 2004

	October	November	December
Payments of prior month's expense[1]	$18,400	$ 27,330	$ 33,330
Payment of current month's expense[2]	63,770	77,770	90,650
Total payment	$82,170	$105,100	$123,980

[1] $18,400, given as Accrued Expenses Payable, October 1.
$27,330 = ($105,600 − $14,500) × 30%
$33,330 = ($125,600 − $14,500) × 30%

[2] $63,770 = ($105,600 − $14,500) × 70%
$77,770 = ($125,600 − $14,500) × 70%
$90,650 = ($144,000 − $14,500) × 70%

Note: Insurance and depreciation are expenses that do not result in cash payments in October, November, and December.

Ex. 20–18

MINTER MANUFACTURING COMPANY
Capital Expenditures Budget
For the Four Years Ending December 31, 2002–2005

	2002	2003	2004	2005
Building	$6,000,000	$4,000,000		$4,000,000[1]
Equipment		1,600,000	$ 300,000	1,000,000
Information systems			1,152,000[2]	
Total	$6,000,000	$5,600,000	$ 1,452,000	$5,000,000

[1] $10,000,000 × 0.40 = $4,000,000
[2] $1,800,000 × 0.80 × 0.80 = $1,152,000

PROBLEMS

Prob. 20–1A

1.

| | Unit Sales, Year Ended 2003 | | Increase (Decrease) Actual Over Budget | |
	Budget	Actual Sales	Amount	Percent
8" × 10" Frame:				
East..................................	25,000	26,125	1,125	4.50 %
Central.............................	32,000	32,640	640	2.00 %
West.................................	12,000	11,448	(552)	(4.60)%
12" × 16" Frame:				
East..................................	20,000	20,600	600	3.00 %
Central.............................	25,000	26,375	1,375	5.50 %
West.................................	10,000	9,500	(500)	(5.00)%

2.

	2003 Actual Units	Percentage Increase (Decrease)	2004 Budgeted Units
8" × 10" Frame:			
East..	26,125	4.5 %	27,000
Central......................................	32,640	2.0 %	33,000
West..	11,448	(4.6)%	11,000
12" × 16" Frame:			
East..	20,600	3.0 %	21,000
Central......................................	26,375	5.5 %	28,000
West..	9,500	(5.0)%	9,000

3.

RENOIR FRAME COMPANY
Sales Budget
For the Year Ending December 31, 2004

Product and Area	Unit Sales Volume	Unit Selling Price	Total Sales
8" × 10" Frame:			
East..	27,000	$ 9.00	$ 243,000
Central......................................	33,000	9.00	297,000
West..	11,000	9.00	99,000
Total	71,000		$ 639,000
12" × 16" Frame:			
East..	21,000	$13.00	$ 273,000
Central......................................	28,000	13.00	364,000
West..	9,000	13.00	117,000
Total	58,000		$ 754,000
Total revenue from sales			$1,393,000

Prob. 20–2A

1.

SUMMERTIME GRILL COMPANY
Sales Budget
For the Month Ending May 31, 2003

Product and Area	Unit Sales Volume	Unit Selling Price	Total Sales
Backyard Chef:			
Maine	3,500	$ 550	$ 1,925,000
Vermont...	2,800	500	1,400,000
New Hampshire	4,000	600	2,400,000
Total	10,300		$ 5,725,000
Master Chef:			
Maine	1,800	$1,300	$ 2,340,000
Vermont...	1,500	1,200	1,800,000
New Hampshire	2,900	1,500	4,350,000
Total	6,200		$ 8,490,000
Total revenue from sales			$14,215,000

2.

SUMMERTIME GRILL COMPANY
Production Budget
For the Month Ending May 31, 2003

	Units	
	Backyard Chef	Master Chef
Expected units to be sold	10,300	6,200
Plus desired inventory, May 31, 2003	1,200	500
Total..	11,500	6,700
Less estimated inventory, May 1, 2003	1,500	400
Total units to be produced..	10,000	6,300

3.

SUMMERTIME GRILL COMPANY
Direct Materials Purchases Budget
For the Month Ending May 31, 2003

	Direct Materials				
	Grates (units)	Stainless Steel (lbs.)	Burner Sub-assemblies (units)	Shelves (units)	Total
Required units for production:					
Backyard Chef.........	20,000[1]	250,000[2]	10,000[3]	20,000[4]	
Master Chef	37,800[5]	409,500[6]	25,200[7]	18,900[8]	
Plus desired inventory,					
May 31, 2003............	800	1,900	800	480	
Total.............................	58,600	661,400	36,000	39,380	
Less estimated inventory,					
May 1, 2003..............	1,000	2,500	600	400	
Total units to be					
purchased................	57,600	658,900	35,400	38,980	
Unit price.......................	× $15.00	× $3.00	× $72.00	× $7.00	
Total direct materials					
to be purchased	$864,000	$1,976,700	$2,548,800	$272,860	$5,662,360

[1] 10,000 × 2 grates = 20,000 grates

[2] 10,000 × 25 lbs. = 250,000 lbs.

[3] 10,000 × 1 subassembly = 10,000 subassemblies

[4] 10,000 × 2 shelves = 20,000 shelves

[5] 6,300 × 6 grates = 37,800 grates

[6] 6,300 × 65 lbs. = 409,500 lbs.

[7] 6,300 × 4 subassemblies = 25,200 subassemblies

[8] 6,300 × 3 shelves = 18,900 shelves

Prob. 20–2A   Concluded

4.

SUMMERTIME GRILL COMPANY
Direct Labor Cost Budget
For the Month Ending May 31, 2003

	Stamping Department	Forming Department	Assembly Department	Total
Hours required for production:				
Backyard Chef[1]	5,000	7,500	15,000	
Master Chef[2]	3,780	9,450	15,750	
Total	8,780	16,950	30,750	
Hourly rate..................................	× $12.00	× $10.00	× $9.00	
Total direct labor cost..............	$105,360	$169,500	$276,750	$551,610

[1] This line is calculated as 10,000 Backyard Chef units from the production budget multiplied by the hours per unit in each department estimated for the Backyard Chef. 5,000 = 10,000 × 0.50; 7,500 = 10,000 × 0.75; 15,000 = 10,000 × 1.50

[2] This line is calculated as 6,300 Master Chef units from the production budget multiplied by the hours per unit in each department estimated for the Master Chef. 3,780 = 6,300 × 0.60; 9,450 = 6,300 × 1.50; 15,750 = 6,300 × 2.50

Prob. 20–3A

1.

INSTANT MEMORIES FILM COMPANY
Sales Budget
For the Month Ending October 31, 2003

	Unit Sales Volume	Unit Sales Price	Total Sales
Instant Image	26,800	$65.00	$1,742,000
Pro Image	20,400	90.00	1,836,000
Total revenue from sales			$3,578,000

2.

INSTANT MEMORIES FILM COMPANY
Production Budget
For the Month Ending October 31, 2003

	Units	
	Instant Image	Pro Image
Expected units to be sold	26,800	20,400
Plus desired inventory, October 31, 2003	5,400	1,900
Total	32,200	22,300
Less estimated inventory, October 1, 2003......................	4,800	2,400
Total units to be produced.......................................	27,400	19,900

3.

INSTANT MEMORIES FILM COMPANY
Direct Materials Purchases Budget
For the Month Ending October 31, 2003

	Celluloid	Silver	Total
Units required for production:			
Instant Image	10,960[1]	68,500[2]	
Pro Image..	11,940[3]	79,600[4]	
Plus desired units of inventory,			
October 31, 2003	3,400	2,900	
Total...	26,300	151,000	
Less estimated units of inventory,			
October 1, 2003	2,700	3,000	
Total units to be purchased................	23,600	148,000	
Unit price..	× $1.50	× $6.00	
Total direct materials to be			
purchased......................................	$ 35,400	$888,000	$923,400

[1] 27,400 × 0.40 lb.   [2] 27,400 × 2.50 ozs.   [3] 19,900 × 0.60 lb.   [4] 19,900 × 4.00 ozs.

Prob. 20–3A   **Continued**

4.

INSTANT MEMORIES FILM COMPANY
Direct Labor Cost Budget
For the Month Ending October 31, 2003

	Coating Department	Slitting Department	Total
Hours required for production:			
Instant Image	5,480[1]	6,850[2]	
Pro Image..	7,960[3]	5,970[4]	
Total	13,440	12,820	
Hourly rate..	× $14.00	× $16.00	
Total direct labor cost..........................	$188,160	$205,120	$393,280

[1] 27,400 × 0.20 hour
[2] 27,400 × 0.25 hour
[3] 19,900 × 0.40 hour
[4] 19,900 × 0.30 hour

5.

INSTANT MEMORIES FILM COMPANY
Factory Overhead Cost Budget
For the Month Ending October 31, 2003

Indirect factory wages...	$525,000
Depreciation of plant and equipment	145,000
Power and light..	46,000
Insurance and property tax	18,400
Total..	$734,400

6.

INSTANT MEMORIES FILM COMPANY
Cost of Goods Sold Budget
For the Month Ending October 31, 2003

Finished goods inventory, October 1, 2003 ..			$ 300,000[1]
Work in process, October 1, 2003		$ 28,500	
Direct materials:			
Direct materials inventory, October 1, 2003	$ 22,050[2]		
Direct materials purchases	923,400		
Cost of direct materials available for use	$945,450		
Less direct materials inventory, October 31, 2003	22,500[3]		
Cost of direct materials placed in production	$922,950		
Direct labor...	393,280		
Factory overhead..	734,400		
Total manufacturing costs............................		2,050,630	
Total work in process during period..............		$2,079,130	
Less work in process, October 31, 2003		34,200	
Cost of goods manufactured.........................			2,044,930
Cost of finished goods available for sale......			$ 2,344,930
Less finished goods inventory, October 31, 2003			293,500[4]
Cost of goods sold			$ 2,051,430

[1] Instant Image (4,800 × $35)	$	168,000
Pro Image (2,400 × $55)..		132,000
Total	$	300,000
[2] Celluloid (2,700 × $1.50)..	$	4,050
Silver (3,000 × $6.00)		18,000
Total	$	22,050
[3] Celluloid (3,400 × $1.50)..	$	5,100
Silver (2,900 × $6.00)		17,400
Total	$	22,500
[4] Instant Image (5,400 × $35)	$	189,000
Pro Image (1,900 × $55)..		104,500
Total	$	293,500

Prob. 20–3A   Concluded

7.

INSTANT MEMORIES FILM COMPANY
Selling and Administrative Expenses Budget
For the Month Ending October 31, 2003

Selling expenses:		
Sales salaries expense	$225,000	
Advertising expense	146,500	
Telephone expense—selling	5,000	
Travel expense—selling	38,500	
Total selling expenses		$415,000
Administrative expenses:		
Office salaries expense	$120,800	
Depreciation expense—office equipment	5,300	
Telephone expense—administrative	1,900	
Office supplies expense	3,000	
Miscellaneous administrative expense	4,200	
Total administrative expenses		135,200
Total operating expenses		$550,200

8.

INSTANT MEMORIES FILM COMPANY
Budgeted Income Statement
For the Month Ending October 31, 2003

Revenue from sales		$3,578,000
Cost of goods sold		2,051,430
Gross profit		$1,526,570
Operating expenses:		
Selling expenses	$415,000	
Administrative expenses	135,200	
Total operating expenses		550,200
Income from operations		$ 976,370
Other income:		
Interest revenue	$ 16,700	
Other expenses:		
Interest expense	12,300	4,400
Income before income tax		$ 980,770
Income tax expense		392,308
Net income		$ 588,462

Prob. 20–4A

1.

BUTLER BOAT COMPANY
Cash Budget
For the Three Months Ending October 31, 2003

	August	September	October
Estimated cash receipts from:			
Cash sales	$ 59,000	$ 65,000	$ 75,000
Collection of accounts receivable[1]	417,200	495,400	563,400
Dividends	1,500		
Total cash receipts	$477,700	$560,400	$ 638,400
Estimated cash payments for:			
Manufacturing costs[2]	$276,000	$302,000	$ 350,000
Selling and administrative expenses .	150,000	170,000	200,000
Capital expenditures			120,000
Other purposes:			
Note payable (including interest) ..			102,500
Income tax		42,000	
Dividends			15,000
Total cash payments	$426,000	$514,000	$ 787,500
Cash increase or (decrease)	$ 51,700	$ 46,400	$ (149,100)
Cash balance at beginning of month	55,000	106,700	153,100
Cash balance at end of month	$106,700	$153,100	$ 4,000
Minimum cash balance	45,000	45,000	45,000
Excess or (deficiency)	$ 61,700	$108,100	$ (41,000)

Computations:

[1] Collections of accounts receivable:	August	September	October
June sales	$152,000		
July sales	265,200*	$176,800**	
August sales		318,600	$ 212,400
September sales			351,000
Total	$417,200	$495,400	$ 563,400

*$442,000 × 60% = $265,200
**$442,000 × 40% = $176,800

[2] Payments for manufacturing costs:			
Payment of accounts payable, beginning of month balance	$ 60,000	$ 54,000**	$ 62,000
Payment of current month's cost	216,000*	248,000	288,000
Total	$276,000	$302,000	$ 350,000

*($300,000 – $30,000) × 80% = $216,000
**($300,000 – $30,000) × 20% = $54,000

Prob. 20–4A   Concluded

2. The budget indicates that the minimum cash balance will not be maintained in October. This is due to the capital expenditures and note repayment requiring significant cash outflows during this month. This situation can be corrected by borrowing and/or by the sale of the marketable securities, if they are held for such purposes. At the end of August and September, the cash balance will exceed the minimum desired balance, and the excess could be considered for temporary investment.

Prob. 20–5A

1.

LITTLE SUZIE CAKE COMPANY
Budgeted Income Statement
For the Year Ending December 31, 2004

Sales			$ 1,050,000[1]
Cost of goods sold:			
Direct materials		$300,000[2]	
Direct labor		112,500[3]	
Factory overhead		92,000[4]	
Cost of goods sold			504,500
Gross profit			$ 545,500
Operating expenses:			
Selling expenses:			
Sales salaries and commissions	$120,000[5]		
Advertising	60,000		
Miscellaneous selling expense	29,300[6]		
Total selling expenses		$209,300	
Administrative expenses:			
Office and officers salaries	$102,600[7]		
Supplies	16,500[8]		
Miscellaneous administrative expense	20,500[9]		
Total administrative expenses		139,600	
Total operating expenses			348,900
Income before income tax			$ 196,600
Income tax expense			65,000
Net income			$ 131,600

[1] 250,000 units × $4.20
[2] 250,000 units × $1.20
[3] 250,000 units × $0.45
[4] (250,000 units × $0.28) + $14,000 + $8,000
[5] (250,000 units × $0.30) + $45,000
[6] (250,000 units × $0.10) + $4,300
[7] (250,000 units × $0.15) + $65,100
[8] (250,000 units × $0.05) + $4,000
[9] (250,000 units × $0.07) + $3,000

2.

LITTLE SUZIE CAKE COMPANY
Budgeted Balance Sheet
December 31, 2004

Assets

Current assets:

Cash		$140,600[1]	
Accounts receivable		104,700	
Inventories:			
Finished goods	$74,800		
Work in process.............................	25,600		
Materials	46,700	147,100	
Prepaid expenses.................................		2,400	
Total current assets........................			$ 394,800
Property, plant, and equipment:			
Plant and equipment.............................		$390,000	
Less accumulated depreciation...............		149,200	240,800
Total assets...			$ 635,600

Liabilities

Current liabilities:

Accounts payable		$ 59,000

Stockholders' Equity

Common stock.......................................	$200,000	
Retained earnings	376,600[2]	
Total stockholders' equity.......................		576,600
Total liabilities and stockholders' equity.......		$635,600

[1] Cash balance, December 31, 2004:

Balance, January 1, 2004..		$ 85,000
Cash from operations:		
Net income	$131,600	
Depreciation of plant and equipment........................	14,000	145,600
Less: Dividends to be paid 2004	$ 40,000	
Plant and equipment to be acquired in 2004 ...	50,000	(90,000)
Balance, December 31, 2004		$140,600

[2] Retained earnings balance, December 31, 2004:

Balance, January 1, 2004..	$285,000
Plus net income for 2004	131,600
	$416,600
Less dividends to be declared in 2004.............................	40,000
Balance, December 31, 2004	$376,600

Prob. 20–1B

1.

	Unit Sales, Year Ended 2003		Increase (Decrease) Actual Over Budget	
	Budget	Actual Sales	Amount	Percent
Home Alert System:				
United States	18,500	19,055	555	3.00 %
Europe.............................	5,400	5,022	(378)	(7.00)%
Asia..................................	3,700	3,885	185	5.00 %
Business Alert System:				
United States	10,500	10,752	252	2.40 %
Europe.............................	8,600	8,987	387	4.50 %
Asia..................................	4,200	4,011	(189)	(4.50)%

2.

	2003 Actual Units	Percentage Increase (Decrease)	2004 Budgeted Units
Home Alert System:			
United States	19,055	3.00 %	20,000
Europe...	5,022	(7.00)%	5,000
Asia...	3,885	5.00 %	4,000
Business Alert System:			
United States	10,752	2.40 %	11,000
Europe...	8,987	4.50 %	9,000
Asia...	4,011	(4.50)%	4,000

Prob. 20–1B   Concluded

3.

HOME GUARD SECURITY DEVICES INC.
Sales Budget
For the Year Ending December 31, 2004

Product and Area	Unit Sales Volume	Unit Selling Price	Total Sales
Home Alert System:			
United States	20,000	$280	$ 5,600,000
Europe..	5,000	280	1,400,000
Asia...	4,000	280	1,120,000
Total	29,000		$ 8,120,000
Business Alert System:			
United States	11,000	$870	$ 9,570,000
Europe..	9,000	870	7,830,000
Asia...	4,000	870	3,480,000
Total	24,000		$20,880,000
Total revenue from sales			$29,000,000

Prob. 20–2B

1.

DALEN FURNITURE COMPANY
Sales Budget
For the Month Ending July 31, 2003

Product and Area	Unit Sales Volume	Unit Selling Price	Total Sales
King:			
Northern Domestic...........................	7,300	$450	$ 3,285,000
Southern Domestic	6,400	430	2,752,000
International....................................	1,500	500	750,000
Total	15,200		$ 6,787,000
Prince:			
Northern Domestic...........................	5,250	$310	$ 1,627,500
Southern Domestic	5,100	300	1,530,000
International....................................	900	350	315,000
Total	11,250		$ 3,472,500
Total revenue from sales			$10,259,500

2.

DALEN FURNITURE COMPANY
Production Budget
For the Month Ending July 31, 2003

	Units	
	King	Prince
Expected units to be sold	15,200	11,250
Plus desired inventory, July 31, 2003................................	700	300
Total...	15,900	11,550
Less estimated inventory, July 1, 2003	840	280
Total units to be produced...	15,060	11,270

Prob. 20–2B   Continued

3.

DALEN FURNITURE COMPANY
Direct Materials Purchases Budget
For the Month Ending July 31, 2003

	Direct Materials				
	Fabric (sq. yds.)	Wood (lineal ft.)	Filler (cu. ft.)	Springs (units)	Total
Required units for production:					
King.................................	60,240[1]	451,800[2]	52,710[3]	180,720[4]	
Prince..............................	36,064[5]	225,400[6]	33,810[7]	112,700[8]	
Plus desired inventory,					
July 31, 2003....................	4,500	5,700	2,700	7,000	
Total.......................................	100,804	682,900	89,220	300,420	
Less estimated inventory,					
July 1, 2003......................	4,300	6,300	2,500	7,500	
Total units to be purchased..	96,504	676,600	86,720	292,920	
Unit price..............................	× $7.00	× $2.50	× $3.00	× $2.00	
Total direct materials					
to be purchased...............	$675,528	$1,691,500	$260,160	$585,840	$3,213,028

[1] 15,060 × 4 sq. yds. = 60,240 sq. yds.

[2] 15,060 × 30 lineal ft. = 451,800 lineal ft.

[3] 15,060 × 3.5 cu. ft. = 52,710 cu. ft.

[4] 15,060 × 12 springs = 180,720 springs

[5] 11,270 × 3.2 sq. yds. = 36,064 sq. yds.

[6] 11,270 × 20 lineal ft. = 225,400 lineal ft.

[7] 11,270 × 3.0 cu. ft. = 33,810 cu. ft.

[8] 11,270 × 10 springs = 112,700 springs

4.

DALEN FURNITURE COMPANY
Direct Labor Cost Budget
For the Month Ending July 31, 2003

	Framing Department	Cutting Department	Upholstery Department	Total
Hours required for production:				
King[1]	30,120	7,530	37,650	
Prince[2]	16,905	4,508	20,286	
Total.....................................	47,025	12,038	57,936	
Hourly rate...............................	× $10.00	× $12.00	× $15.00	
Total direct labor cost..............	$470,250	$144,456	$869,040	$1,483,746

[1] This line is calculated as 15,060 King units from the production budget multiplied by the hours per unit in each department estimated for the King chairs. $30,120 = 15,060 × 2.0$; $7,530 = 15,060 × 0.5$; $37,650 = 15,060 × 2.5$

[2] This line is calculated as 11,270 Prince units from the production budget multiplied by the hours per unit in each department estimated for the Prince chairs. $16,905 = 11,270 × 1.50$; $4,508 = 11,270 × 0.4$; $20,286 = 11,270 × 1.8$

Prob. 20–3B

1.

SAFETY SPORTS INC.
Sales Budget
For the Month Ending August 31, 2003

	Unit Sales Volume	Unit Sales Price	Total Sales
Batting helmet..	25,800	$40.00	$1,032,000
Football helmet...	54,100	75.00	4,057,500
Total revenue from sales			$5,089,500

2.

SAFETY SPORTS INC.
Production Budget
For the Month Ending August 31, 2003

	Units	
	Batting Helmet	Football Helmet
Expected units to be sold	25,800	54,100
Plus desired inventory, August 31, 2003............................	2,400	3,500
Total...	28,200	57,600
Less estimated inventory, August 1, 2003	2,450	3,900
Total units to be produced...	25,750	53,700

3.

SAFETY SPORTS INC.
Direct Materials Purchases Budget
For the Month Ending August 31, 2003

	Plastic	Foam Lining	Total
Units required for production:			
Batting helmet	36,050[1]	15,450[2]	
Football helmet......................................	171,840[3]	64,440[4]	
Plus desired units of inventory,			
August 31, 2003....................................	11,400	4,500	
Total...	219,290	84,390	
Less estimated units of inventory,			
August 1, 2003.....................................	9,500	4,700	
Total units to be purchased......................................	209,790	79,690	
Unit price...	× $6.50	× $3.00	
Total direct materials to be purchased....	$1,363,635	$239,070	$1,602,705

[1] 25,750 × 1.4 lbs.   [2] 25,750 × 0.60 lb.   [3] 53,700 × 3.20 lbs.   [4] 53,700 × 1.20 lb.

Prob. 20–3B   **Continued**

4.

SAFETY SPORTS INC.
Direct Labor Cost Budget
For the Month Ending August 31, 2003

	Molding Dept.	Assembly Dept.	Total
Hours required for production:			
Batting helmet	4,120[1]	10,300[2]	
Football helmet	13,425[3]	32,220[4]	
Total	17,545	42,520	
Hourly rate	× $14	× $12	
Total direct labor cost	$245,630	$510,240	$755,870

[1] 25,750 × 0.16 hour
[2] 25,750 × 0.40 hour
[3] 53,700 × 0.25 hour
[4] 53,700 × 0.60 hour

5.

SAFETY SPORTS INC.
Factory Overhead Cost Budget
For the Month Ending August 31, 2003

Indirect factory wages	$250,000
Depreciation of plant and equipment	63,000
Power and light	24,000
Insurance and property tax	9,700
Total	$346,700

6.
SAFETY SPORTS INC.
Cost of Goods Sold Budget
For the Month Ending August 31, 2003

Finished goods inventory, August 1, 2003....			$ 207,450[a]
Work in process, August 1, 2003		$ 43,600	
Direct materials:			
Direct materials inventory, August 1, 2003	$ 75,850[b]		
Direct materials purchases...........................	1,602,705		
Cost of direct materials available for use...	$ 1,678,555		
Less direct materials inventory,			
August 31, 2003	87,600[c]		
Cost of direct materials placed in production	$ 1,590,955		
Direct labor...	755,870		
Factory overhead...	346,700		
Total manufacturing costs.............................		2,693,525	
Total work in process during period..............		$ 2,737,125	
Less work in process, August 31, 2003.........		37,800	
Cost of goods manufactured..........................			2,699,325
Cost of finished goods available for sale......			$ 2,906,775
Less finished goods inventory,			
August 31, 2003			190,400[d]
Cost of goods sold			$ 2,716,375

[a] Batting helmet (2,450 × $21)	$ 51,450	
Football helmet (3,900 × $40).....................................	156,000	
Total	$207,450	
[b] Plastic (9,500 × $6.50)...	$ 61,750	
Foam lining (4,700 × $3.00)	14,100	
Total	$ 75,850	
[c] Plastic (11,400 × $6.50)...	$ 74,100	
Foam lining (4,500 × $3.00)	13,500	
Total	$ 87,600	
[d] Batting helmet (2,400 × $21)	$ 50,400	
Football helmet (3,500 × $40).....................................	140,000	
Total	$190,400	

Prob. 20–3B   Concluded

7.

SAFETY SPORTS INC.
Selling and Administrative Expenses Budget
For the Month Ending August 31, 2003

Selling expenses:		
Sales salaries expense	$505,700	
Advertising expense	350,800	
Telephone expense—selling	4,700	
Travel expense—selling	42,100	
Total selling expenses		$ 903,300
Administrative expenses:		
Office salaries expense	$145,800	
Depreciation expense—office equipment	6,200	
Telephone expense—administrative	900	
Office supplies expense	4,000	
Miscellaneous administrative expense	5,000	
Total administrative expenses		161,900
Total operating expenses		$1,065,200

8.

SAFETY SPORTS INC.
Budgeted Income Statement
For the Month Ending August 31, 2003

Revenue from sales		$5,089,500
Cost of goods sold		2,716,375
Gross profit		$2,373,125
Operating expenses:		
Selling expenses	$903,300	
Administrative expenses	161,900	
Total operating expenses		1,065,200
Income from operations		$1,307,925
Other income:		
Interest revenue	$ 12,500	
Other expenses:		
Interest expense	15,700	(3,200)
Income before income tax		$1,304,725
Income tax expense		521,890
Net income		$ 782,835

Prob. 20–4B

1.

LIGHTNING BLADE N'SKATE COMPANY
Cash Budget
For the Three Months Ending June 30, 2003

	April	May	June
Estimated cash receipts from:			
Cash sales	$ 30,000	$ 36,000	$ 38,000
Collection of accounts receivable[1]	286,000	273,000	307,800
Dividends	3,000		
Total cash receipts	$319,000	$309,000	$ 345,800
Estimated cash payments for:			
Manufacturing costs[2]	$129,000	$154,000	$ 176,000
Selling and administrative expenses	100,000	120,000	125,000
Capital expenditures			90,000
Other purposes:			
Note payable (including interest)			51,500
Income tax		32,000	
Dividends			10,000
Total cash payments	$229,000	$306,000	$ 452,500
Cash increase or (decrease)	$ 90,000	$ 3,000	$ (106,700)
Cash balance at beginning of month	40,000	130,000	133,000
Cash balance at end of month	$130,000	$133,000	$ 26,300
Minimum cash balance	35,000	35,000	35,000
Excess or (deficiency)	$ 95,000	$ 98,000	$ (8,700)

Computations:

[1] Collections of accounts receivable:	April	May	June
February sales	$ 90,000		
March sales	196,000*	$ 84,000**	
April sales		189,000	$ 81,000
May sales			226,800
Total	$286,000	$ 273,000	$ 307,800

    *$280,000 × 70% = $196,000
    **$280,000 × 30% = $84,000

[2] Payments for manufacturing costs:

Payment of accounts payable, beginning of			
month balance	$ 25,000	$ 26,000**	$ 32,000
Payment of current month's cost	104,000*	128,000	144,000
Total	$129,000	$ 154,000	$ 176,000

    *($150,000 – $20,000) × 80% = $104,000
    **($150,000 – $20,000) × 20% = $26,000

Prob. 20–4B   Concluded

2. The budget indicates that the minimum cash balance will not be maintained in June. This is due to the capital expenditures and note repayment requiring significant cash outflows during this month. This situation can be corrected by borrowing and/or by the sale of the marketable securities, if they are held for such purposes. At the end of April and May, the cash balance will exceed the minimum desired balance, and the excess could be considered for temporary investment.

Prob. 20–5B

1.

CODY CAMERA COMPANY
Budgeted Income Statement
For the Year Ending December 31, 2004

Sales			$3,600,000[1]
Cost of goods sold:			
Direct materials		$1,050,000[2]	
Direct labor		375,000[3]	
Factory overhead		231,000[4]	
Cost of goods sold			1,656,000
Gross profit			$1,944,000
Operating expenses:			
Selling expenses:			
Sales salaries and commissions	$408,500[5]		
Advertising	105,800		
Miscellaneous selling expense	86,500[6]		
Total selling expenses		$ 600,800	
Administrative expenses:			
Office and officers salaries	$276,500[7]		
Supplies	49,700[8]		
Miscellaneous administrative expense.	35,000[9]		
Total administrative expenses		361,200	
Total operating expenses			962,000
Income before income tax			$ 982,000
Income tax expense			235,800
Net income			$ 746,200

[1] 30,000 units × $120
[2] 30,000 units × $35
[3] 30,000 units × $12.50
[4] (30,000 units × $5.20) + $55,000 + $20,000
[5] (30,000 units × $10.80) + $84,500
[6] (30,000 units × $2.50) + $11,500
[7] (30,000 units × $6.40) + $84,500
[8] (30,000 units × $1.50) + $4,700
[9] (30,000 units × $1.10) + $2,000

Prob. 20–5B   Continued

2.

CODY CAMERA COMPANY
Budgeted Balance Sheet
December 31, 2004

Assets

Current assets:			
Cash		$443,700[1]	
Accounts receivable		246,700	
Inventories:			
Finished goods	$157,800		
Work in process..................................	37,800		
Materials	57,800	253,400	
Prepaid expenses....................................		4,500	
Total current assets..............................			$ 948,300
Property, plant, and equipment:			
Plant and equipment................................		$800,000	
Less accumulated depreciation................		322,000	478,000
Total assets..			$1,426,300

Liabilities

Current liabilities:			
Accounts payable			$ 184,500

Stockholders' Equity

Common stock..		$450,000	
Retained earnings		791,800[2]	
Total stockholders' equity			1,241,800
Total liabilities and stockholders' equity.......			$1,426,300

[1] Cash balance, December 31, 2004:

Balance, January 1, 2004...			$ 122,500
Cash from operations:			
Net income	$746,200		
Depreciation of plant and equipment............................	55,000		801,200
Less: Dividends to be paid in 2004...............................	$300,000		
Plant and equipment to be acquired in 2004 ...	180,000		(480,000)
Balance, December 31, 2004			$ 443,700

[2] Retained earnings balance, December 31, 2004:

Balance, January 1, 2004...		$ 345,600
Plus net income for 2004...		746,200
		$1,091,800
Less dividends to be declared in 2004............................		300,000
Balance, December 31, 2004		$ 791,800

SPECIAL ACTIVITIES

Activity 20–1

Josh should reject Connie's request to charge the convention-related costs against July's budget. This is just one example of many attempts to slide expenses into different budget periods than when actually incurred. This is a common issue that controllers face. Often, operating managers will attempt to accelerate future expenditures into low-expenditure months or delay present expenditures into future periods in order to avoid going over budget. These attempts to "slide" expenditures should not be supported, or else the whole concept of the budget will begin to become an accounting game. The integrity of the budget process must be defended by the controller. Thus, expenditures should be accrued to the period in which the benefit is received. Allowing Connie to slide expenditures into chosen periods will open a Pandora's box that will be difficult to close in the future. Josh should reassure Connie that management will not take a single month's results as an indication of either good or poor management. Month-to-month variation should be expected. Rather, management will take a long-term perspective and evaluate whether the department is staying within budget over a longer period of time. Abnormal month-to-month variations from budget can "wash out" over time.

Activity 20–2

Holding department managers responsible for costs that are not under their control is likely to produce a frustrating environment that will not be healthy for the firm. In the case of Elgin, the inclusion of such expenses caused responsibility center managers to avoid ownership for their cost performance. As a result, there was little cost consciousness in the organization. Part of developing a cost-conscious culture is reporting and accumulating costs to responsibility centers, for which senior management can logically assume there is control and authority. Authority and responsibility must go hand-in-hand.

Elgin appeared to be using a static budgeting approach prior to the change. The old approach did not distinguish between fixed and variable costs and therefore did not allow for the budget to flex to volume changes. As a result, the volume adjustments had to be done *ad hoc*, by judgment adjustments. The new system will be a flexible budget system that adjusts the variable portion of the budget by changes in an activity driver.

Activity 20–3

a. The budget information indicates that the actual expenditures by the Operations Department exceeded what was planned by $7,000. The bank manager may ask the operations manager why the travel and training expenditures exceeded the plan by a total of $15,000. It may be that the additional expenditures were necessary, but an explanation is in order.

b. The bank manager does not know if the actual resources consumed by the Operations Department are the right amount of resources for doing the right things. In other words, this budget doesn't say anything about the actual work of the Operations Department and how much cost this work consumes. The bank manager doesn't have a good sense if there is waste in the department or not. The $7,000 excess expenditure over budget raises several questions. If the department did twice as much work as planned, then the $7,000 is a bargain. If, on the other hand, the department did much less work than planned, then the $7,000 understates how poorly the department used resources. Again, how much work the department actually did is unknown, so these questions cannot be answered. Examples of the kind of work conducted by the department might include processing credit card statements, processing checking statements, processing loan repayments, and correcting errors.

The budget doesn't indicate why there was more travel and training than expected. Maybe the department introduced a new computer system, and all employees needed off-site training in order to use the system. This would explain the additional spending on travel and training. The training needed to be done, regardless of the budget.

Activity 20–4

Webvan could use a master budget to plan operations consistent with its sales growth. The sales projections could be used to develop the food purchases budget for the prepared meals, groceries, and other items. Sales projections could also be used to develop the direct labor budget for chefs and drivers. In addition, portions of the overhead budget can be associated with the sales projections. For example, the number of warehouse employees, number of vans, and fuel for serving a city should be related to the sales for that city. Thus, Webvan would be able to plan its costs and keep them aligned with sales projections. In addition, the budget process could be used to direct and coordinate all the various metropolitan areas within the company. In this way, the areas would be "playing from the same gamebook." This would avoid various cities engaging in activities that are not consistent with the overall company objectives. The actual performance of the company could be compared with the budget in order to provide all levels of the organization appropriate feedback and control. This feedback can be used to adjust operations to any changes that may be occurring. Thus, if sales are expanding faster or slower than planned, costs could be brought into line rapidly. This would help prevent the company from becoming either short of drivers and food due to sales outpacing projections or overbuilding a delivery infrastructure before the sales have materialized in sufficient volume to justify the cost.

As of this writing, Webvan has lost over $100 million in its first year of operations. This is because of significant start-up costs incurred by the company, including advertising and costs for building the delivery infrastructure. The fixed costs associated with warehouses, kitchens, and a minimal number of delivery vans require a significant "up-front" commitment before the sales reach break-even.

Activity 20–5

This particular excerpt reflects an emerging theme in business. Namely, drive financial accountability down to line employees. Traditionally, financial accountability has been the domain of management. The line employees were not given financial information, so they were not accountable or informed about financial performance. The Bottom Line Powered Management (BLPM) approach first trains employees on how to understand financial numbers. Second, once the employees are trained, the financial performance information and budgeted target information is driven down to the line employees. This means that the financial information is broken down by work group so that the team can be working with numbers that they actually influence. Thus, the financial information is made widely available to all employees and is not reserved only for management. This is a key ingredient. Third, this information is made available often and rapidly. The excerpt indicates that the financial information is made available weekly. This allows employees to discover and respond to problems quickly. Fourth, the type of financial data provided to the employees is expressed in terms that are intuitive, understandable, and actionable. Thus, the information that is provided to employees can lead to direct cost reduction effort because the employees know how their jobs impact financial performance.

Activity 20–6

1. The budget suggests that Ben's planned cash inflows will be insufficient to meet anticipated school-related and living costs. Ben needs to begin making plans now in order to avoid a difficult situation as the school year progresses. Some decisions can be made now that might avoid a potential hardship. The budget information is useful for planning. Planning will allow Ben to make more informed decisions about incurring expenses, part-time job hours required, acceptable summer pay, rental constraints, and scholarship needs. To summarize, the budget is a planning tool that highlights potential problem areas and indicates possible courses of action to avoid the shortfall.

2. a. The issue of certainty is an important one. Each line on the budget has a dollar amount. However, some dollars are more certain than others. The following table summarizes the relative certainty of each of the items:

	Certain	Moderate	Uncertain
Part-time salary..............			X
Summer job salary.........			X
Tuition...........................	X		
Books.............................		X	
Rent...............................	X		
Food..............................		X	
Utilities..........................		X	
Entertainment................		X	

Unfortunately, all the payments are certain, or moderately certain, while the receipts are uncertain. The income from the summer and part-time jobs is dependent on getting jobs and being able to hold the jobs during school. The expenses, however, are relatively certain. The school-related costs and the costs of food and shelter must be paid. This means that the budget may be a "best case scenario." If the salaries do not happen as anticipated, then the whole plan will be moot.

Activity 20–6   Concluded

b. Controllable (discretionary) items are ones that Ben has some control over and that he could change. Noncontrollable items are those that Ben has little control over. These payments will be incurred regardless of actions on his part. The following table summarizes the controllable nature of the expenses:

	Controllable	Partially Controllable	Not Controllable
Tuition			X
Books		X	
Rent		X	
Food		X	
Utilities		X	
Entertainment	X		

Tuition is not controllable, once it is decided that school is part of the plan. Adjustments should focus on the partially controllable and controllable items in the budget.

3. Reference to 2(b) gives clues as to where the leverage points are. The book budget could be reduced by buying used books or reselling books back to the bookstore. Rent could be adjusted downward. The budgeted rent is approximately $290 per month. This is not high, but there may be possibilities with respect to campus housing or finding a roommate to share the rent that may allow this figure to be reduced. The food budget is assumed to be required, but it is partially controllable by selecting lower-cost items. Ben must eat. Utilities are budgeted at $67 per month. Utilities can be reduced by judicious use of power, fewer long distance phone calls, basic or no cable TV, splitting utilities with a roommate, etc. The entertainment budget is the most controllable. The weekly budget calls for approximately $75 in entertainment. This is a pretty healthy amount. A good area for savings is in the entertainment area of the budget.

4. The budget fails to account for the possibility of unforeseen expenditures during the year. The budget should have some slack to guard against surprise payments. Some common sources of surprises would be medical expenses and repair costs. Naturally, there are good surprises also, e.g., a gift from parents or a scholarship. A second omission in the budget is a failure to account for "asset" purchases. This budget is only for maintenance. There is no budget for clothes, transportation, loan payments, savings, or other cash outflows associated with the longer-term concerns of life.

Activity 20–7

Most states have home pages and budget information available online. The budget information will usually be fairly easy to identify. If the students are unable to find budget information for their own state, the solution to the activity for Ohio for 2000 and 2001 is as follows. (The students should be using more recent information; so this is only a guide.)

1. Total GRF – Estimated Revenues for FYs 2000 and 2001

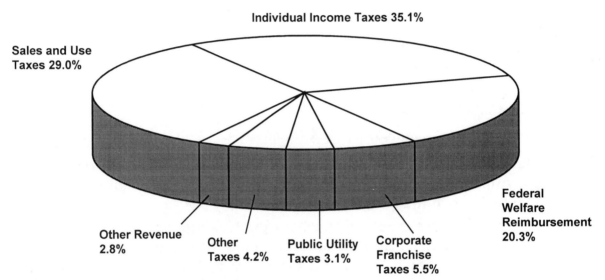

Individual Income Taxes 35.1%

Sales and Use Taxes 29.0%

Federal Welfare Reimbursement 20.3%

Other Revenue 2.8%

Other Taxes 4.2%

Public Utility Taxes 3.1%

Corporate Franchise Taxes 5.5%

What Does This Chart Show?

This pie chart shows the proportional contribution that each revenue source makes toward the state's General Revenue Fund (GRF). All revenues coming into the state treasury that are not specifically authorized by law to be placed in a separate fund are deposited in the GRF.

Estimated GRF Revenues (dollars in millions)			
Revenue Source	FY 2000	FY 2001	Total
Individual Income Taxes	$6,654.4	$7,360.7	$14,015.1
Sales and Use Taxes	$5,670.0	$5,896.0	$11,566.0
Federal Welfare Reimbursement	$3,946.0	$4,164.8	$8,110.8
Corporate Franchise Taxes	$1,077.3	$1,109.6	$2,186.9
Public Utility Taxes	$630.0	$625.0	$1,255.0
Other Taxes	$848.0	$838.5	$1,686.5
Other Revenue	$755.8	$374.5	$1,130.3
Total	$19,581.5	$20,369.1	$39,950.6
Source: Ohio Office of Budget and Management, March 1999			

Activity 20–7   Continued

2. Total GRF – Recommended Appropriations for FYs 2000 and 2001

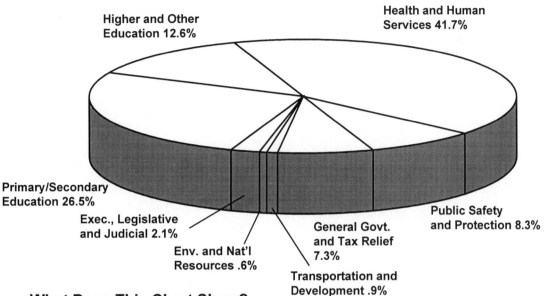

Higher and Other Education 12.6%

Health and Human Services 41.7%

Primary/Secondary Education 26.5%

Exec., Legislative and Judicial 2.1%

Env. and Nat'l Resources .6%

General Govt. and Tax Relief 7.3%

Transportation and Development .9%

Public Safety and Protection 8.3%

What Does This Chart Show?

This pie chart shows the share of the state's General Revenue Fund (GRF) that is used for each major function of state government. The GRF is the state's largest single source of revenue and it finances about one-half of all state government activities.

Recommended GRF Appropriations (dollars in millions)			
Function	FY 2000	FY 2001	Total
Primary/Secondary Education	$5,107.8	$5,476.6	$10,586.4
Higher and Other Education	$2,464.4	$2,563.8	$5,028.2
Health and Human Services	$8,138.8	$8,532.1	$16,670.9
Public Safety and Protection	$1,617.9	$1,694.0	$3,311.9
Gen'l Government/Tax Relief	$1,404.6	$1,521.2	$2,925.8
Transportation and Development	$178.6	$177.8	$356.4
Environment and Nat'l Resources	$128.9	$128.6	$257.5
Executive, Legislative and Judicial	$413.9	$432.2	$846.1
Total	$19,454.8	$20,528.5	$39,983.1
Note: Numbers may not add to total due rounding			
Source: Ohio Office of Budget and Management, March 1999			

Activity 20–7   Concluded

3. For 2000 and 2001, the Ohio state budget is balanced. The two-year total budgeted revenues are $39.95 billion, while the budgeted expenditures are $39.98 billion. While most state budgets will be in balance due to state constitutional constraints, the FY 2001 Ohio state budget is slightly over appropriated relative to budgeted revenues.

CHAPTER 21
PERFORMANCE EVALUATION USING VARIANCES
FROM STANDARD COSTS

CLASS DISCUSSION QUESTIONS

1. Standard costs assist management in controlling costs and in motivating employees to focus on costs.

2. Management can use standards to assist in achieving control over costs by investigating significant deviations of performance (variances) from standards and taking corrective action.

3. Reporting by the "principle of exceptions" is the reporting of only variances (or "exceptions") between standard and actual costs to the individual responsible for cost control.

4. There is no set time period for the revision of standards. They should be revised when prices, product design, labor rates, and manufacturing methods change to such an extent that current standards no longer represent a useful measure of performance.

5. Standard costs for direct materials, direct labor, and factory overhead per unit of product are used in budgetary performance evaluation. Product standard costs are multiplied by the planned production volumes. Budget control is achieved by comparing actual results with the standard costs at actual volumes.

6. a. The two variances in direct materials cost are:
    (1) Price
    (2) Quantity or usage
   b. The price variance is the result of a difference between the actual price and the standard price. It may be caused by such factors as a change in market prices or inefficient purchasing procedures. The quantity or usage variance results from using more or less materials than the standard quantity. It can be caused by such factors as excessive spoilage, carelessness in the production processes, and the use of inferior materials.

7. The offsetting variances might have been caused by the purchase of low-priced, inferior materials. The low price of the materials would generate a favorable materials price variance, while the inferior quality of the materials would cause abnormal spoilage and waste, thus generating an unfavorable materials quantity variance.

8. a. The two variances in direct labor costs are:
    (1) Rate (price or wage)
    (2) Time (usage or efficiency)
   b. The direct labor cost variance is usually under the control of the production supervisor.

9. No. Even though the assembly workers are covered by union contracts, direct labor cost variances still might result. For example, direct labor rate variances could be caused by scheduling overtime to meet production demands or by assigning higher-paid workers to jobs normally performed by lower-paid workers. Likewise, direct labor time variances could result during the training of new workers.

10. a. The variable factory overhead controllable variance results from incurring a total amount of variable factory overhead cost greater or less than the amount budgeted for the level of operations achieved. The fixed factory overhead volume variance results from operating at a level above or below 100% of normal capacity.
    b. The factory overhead cost variance report presents the standard factory overhead cost variance data, that is, the volume and the controllable variances.

11. The budgeted fixed costs at normal volume are the amount of fixed costs expected to be incurred for a volume of activity that has been the historical norm. Actual volume that

exceeds or is less than the historical norm gives rise to a volume variance.

12. Net unfavorable direct materials price variance

13. Net favorable direct materials quantity variance

14. No

15. Cost of Goods Sold

16. Standards can be very appropriate in repetitive service operations. Fast food restaurants can use standards for evaluating the productivity of the counter and food preparation employees. In addition, standards could be used to plan staffing patterns around various times of the day (e.g., increasing staff during the lunch hour).

17. Nonfinancial performance measures provide managers additional measures beyond the dollar impact of decisions. Nonfinancial considerations may help the organization include external customer perspectives about quality and service in performance measurements.

EXERCISES

Ex. 21–1

Ingredient	Quantity	×	Price	Total
Cocoa	260 pounds	×	$0.25 per pound	$ 65.00
Sugar	100 pounds	×	$0.45 per pound	45.00
Milk	60 gallons	×	$1.50 per gallon	90.00
Total cost				$ 200.00

Standard direct materials cost per bar of chocolate:

$$\frac{\$200 \text{ per batch}}{1,000 \text{ bars}} = \$0.20 \text{ per bar}$$

Ex. 21–2

Direct labor..	$12.00	× 4.80 hours	$ 57.60
Direct materials....................................	$24.00	× 20 board ft.	480.00
Variable factory overhead............................	$4.00	× 4.80 hours	19.20
Fixed factory overhead	$1.50	× 4.80 hours	7.20
Total cost per unit.......................................			$564.00

Ex. 21–3

a.

BAKER BOTTLE COMPANY
Manufacturing Cost Budget
For the Month Ended May 31, 2003

	Standard Cost at Planned Volume (400,000 Bottles)
Manufacturing costs:	
Direct labor	$ 7,200
Direct materials	28,800
Factory overhead	2,000
Total	$38,000

$1.80 \times (400{,}000 \div 100) = \$7{,}200$

$7.20 \times (400{,}000 \div 100) = \$28{,}800$

$0.50 \times (400{,}000 \div 100) = \$2{,}000$

Note: The cost standards are expressed as "per 100 bottles."

b.

BAKER BOTTLE COMPANY
Manufacturing Costs—Budget Performance Report
For the Month Ended May 31, 2003

	Actual Costs	Standard Cost at Actual Volume (450,000 bottles)	Cost Variance— (Favorable) Unfavorable
Manufacturing costs:			
Direct labor..............................	$ 7,950	$ 8,100	$ (150)
Direct materials.........................	33,100	32,400	700
Factory overhead......................	2,500	2,250	250
Total manufacturing cost ...	$43,550	$42,750	$ 800

$1.80 \times (450{,}000 \div 100) = \$8{,}100$

$7.20 \times (450{,}000 \div 100) = \$32{,}400$

$0.50 \times (450{,}000 \div 100) = \$2{,}250$

c. BBC's actual costs were $800 more than budgeted. An unfavorable direct materials cost variance and factory overhead cost variance more than offset a smaller favorable direct labor cost variance. The unfavorable variances should be investigated further to discover the cause. *Note:* The budget prepared in (a) at the beginning of the month should not be used in the budget performance report because actual volumes were greater than planned (450,000 vs. 400,000).

a.

Price variance:

Actual price...................................	$ 1.90	per pound
Standard price................................	2.00	per pound
Variance—favorable	$(0.10)	per pound
	× actual quantity, 126,800	$(12,680)

Quantity variance:

Actual quantity	126,800	pounds
Standard quantity............................	125,000	pounds
Variance—unfavorable..............	1,800	pounds
	× standard price, $2.00	3,600

Total direct materials cost variance—favorable .... $ (9,080)

b. The direct materials price variance should normally be reported to the Purchasing Department, which may or may not be able to control this variance. If materials of the same quality were purchased from another supplier at a price lower than the standard price, the variance was controllable. On the other hand, if the variance resulted from a marketwide price decrease, the variance was not subject to control.

The direct materials quantity variance should be reported to the proper level of operating management for possible corrective action. For example, if excessive amounts of direct materials had been used because of the malfunction of equipment that had not been properly maintained or operated, the variance would be reported to the production supervisor. On the other hand, if the excess usage of materials had been caused by the use of inferior raw materials, the Purchasing Department should be held responsible.

The total materials cost variance should be reported to senior plant management, such as the plant manager or materials manager.

Ex. 21–5

Product finished	6,000	units
Standard finished product for direct materials used		
(40,000 lbs. ÷ 6.25 lbs.)	6,400	units
Deficiency of finished product for materials used	(400)	units

Standard cost for direct materials:
   Quantity variance divided by deficiency of product
      for materials used ($3,400 ÷ 400 units) .... $ 8.50

Alternate solution:

Materials used	40,000	lbs.
Price variance..	$1,600	
Price variance per pound (price variance divided		
by materials used)	$ 0.04	

Unit price of direct materials...	$ 1.40
Less price variance per pound	0.04
Standard price per pound...	$ 1.36
Pounds per unit of product	× 6.25
Standard direct materials cost per unit of product......	$ 8.50

Ex. 21–6

a.

	Standard Quantity	×	Standard Price	=	Standard Cost per Batch
Whole tomatoes	2,000		$0.35		$ 700.00
Vinegar	104		2.50		260.00
Corn syrup	15		8.50		127.50
Salt	50		2.25		112.50
					$ 1,200.00
Pounds per batch				÷	1,500 pounds
					$ 0.80 per pound

b.

Actual Quantity for Batch A-24	Standard Quantity per Batch	Quantity Difference	×	Standard Price	=	Materials Quantity Variance
2,050	2,000	50		$0.35		$17.50 U
100	104	(4)		2.50		(10.00) F
16	15	1		8.50		8.50 U
48	50	(2)		2.25		(4.50) F
2,214	2,169					$11.50 U

Ex. 21–7

a. Rate variance:

Actual rate	$16.40	per hour
Standard rate	16.00	per hour
Variance—unfavorable	$ 0.40	per hour × actual time,
		8,400 hours $ 3,360

Time variance:

Actual time	8,400	hours
Standard time	9,000	hours
Variance—favorable	(600)	hours
	× standard rate, $16.00	(9,600)

Total direct labor cost variance—favorable .... $ (6,240)

b. The employees may have been more experienced or better trained, thereby requiring a higher labor rate than planned. The higher level of experience or training may have resulted in more efficient performance. Thus, the actual time required was less than standard. Fortunately, the gained efficiency offset the higher labor rate.

Ex. 21–8

a. Rate variance:

Actual rate	$ 13.00
Standard rate	12.50
Difference	$ 0.50
Actual hours used	× 1,860
Rate variance—unfavorable	$ 930

Time variance:

Actual hours	1,860
Standard hours (7.60 hours × 250 units)	1,900
Difference	(40)
Standard rate	×$12.50
Time variance—favorable	(500)
Direct labor cost variance—unfavorable	$ 430

b. Debit to work in process:

Standard hours at actual production	1,900
Standard rate	× $12.50
Standard direct labor cost	$ 23,750

Ex. 21–9

Step 1: Determine the standard direct materials and direct labor per unit.

Standard direct materials quantity per unit:

Direct materials pounds budgeted for September:

$$\frac{\$28,600}{\$0.50 \text{ per pound}} = 57,200 \text{ pounds}$$

Standard pounds per unit:

$$\frac{57,200 \text{ pounds}}{22,000 \text{ units}} = 2.60 \text{ standard pounds per unit}$$

Standard direct labor time per unit:

Direct labor hours budgeted for September:

$$\frac{\$24,200}{\$11.00 \text{ per hour}} = 2,200 \text{ direct labor hours}$$

Standard direct labor hours per unit:

$$\frac{2,200 \text{ hours}}{22,000 \text{ units}} = 0.10 \text{ standard direct labor hour per unit}$$

Step 2: Using the standard quantity and time rates in Step 1, determine the standard costs for the actual September production.

Standard direct materials at actual volume: 25,000 units × 2.60 pounds per unit × $0.50 = ...	$ 32,500
Standard direct labor at actual volume: 25,000 units × 0.1 direct labor hour per unit × $11.00 = ...	27,500
Total...	$ 60,000

Step 3: Determine the direct materials quantity and direct labor time variances, assuming no direct materials price or direct labor rate variances.

Actual direct materials used in production	$ 31,250
Standard direct materials (Step 2)..	32,500
Direct materials quantity variance—favorable	$ (1,250)
Actual direct labor..	$ 28,100
Standard direct labor (Step 2)	27,500
Direct labor time variance—unfavorable	$ 600

Ex. 21–10

PAUL BUNYAN WOOD PRODUCTS COMPANY
Factory Overhead Cost Budget—Press Department
For the Month Ended September 30, 2003

Direct labor hours..	4,000	6,000	8,000
Variable overhead cost:			
Indirect factory labor	$11,200	$16,800	$22,400
Power and light	1,800	2,700	3,600
Indirect materials	8,800	13,200	17,600
Total variable factory overhead.............	$21,800	$32,700	$43,600
Fixed factory overhead cost:			
Supervisory salaries.....................................	$21,600	$21,600	$21,600
Depreciation of plant and equipment.........	18,000	18,000	18,000
Insurance and property taxes	4,800	4,800	4,800
Total fixed factory overhead...................	$44,400	$44,400	$44,400
Total factory overhead	$66,200	$77,100	$88,000

Ex. 21–11

Variable factory overhead controllable variance:		
Actual variable factory overhead cost incurred	$448,000	
Budgeted variable factory overhead for 30,000 hrs.		
[30,000 × ($18.80 − $3.20)]....................................	468,000	
Variance—favorable		$(20,000)
Fixed factory overhead volume variance:		
Productive capacity at 100%.....................................	36,000 hours	
Standard for amount produced..............................	30,000 hours	
Productive capacity not used	6,000 hours	
Standard fixed factory overhead rate......................	× $3.20	
Variance—unfavorable		19,200
Total factory overhead cost variance—favorable.........		$ (800)*

*Proof: ($448,000 + $115,200) − $564,000

Ex. 21–12

a. Controllable variance:

Actual variable factory overhead ($262,400 − $77,500)		$184,900
Standard variable factory overhead at actual production:		
Standard hours at actual production	45,000	
Variable factory overhead rate[1]	× $4.10	
Standard variable factory overhead		184,500
Controllable variance—unfavorable		$ 400

b. Volume variance:

Volume at 100% of normal capacity	50,000	
Less: Standard hours	45,000	
Idle capacity	5,000	
Fixed overhead rate[2]	× $1.55	
Volume variance—unfavorable		7,750
Total factory overhead cost variance—unfavorable		$8,150[3]

[1] Variable factory overhead rate: $\dfrac{\$164,000}{40,000\ \text{hours}} = \$4.10$ per hour

[2] Fixed factory overhead rate: $\dfrac{\$77,500}{50,000\ \text{hours}} = \$1.55$ per hour

[3] Proof: $262,400 − [($4.10 + $1.55) × 45,000 hours] = $8,150

Ex. 21–13

MURPHY MOLDED PRODUCTS INC.
Factory Overhead Cost Variance Report—Trim Department
For the Month Ended May 31, 2003

Productive capacity for the month.. 20,000 hou

Actual productive capacity used for the month............................... 15,000 hou

	Budget (at actual production)	Actual	Variances Favorable	Variances Unfavorable
Variable factory overhead costs:[1]				
Indirect factory labor	$ 42,000	$ 35,200	$ 6,800	
Power and light	5,250	4,000	1,250	
Indirect materials	27,750	22,500	5,250	
Total variable factory overhead cost	$ 75,000	$ 61,700		
Fixed factory overhead costs:				
Supervisory salaries	$ 114,200	$ 114,200		
Depreciation of plant and equipment...........................	39,200	39,200		
Insurance and property taxes	6,600	6,600		
Total fixed factory over-head cost........................	$ 160,000	$ 160,000		
Total factory overhead cost.........	$ 235,000	$ 221,700		
Total controllable variances			$ 13,300	$ 0
Net controllable variance—favorable				$ (13,300)
Volume variance—unfavorable:				
Idle hours at the standard rate for fixed factory overhead—5,000 hours × $8.00[2]				40,000
Total factory overhead cost variance—unfavorable				$ 26,700

[1] The budgeted variable factory overhead costs are determined by multiplying 15,000 hours by the variable factory overhead cost rate for each variable cost category. These rates are determined by dividing each budgeted amount (estimated at the beginning of the month) by the planned (budgeted) volume of 12,000 hours.

[2] Fixed factory overhead rate: $\dfrac{\$160,000}{20,000 \text{ hours}} = \$8.00$

Ex. 21–14

a. Materials (800 × $41)... 32,800
   Direct Materials Price Variance (800 × $1.50).............. 1,200
      Accounts Payable (800 × $42.50) 34,000

b. Work in Process (540 × $41) 22,140
      Direct Materials Quantity Variance (20 × $41)........ 820
      Materials (520 × $41) 21,320

Ex. 21–15

CUMBERLAND COMPANY
Income Statement
For the Month Ended January 31, 2003

	Favorable	Unfavorable	
Sales			$960,000
Cost of goods sold—at standard			650,000
Gross profit—at standard			$310,000
Less variances from standard cost:			
Direct materials price.................................	$1,200		
Direct materials quantity	2,200		
Direct labor rate.......................................		$ 800	
Direct labor time.......................................		3,000	
Factory overhead controllable....................	3,800		
Factory overhead volume..........................		8,000	4,600
Gross profit..			$305,400
Operating expenses:			
Selling expenses.......................................		$91,500	
Administrative expenses...........................		44,000	135,500
Income from operations................................			$169,900
Other expense:			
Interest expense.......................................			1,900
Income before income tax			$168,000

Ex. 21–16

In determining the volume variance, the productive capacity not used (20,000 hours) should be multiplied by the standard fixed factory overhead rate of $3.50 ($10.00 – $6.50) to yield an unfavorable variance of $70,000.

A correct determination of the factory overhead cost variances is as follows:

Variable factory overhead controllable variance:

Actual variable factory overhead cost incurred	$ 385,700	
Budgeted variable factory overhead for 60,000 hours (60,000 × $6.50)...	390,000	
Variance—favorable...		$ (4,300)

Fixed factory overhead volume variance:

Productive capacity at 100%.....................................	80,000 hours	
Standard for amount produced................................	60,000 hours	
Productive capacity not used	20,000 hours	
Standard fixed factory overhead rate......................	× $3.50	
Variance—unfavorable		70,000

Total factory overhead cost variance—unfavorable	$65,700

Ex. 21–17

a. Actual weekly expenditure: 2 people × $15.00 per hour × 40 hours per week = $1,200

b. Standard time used for the volume of admissions:

	Unscheduled	Scheduled	Total
Number of admissions....	45	180	
Standard time	× 36 minutes	× 18 minutes	
Total................................	1,620 minutes	3,240 minutes	4,860 minutes
			or
			81 hours

c. Productive minutes available
   (2 employees × 40 hours × 60 minutes) 4,800
   Less: Standard minutes used at actual volume..................... 4,860
   Time difference from standard .... (60)
   Standard rate per minute .... × $0.25[1]
   Direct labor time (efficiency) variance—favorable................. $ (15)

or

$1,200 (a) – $1,215[2] = $(15)

[1] Standard direct labor rate:

$15 ÷ 60 min. = $0.25 per minute

[2] Standard labor cost at actual volume:

Productive time (4,860/60) × $15 = $1,215

The Admissions Department was slightly more efficient than standard. However, administrative processes are much less repetitive than manufacturing processes; thus, the reported variance may merely be an error in measuring time.

Ex. 21–18

a. Standard sorts per minute × Standard minutes per hour = Standard sorts per hour (per employee)

60 sorts per minute × 60 minutes per hour = 3,600 standard sorts per hour

Pieces of mail ÷ Standard sorts per hour = Number of hours planned

25,920,000 letters ÷ 3,600 sorts per hour = 7,200 hours planned

Number of hours planned ÷ Hours per temporary employee per month = Number of hires

7,200 hours ÷ 160 hours = 45 temporary hires for December

b. Actual pieces sorted = 25,200,000

Actual pieces of mail sorted ÷ Standard sorts per hour = Standard number of hours for actual production

25,200,000 ÷ 3,600 standard sorts per hour = 7,000 standard hours for actual production

Actual hours staffed	7,200
Standard hours for actual production	7,000
Excess of actual over standard hours	200
Standard hourly rate	× $16
Direct labor time variance—unfavorable	$ 3,200

Ex. 21–19

a. <u>Possible Input Measures</u>

Registration staffing per student

Technology investment per period for registration process

Training hours per registration personnel

Amount of faculty staffing short of demand

Amount of technology capacity (size of computer, number of input lines) for registration process

Maintenance dollars spent on the registration system

Employee satisfaction score

Number of hours per day registration is available

<u>Possible Output Measures</u>

Cycle time for a student to register for classes

Number of times a course is unavailable

Number of separate registration events or steps (log-ons or line waits) per student

Number of times a replacement course was used by a student

Number of registration errors

Student satisfaction score with the registration process

Number of student complaints about registration process

Number of registration rework steps per student

Cost of registration per student

Number of personnel overtime hours during registration

Labor time variance for registration process (standard hours less actual hours at standard labor rate)

Reliability of registration system (computer uptime, number of downtime events)

b. The university is interested in not only the efficiency of the process but also the quality of the process. This means that the process must meet multiple objectives. The university wants this process to meet the needs of students, which means it should not pose a burden to students. Students should be able to register for classes quickly, get the courses they want, and avoid registration errors, hassles, and problems. Thus, the nonfinancial measures are used to balance the need for a cost-efficient process with one that will meet the needs of the student.

Ex. 21–20

	Input Measure	Output Measure	Explanation
Number of misfilled orders		X	Incorrectly filled orders reduce the customer's satisfaction with the order process. A measure of output quality of the process.
Average computer response time to customer "clicks"		X	A measure of the speed of the ordering process. If the speed is too slow, we may lose customers.
System capacity divided by customer demands	X		The system capacity relative to the demands on the system will drive the response time and customer satisfaction with ordering.
Elapsed time between customer order and product delivery		X	An important overall measure of process responsiveness. If the company is too slow in providing product, we may lose customers.
Number of page faults or errors due to software programming errors		X	The page errors will negatively impact the customer's ordering experience. It's a measure of process output quality.
Server (computer) downtime		X	A measure of ordering system reliability.
Training dollars per programmer	X		Trained programmers should enhance the software's responsiveness and reliability.
Dollar amount of returned goods		X	An important measure of customer satisfaction with the final product that was ordered.
Number of orders per warehouse employee	X		This measure is related to the capacity of the warehouse relative to the demands placed upon it. This relationship will impact the delivery cycle time.
Number of customer complaints divided by the number of orders		X	An extreme measure of customer dissatisfaction with the ordering process.
Maintenance dollars divided by hardware investment	X		A driver of the ordering system's reliability and downtime. The maintenance dollars should be scaled to the amount of hardware in order to facilitate comparison across time.

PROBLEMS

Prob. 21–1A

a.

	Standard Materials and Labor Cost per Dress
Direct materials ($6.00 × 4.2 yards)	$25.20
Direct labor [$10 × (18 min. ÷ 60 min.)]	3.00
	$28.20

b.   **Direct Materials Cost Variance**

Price variance:

Actual price..................................	$6.20	
Standard price	6.00	
Variance—unfavorable	$0.20	
	× actual quantity, 6,100 yards	$1,220

Quantity variance:

Actual quantity	6,100	yards
Standard quantity (4.2 yds. × 1,500)	6,300	yards
Variance—favorable...............	(200)	yards
	× standard price, $6.00	(1,200)

Total direct materials cost variance—unfavorable.............................. $ 20

c.   **Direct Labor Cost Variance**

Rate variance:

Actual wage per hour	$ 10.75	
Standard wage per hour	10.00	
Variance—unfavorable	$ 0.75 × 468 hours actual time (13 employees × 36 hrs.)	$ 351

Time variance:

Actual productive time (13 employees × 36 hours)	468	hours
Standard time for actual dresses [1,500 × (18 min. ÷ 60 min.)]..................	450	hours
Variance—unfavorable	18	hours
	× standard rate, $10	180

Total direct labor cost variance—unfavorable .... $ 531

Prob. 21–2A

1. a.

Direct Materials Variance	Cocoa		Sugar		Total	
Price variance:						
Actual price..	$ 9.50		$ 3.20			
Standard price	10.00		3.00			
Variance	$ (0.50)		$ 0.20			
Actual quantity	× 80,900		× 125,700			
Direct materials price variance......	$ (40,450)	F	$ 25,140	U	$ (15,310)	F
Quantity variance:						
Actual quantity used............................	80,900		125,700			
Standard quantity used[1]	81,600		124,000			
Variance	(700)		1,700			
Standard price......................................	× $10.00		× $3.00			
Direct materials quantity variance	$ (7,000)	F	$ 5,100	U	(1,900)	F
Total direct materials cost variance					$ (17,210)	F
Total direct materials cost variance:						
Actual cost[2]...	$ 768,550		$ 402,240			
Standard cost[3]	816,000		372,000			
Total direct materials cost variance	$ (47,450)	F	$ 30,240	U	$ (17,210)	F

[1] 81,600 = (12 lbs. × 2,800 actual production of dark chocolate) + (8 lbs. × 6,000 actual production of light chocolate)

124,000 = (10 lbs. × 2,800 actual production of dark chocolate) + (16 lbs. × 6,000 actual production of light chocolate)

[2] $768,550 = 80,900 lbs. × $9.50

$402,240 = 125,700 lbs. × $3.20

[3] $816,000 = 81,600 lbs. × $10.00

$372,000 = 124,000 lbs. × $3.00

Prob. 21–2A **Concluded**

b.

Direct Labor Variance		Dark Chocolate		Light Chocolate		Total	
Rate variance:							
Actual rate..	$	14.40		$	14.40		
Standard rate......................................		14.00			14.00		
Variance..	$	0.40		$	0.40		
Actual time...	×	725		×	2,310		
Direct labor rate variance.............	$	290	U	$	924	U	$ 1,214 U
Time variance:							
Actual time...		725			2,310		
Standard time[1]		700			2,400		
Variance..		25			(90)		
Standard rate......................................	×	$14.00		×	$14.00		
Direct labor time variance.............	$	350	U	$	(1,260)	F	(910) F
Total direct labor cost variance							$ 304 U
Total direct labor cost variance:							
Actual cost[2]..	$	10,440		$	33,264		
Standard cost[3]		9,800			33,600		
Total direct labor cost variance...	$	640	U	$	(336)	F	$ 304 U

[1] 700 = 0.25 hr. × 2,800 actual production of dark chocolate
   2,400 = 0.40 hr. × 6,000 actual production of light chocolate

[2] $10,440 = 725 hrs. × $14.40
   $33,264 = 2,310 hrs. × $14.40

[3] $9,800 = 700 hrs. × $14.00
   $33,600 = 2,400 hrs. × $14.00

2. The variance analyses should be based on the standard amounts at actual volumes. The budget must flex with the volume changes. If the actual volume is different from the planned volume, as it was in this case, then the budget used for performance evaluation should reflect the change in direct materials and direct labor that will be required for the actual production. In this way, spending from volume changes can be separated from efficiency and price variances.

Prob. 21–3A

a. <u>Direct Materials Cost Variance</u>

Price variance:
Actual price......................................	$ 3.50 per pound	
Standard price	<u>3.40</u> per pound	
Variance—unfavorable	$ 0.10 per pound	
	× actual quantity, 5,930	$593

Quantity variance:
Actual quantity	5,930 pounds	
Standard quantity...........................	<u>6,000</u> pounds	
Variance—favorable...................	(70) pounds	
	× standard price, $3.40	<u>(238)</u>

Total direct materials cost variance—unfavorable................................. <u>$355</u>

b. <u>Direct Labor Cost Variance</u>

Rate variance:
Actual rate.......................................	$18.50	
Standard rate	<u>18.00</u>	
Variance—unfavorable	$ 0.50 per hour	
	× actual time, 1,140	$570

Time variance:
Actual time......................................	1,140 hours	
Standard time	<u>1,125</u> hours	
Variance—unfavorable	15 hours	
	× standard rate, $18	<u>270</u>

Total direct labor cost variance—unfavorable...................................... <u>$840</u>

c. <u>Factory Overhead Cost Variance</u>

Variable factory overhead controllable variance:
Actual variable factory overhead cost incurred..........	$ 5,250	
Budgeted variable factory overhead for 1,125 hrs......	<u>5,400</u>	
Variance—favorable		$(150)

Fixed factory overhead volume variance:
Normal capacity at 100%..	1,100 hours	
Standard for amount produced	<u>1,125</u>	
Productive capacity used...	(25) hours	
Standard fixed factory overhead cost rate	×$12.00	
Variance—favorable		<u>(300)</u>

Total factory overhead cost variance—favorable.............. <u>$(450)</u>

Prob. 21–4A

WELLS INC.
Factory Overhead Cost Variance Report—Welding Department
For the Month Ended May 31, 2003

Normal capacity for the month.. 3,000 hours
Actual production for the month .... 3,100 hours

	Budget [1]	Actual	Variances Favorable	Variances Unfavorable
Variable costs:				
Indirect factory wages	$ 23,560	$ 23,450	$(110)	
Power and light	3,875	3,980		$ 105
Indirect materials	10,540	10,600		60
Total variable cost..................	$ 37,975	$ 38,030		
Fixed costs:				
Supervisory salaries..................	$ 67,500	$ 67,500		
Depreciation of plant and equipment................................	26,400	26,400		
Insurance and property taxes ...	5,100	5,100		
Total fixed cost........................	$ 99,000	$ 99,000		
Total factory overhead cost............	$ 136,975	$ 137,030		
Total controllable variances			$(110)	$ 165
Net controllable variance—unfavorable.............................				$ 55

Volume variance—favorable:
Idle hours at standard rate for fixed factory overhead
(3,000 hrs. – 3,100 hrs.) × $33[2] .... (3,300)

Total factory overhead cost variance—favorable.............. $ (3,245)

[1] The budgeted variable costs are determined by multiplying the variable over-head rate (the May budget divided by 3,000 hours for each variable overhead cost) by 3,100 actual hours.

[2] $99,000 ÷ 3,000 hours = $33

Prob. 21–4A   Concluded

This solution is applicable only if the GENERAL LEDGER SOFTWARE that accompanies the text is used.

WELLS INC.
Budget Report
For the Month Ended May 31, 2003

	Budget	Actual	Difference from Budget	%
Operating revenue............................	175,000	178,000	3,000	(1.71)
Operating expenses:				
Indirect factory wages	23,560	23,450	(110)	(0.47)
Power and light	3,875	3,980	105	2.71
Indirect materials	10,540	10,600	60	0.57
Supervisory salaries...................	67,500	67,500		
Depreciation of plant and				
equipment.............................	26,400	26,400		
Insurance and property taxes ...	5,100	5,100		
Total operating expenses.....	136,975	137,030	55	0.04
Net income	38,025	40,970	2,945	7.74

Note: The difference from budget for the operating expenses is unfavorable, so it is subtracted from the positive (favorable) difference from budget for revenue.

Prob. 21–5A

1. | Actual hours provided (4 × 40 hours) | 160 |
    | Standard hours required for the original plan | 150* |
    | Labor time difference | 10 |
    | Standard labor rate | × $20.00 |
    | Direct labor time variance—unfavorable | $ 200.00 |

    $$*\frac{4{,}500 \text{ lines}}{30 \text{ lines per hour}} = 150 \text{ hours}$$

2. | Actual hours provided (4 × 40 hours) | 160 |
    | Standard hours required for the actual results | 176* |
    | Labor time difference | (16) |
    | Standard labor rate | × $20.00 |
    | Direct labor time variance—favorable | $ (320.00) |

    $$*\frac{5{,}280 \text{ lines}}{30 \text{ lines per hour}} = 176 \text{ hours}$$

3. | Actual labor rate | $ 26.00 |
    | Standard labor rate | 20.00 |
    | Difference | $ 6.00 |
    | Actual hours provided (4 × 40 hours) | × 160 |
    | Direct labor rate variance—unfavorable | $ 960.00 |

    The labor cost variance is $640 unfavorable
    ($960 unfavorable rate variance – $320 favorable time variance).

4. | Actual hours provided (5 × 40 hours) | 200 |
    | Standard hours required for the actual results | 176 |
    | Labor time difference | 24 |
    | Standard labor rate | × $20.00 |
    | Direct labor time variance—unfavorable | $ 480.00 |

5. Hiring an extra employee is less costly than the bonus by $160. The cost variance for paying the bonus was $640 unfavorable, while the cost variance that would result from hiring another employee would have been $480 unfavorable. Note that there will be no labor rate variance if a fifth programmer is hired.

6. The labor rate and time variances fail to consider the number of errors in the code from programmer fatigue. A program that has many errors will require significant time for debugging at a later date. In addition, hidden errors can cause possible field failures with customers. Thus, managers should consider not only the efficiency of doing the work, but also the quality of the work.

Prob. 21–1B

a.

	Standard Materials and Labor Cost per Faucet
Direct materials ($8.50 × 2.5 pounds).....................................	$21.25
Direct labor ($13.00) × (12 min. ÷ 60 min.)	2.60
	$23.85

b. <u>Direct Materials Cost Variance</u>

Price variance:
Actual price.................................	$ 8.25	
Standard price	8.50	
Variance—favorable..............	$ (0.25)	
	× actual quantity, 8,140 pounds	$ (2,035)

Quantity variance:
Actual quantity	8,140 pounds	
Standard quantity		
(2.5 lbs. × 3,200)	8,000	
Variance—unfavorable	140 pounds	
	× standard price, $8.50	1,190

Total direct materials cost variance—favorable .... $ (845)

c. <u>Direct Labor Cost Variance</u>

Rate variance:
Actual wage rate.........................	$ 12	
Standard rate	13	
Variance—favorable..............	$ (1) × 520 hours	
	actual time (13 employees	
	× 40 hrs.)	$ (520)

Time variance:
Actual productive time		
13 employees × 40 hours.......	520 hours	
Standard time for actual units		
(3,200) × (12 min. ÷ 60 min.)...	640	
Variance—favorable..............	(120) hours	
	× standard rate, $13	(1,560)

Total direct labor cost variance—favorable .... $ (2,080)

Prob. 21–2B

1. a.

Direct Materials Variance	Filler	Liner	Total
Price variance:			
Actual price...	$ 24.60	$ 8.20	
Standard price	25.00	8.00	
Variance	$ (0.40)	$ 0.20	
Actual quantity	× 15,200	× 34,000	
Direct materials price variance.........	$ (6,080) F	$ 6,800 U	$ 720 U
Quantity variance:			
Actual quantity used..............................	15,200	34,000	
Standard quantity used[1]	14,800	34,600	
Variance	400	(600)	
Standard price	× $25.00	× $8.00	
Direct materials quantity variance ...	$ 10,000 U	$ (4,800) F	5,200 U
Total direct materials cost variance			$ 5,920 U
Total direct materials cost variance:			
Actual cost[2]...	$ 373,920	$ 278,800	
Standard cost[3]	370,000	276,800	
Total direct materials cost variance.	$ 3,920 U	$ 2,000 U	$ 5,920 U

[1] 14,800 = (2 lbs. × 1,800 actual production of women's coats) + (3.5 lbs. × 3,200 actual production of men's coats)

  34,600 = (5 yds. × 1,800) + (8 yds. × 3,200)

[2] $373,920 = 15,200 lbs. × $24.60
  $278,800 = 34,000 yds. × $8.20

[3] $370,000 = 14,800 lbs. × $25.00
  $276,800 = 34,600 yds. × $8.00

Prob. 21–2B Concluded

b.

Direct Labor Variance	Women's Coats	Men's Coats	Total
Rate variance:			
Actual rate..	$ 11.75	$ 12.10	
Standard rate..	12.00	12.00	
Variance..	$ (0.25)	$ 0.10	
Actual time..	× 380	× 950	
Direct labor rate variance....................	$ (95) F	$ 95 U	$ 0 U
Time variance:			
Actual time..	380	950	
Standard time[1]	360	960	
Variance..	20	(10)	
Standard rate..	×$12.00	×$12.00	
Direct labor time variance....................	$ 240 U	$ (120) F	120 U
Total direct labor cost variance			$120 U
Total direct labor cost variance:			
Actual cost[2]..	$ 4,465	$11,495	
Standard cost[3]	4,320	11,520	
Total direct labor cost variance...........	$ 145 U	$ (25) F	$120 U

[1] 360 = 0.20 × 1,800 actual production of women's coats

960 = 0.30 × 3,200 actual production of men's coats

[2] $ 4,465 = 380 hrs. × $11.75

$11,495 = 950 hrs. × $12.10

[3] $ 4,320 = 360 hrs. × $12.00

$11,520 = 960 hrs. × $12.00

2. The variance analyses should be based on the standard amounts at actual volumes. The budget must flex with the volume changes. If the actual volume is different from the planned volume, as it was in this case, then the budget used for performance evaluation should reflect the change in direct materials and direct labor that will be required for the actual production. In this way, spending from volume changes can be isolated from efficiency and price variances.

Prob. 21–3B

a.   Direct Materials Cost Variance

Price variance:

Actual price......................................	$ 3.35 per pound	
Standard price	3.40 per pound	
Variance—favorable.....................	$ (0.05) per pound	
	× actual quantity, 36,500	$(1,825)

Quantity variance:

Actual quantity	36,500 pounds	
Standard quantity............................	36,000 pounds	
Variance—unfavorable	500 pounds	
	× standard price, $3.40	1,700

Total direct materials cost variance—favorable .... $ (125)

b.   Direct Labor Cost Variance

Rate variance:

Actual rate..	$16.20	
Standard rate	16.00	
Variance—unfavorable	$ 0.20 per hour	
	× actual time, 3,580	$ 716

Time variance:

Actual time.......................................	3,580 hours	
Standard time	3,500 hours	
Variance—unfavorable	80 hours	
	× standard rate, $16	1,280

Total direct labor cost variance—unfavorable...................................... $ 1,996

c.   Factory Overhead Cost Variance

Variable factory overhead controllable variance:

Actual variable factory overhead cost incurred	$6,270	
Budgeted variable factory overhead for 3,500 hrs..	6,300	
Variance—favorable...		$ (30)

Fixed factory overhead volume variance:

Normal capacity at 100%	4,000 hours	
Standard for amount produced...............................	3,500	
Productive capacity not used	500 hours	
Standard fixed factory overhead cost rate	× $2.50	
Variance—unfavorable		1,250

Total factory overhead cost variance—unfavorable .... $ 1,220

Prob. 21–4B

HEALTHGUARD COMPANY
Factory Overhead Cost Variance Report—Assembly Department
For the Month Ended July 31, 2003

Normal capacity for the month... 5,000 hours
Actual production for the month... 4,600 hours

	Budget [1]	Actual	Variances Favorable	Variances Unfavorable
Variable costs:				
Indirect factory wages	$ 8,280	$8,150	$(130)	
Power and light	2,300	2,390		$ 90
Indirect materials	5,520	5,500	(20)	
Total variable cost..................	$16,100	$16,040		
Fixed costs:				
Supervisory salaries..................	$16,400	$16,400		
Depreciation of plant and				
equipment.............................	4,800	4,800		
Insurance and property taxes ...	1,800	1,800		
Total fixed cost.......................	$23,000	$23,000		
Total factory overhead cost............	$39,100	$39,040		
Total controllable variances			$(150)	$ 90

Net controllable variance—favorable .... $ (60)

Volume variance—unfavorable:
Idle hours at standard rate for fixed factory overhead
(5,000 hrs. − 4,600 hrs.) × $4.60[2] 1,840

Total factory overhead cost variance—unfavorable $1,780

[1] The budgeted variable costs are determined by multiplying the variable overhead rate (the July budget divided by 5,000 hours for each variable overhead
cost) by 4,600 actual hours.

[2] $23,000 ÷ 5,000 hours = $4.60

Prob. 21–4B   Concluded

This solution is applicable only if the GENERAL LEDGER SOFTWARE that accompanies the text is used.

HEALTHGUARD COMPANY
Budget Report
For the Month Ended July 31, 2003

	Budget	Actual	Difference from Budget	%
Operating revenue............................	89,000	101,000	12,000	13.48
Operating expenses:				
Indirect factory wages	8,280	8,150	(130)	(1.57)
Power and light	2,300	2,390	90	3.91
Indirect materials	5,520	5,500	(20)	(0.36)
Supervisory salaries	16,400	16,400		
Depreciation of plant and				
equipment...............................	4,800	4,800		
Insurance and property taxes ...	1,800	1,800		
Total operating expenses.....	39,100	39,040	(60)	(0.15)
Net income	49,900	61,960	12,060	24.17

Note: The difference from budget for the operating expenses is favorable, so it is added to the positive (favorable) difference from budget for revenue.

Prob. 21–5B

1.

Actual hours provided (3 × 40 hours)	120
Standard hours required for the original plan.............	100*
Labor time difference	20
Standard labor rate..	×$12.00
Direct labor time variance—unfavorable	$240.00

$$*\frac{45{,}000 \text{ lines}}{450 \text{ lines per hour}} = 100 \text{ hours}$$

2.

Actual hours provided (3 × 40 hours)	120
Standard hours required for the actual results...........	126*
Labor time difference	(6)
Standard labor rate..	×$12.00
Direct labor time variance—favorable	$ (72.00)

$$*\frac{56{,}700 \text{ lines}}{450 \text{ lines per hour}} = 126 \text{ hours}$$

3.

Actual labor rate..	$ 15.00
Standard labor rate..	12.00
Difference	$ 3.00
Actual hours provided (3 × 40 hours)	× 120
Direct labor rate variance—unfavorable......................	$360.00

The labor cost variance is $288 unfavorable ($360 unfavorable rate variance – $72 favorable time variance).

4.

Actual hours provided (4 × 40 hours)	160
Standard hours required for the actual results...........	126
Labor time difference	34
Standard labor rate..	×$12.00
Direct labor time variance—unfavorable	$408.00

5. The bonus is the better approach by $120. The cost variance for paying the bonus was $288 unfavorable, while the cost variance that would result from hiring another employee would have been $408 unfavorable. Note that there will be no labor rate variance if a fourth transcriptionist is hired.

6. The labor rate and time variances fail to consider the number of errors in the report from typist fatigue. A report that has many errors will require significant time for correction at a later date. In addition, report errors can cause doctors to draw incorrect conclusions from the test analyses. Thus, managers should consider not only the efficiency of doing the work but also the quality of the work.

SPECIAL ACTIVITIES

Activity 21–1

The use of theoretical standards is a legitimate concern for Angie. It is likely that such standards are too tight and do not include the necessary fatigue factors that are likely in this type of operation. It seems as though Angie is arguing for practical standards that can be attained if the operation is running well. Maybe some standard in between is warranted, but that is not the issue. The issue is Dan's method of operation. Dan has effectively agreed to have this dispute arbitrated with a senior official. However, Dan is trying to seal the fate of the argument behind the scenes, before the issue is discussed openly, as agreed. Moreover, Dan is attributing poor motives to Angie behind her back. Dan may get away with this method of operation in the short run, but in the long term he will likely alienate himself within the organization. He may create a distrustful environment that may eventually hamper his ability to provide open, honest feedback. People may eventually avoid him and hide the truth from him.

Activity 21–2

Although the Lang Company performance measurement system uses both financial and nonfinancial measures, there may still be some serious performance omissions. The financial measures are good measures of financial performance. Likewise, employee satisfaction should be measured, since satisfied employees may lead to overall business success. There is, however, at least one major shortcoming to the proposed measures. None of the three measures has a customer orientation. The management of Lang Company should also select a performance measure that reflects how well the business is performing from a customer's perspective. Thus, measures about customer satisfaction, product quality, warranty experience, or on-time delivery would be excellent additions to the three measures already proposed.

Activity 21–3

1. The "orders past due" is a common measure of the aggregate sales value of orders past due. The "buyer's misery index" measures how many customers are waiting for orders to be filled. It is a more pure measure of customer satisfaction. The "buyer's misery index" and the sales value of orders past due can measure two different things but can be used in combination to evaluate process performance. For example, assume that a company has $1,000,000 in sales and 100 customers. The following are two possible scenarios:

Scenario	Sales Value of Orders Past Due	Buyer's Misery Index
1	$150,000	1
2	150,000	50

    In the first scenario, 15% of sales are past due to a single customer. The single customer is probably very upset, but all the other customers are being satisfied. Apparently, one large order was not delivered to the customer. This could be an isolated problem.

    In the second scenario, the same 15% of sales are past due. However, 50% of the customers are experiencing shipping delays. There will be widespread dissatisfaction with the delivery service in the marketplace. This is not an isolated problem but a systemic problem that is affecting half the customers.

    The sales value of orders past due gives an indication of the "depth" of a delivery problem, while the "buyer's misery index" gives an indication of the breadth of delivery problems.

2. The scrap is measured in sales dollars rather than cost in order to communicate the total value of potential lost sales. If an item is scrapped and not sold, then the company not only loses the cost of making the product but also the profit that could have been made from selling the product. The cost plus the profit is the sales value. Such a measure makes the most sense when an operation is producing all that it can sell (100% of capacity) and any scrapped items represent lost sales.

Activity 21-4

This is a case where there is strong evidence that the poor performance that is occurring inside the Assembly Department may be the result of behaviors outside of the department. This is one of the classic problems with variance analysis. Often, the variances reflect causes outside of the responsibility center manager's control. That is what appears to be happening here. The Assembly supervisor complains that both the purchased parts and incoming material from the Fabrication Department have been giving trouble. A review of performance reports reveals the following: (1) the materials price variance is very favorable; (2) the Fabrication Department's labor time variance is also very favorable. A possible explanation is that the Purchasing Department found a low-price supplier. The low price translated into a favorable variance. Unfortunately, it appears the company is "getting what it paid for." Specifically, it appears that the quality of the purchased parts has gone down, thus making assembly much more difficult in the Assembly Department. The Fabrication Department may be performing work faster than standard—again, resulting in a favorable labor time variance. It may be that the department is working too fast. Specifically, the speed is resulting in poor fabrication quality. Again, the Assembly Department is bearing the cost of poorly fabricated parts. The problem in both instances is that the variances measure only productivity and price savings and not quality. As a result, there are strong incentives to purchase from lowest bidders, work fast, cut corners, and push work on through. Unfortunately, the company is worse off, as a whole, due to this set of situations. The sum of the unfavorable variances in Assembly exceeds the favorable variances in the other departments. The analyst will need to confirm these suspicions. If they are supported, the company may wish to introduce quality measures in addition to the variance information in order to avoid the counterproductive behaviors in Purchasing and Fabrication.

Activity 21–5

The plant manager is placing pressure on the controller because the controllable variance is very unfavorable. The claim is that these costs are not really variable at all. This is a very difficult claim to accept. This is a small company, so it purchases its power from the outside. The power and light bill is variable to the amount of energy used in the plant. Energy usage is likely a function of the number of units produced. Likewise, the supplies are likely variable to machine usage, which is also related to the number of units produced. However, these two costs are not where the problem lies. The problem is with the indirect factory wages.

The indirect wages may not be completely variable. However, the variance is $10,000 or 25% higher than the standard. This is much greater than the 10% difference between the existing production volume and full capacity. In other words, even granting the plant manager's position on the indirect wages still does not explain the overall size of the variance. More is being spent on indirect wages than would be implied by even 100% production. Something appears amiss.

The controller should discuss these matters with the plant manager and attempt to discover why the indirect labor costs are so completely out of line with the standards. The plant manager has not complained about the standards yet but may do so in the future. It's very common for the standards to be criticized as too tight.

Activity 21–6

An example of a student response for police performance measures from the Web site is as follows:

	Service Performance	Internal Efficiency	Employee Satisfaction
Hours of patrol	X		X
Responses to calls for service	X		
Crimes investigated	X		
Number of arrests	X		
Persons participating in crime-prevention activities	X		
Deaths and bodily injury resulting from crime	X		
Value of property lost due to crime	X		
Crimes committed per 100,000 population	X		
Percentage of crimes cleared	X	X	
Response time	X		
Citizen satisfaction	X		
Cost per case assigned; cost per crime cleared		X	
Personnel hours per crime cleared		X	

CHAPTER 22
PERFORMANCE EVALUATION FOR DECENTRALIZED OPERATIONS

=52

CLASS DISCUSSION QUESTIONS

1. Cost centers, profit centers, and investment centers.

2. In the cost center, the department manager is responsible for and has authority over costs only. In a profit center, the manager's responsibility and authority extend to costs and revenues.

3. The department manager of a profit center has responsibility for and authority over costs and revenues, while the manager of an investment center has responsibility for and authority over investments in assets as well as costs and revenues.

4. The difference in budget performance reports prepared for department supervisors and plant managers is the amount of detail provided to each. The departmental supervisors require considerable detail to control costs. The report for the plant managers would contain more summarized cost data for the various departments.

5. A cost center manager is not responsible for making decisions concerning sales or the amount of fixed assets invested in the center.

6. A service department is a unit that serves many responsibility centers. The service department cost can be charged to responsibility centers based on the use of services. Responsibility center managers may choose how much service they desire from a service department.

7. The service department charge rate is determined by dividing the service department cost by the total estimated service usage (activity base).

8. Payroll: Number of checks issued. Accounts payable: Number of invoices paid. Accounts receivable: Number of sales invoices collected. Database administration: Number of reports.

9. Rate of return on investment and residual income.

10. The major shortcoming of using income from operations as a measure of investment center performance is that it ignores the amount of investment committed to each center. Since investment center managers also control the amount of assets invested in their centers, they should be held accountable for the use of invested assets.

11. Revenues and expenses are considered in computing the rate of return on investment because they directly impact the determination of income from operations. Invested assets are considered in computing the rate of return on investment because they are the base by which relative profitability is measured.

12.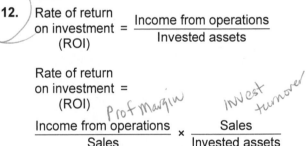

$$\text{Rate of return on investment (ROI)} = \frac{\text{Income from operations}}{\text{Invested assets}}$$

$$\text{Rate of return on investment (ROI)} = \frac{\text{Income from operations}}{\text{Sales}} \times \frac{\text{Sales}}{\text{Invested assets}}$$

Prof margin   Invest turnover

13. Rate of return on investment.

14. A division of a decentralized company could be considered the least profitable, even though it earned the largest amount of income from operations, when its rate of return on investment is the lowest. In this situation, the division would be considered the least profitable per dollar invested in the division.

15. Investment turnover.

16. By dividing income from operations by the amount of invested assets, each division is placed on a comparable basis of income from operations per dollar invested.

17. Division A. Division A will return 20 cents (20%) on each dollar of invested assets, while Divisions B and C will return only 17 cents and 15 cents, respectively. Thus, in expanding operations, Division A should be given priority over Divisions B and C.

18. Residual income = Income from operations − (Invested assets × Minimum acceptable rate of return on invested assets)

19. A balanced scorecard can indicate the underlying causes of financial performance from innovation and learning, customer, internal, and financial perspectives. In addition, a balanced set of measures helps managers consider trade-offs between short-term and long-term financial performance.

20. The objective of transfer pricing is to encourage each division manager to work in the best interests of the company. Thus, transfer prices should encourage managers to transfer goods between divisions if the overall company income can be increased.

21. When unused capacity exists in the supplying division, the negotiated price approach is preferred over the market price approach.

22. The company's management will have to intervene to set the transfer price.

23. The transfer price should be less than the market price but greater than the supplying division's variable cost per unit.

EXERCISES

Ex. 22–1

a.	$151,600	g.	$482,100
b.	$153,900	h.	$484,150
c.	$2,300	i.	$2,050
d.	$482,100	j.	$1,815,800
e.	$484,150	k.	$1,810,750
f.	$2,350	l.	$2,050

Schedules of supporting calculations (answers in italics; the solution requires working from the department level, up to the plant level, then to the vice-president of production level):

HANDY COMPANY
Budget Performance Report—Vice-President, Production
For the Month Ended April 30, 2003

Plant	Budget	Actual	Over Budget	Under Budget
St. Louis Plant	$ 523,700	$ 521,400		$2,300
Tempe Plant	810,000	805,200		4,800
Syracuse Plant	482,100	484,150	$2,050	
	$1,815,800	$1,810,750	$2,050	$7,100

HANDY COMPANY
Budget Performance Report—Manager, Syracuse Plant
For the Month Ended April 30, 2003

Department	Budget	Actual	Over Budget	Under Budget
Compressor Assembly	$151,600	$153,900	$2,300	
Electronic Assembly	125,700	125,750	50	
Final Assembly	204,800	204,500		$300
	$482,100	$484,150	$2,350	$300

Ex. 22–1   **Concluded**

b. MEMO

To: Karen Poling, Vice-President of Production

The Syracuse plant has experienced a $2,050 budget overrun, while the St. Louis and Tempe plants have experienced budget surpluses. The budget of the Syracuse plant reveals that the Compressor Assembly Department causes the majority of the budget overrun. The budget for the Compressor Assembly Department indicates that the budget overrun was caused by a combination of budget overruns in wages, power and light, and maintenance that exceeded a budget surplus in materials. The supervisor of the Compressor Assembly Department should investigate the reasons for the budget overruns in wages, power and light, and maintenance. It is possible that all three of these budget overruns have the same cause, such as a need for unplanned overtime or weekend work to meet schedules.

Ex. 22–2

CIRCLE D ELECTRICAL EQUIPMENT
Divisional Income Statements
For the Year Ended June 30, 2003

	Residential Division	Industrial Division
Net sales	$475,000	$825,000
Cost of goods sold	305,000	425,000
Gross profit	$170,000	$400,000
Administrative expenses	90,500	164,800
Income from operations before service department charges	$ 79,500	$235,200
Service department charges	25,800	75,200
Income from operations	$ 53,700	$160,000

Ex. 22–3

a.

	Residential	Commercial	Highway	Total
Number of payroll checks:				
Weekly payroll × 52......................	6,240	3,120	4,160	
Monthly payroll × 12...................	240	180	300	
Total......................................	6,480	3,300	4,460	14,240
Number of purchase requisitions				
per year......................................	1,600	1,400	1,200	4,200

	Service Dept. Cost	÷	Activity Base	=	Charge Rate
Service department charge rates:					
Payroll...	$149,520	÷	14,240	=	$10.50/check
Purchasing...................................	$59,640	÷	4,200	=	$14.20/req.

	Residential	Commercial	Highway	Total
Service department charges:				
Payroll...	$68,040	$34,650	$46,830	$149,520
Purchasing...................................	22,720	19,880	17,040	59,640
Total...	$90,760	$54,530	$63,870	

The service department charges are determined by multiplying the service department charge rate by the activity base for each division. For example, Residential's service department charges are determined as follows:

Payroll: $10.50 × 6,480 checks = $68,040

Purchasing: $14.20 × 1,600 purchase requisitions = $22,720

b. Residential's service department charge is higher than the other two divisions because Residential is a heavy user of service department services. Residential has many employees on a weekly payroll, which translates into a larger number of check-issuing transactions. This may be because residential jobs are less productive per labor hour, compared to larger commercial and highway jobs. Additionally, Residential uses purchasing services significantly more than the other two divisions. This may be because the division has many different smaller jobs requiring frequent purchase transactions.

Ex. 22–4

Expense	Activity Bases
a. Duplication services	Number of pages
b. Accounts receivable	Number of invoices, number of customers
c. Electronic data processing	Central processing unit (CPU) time, number of printed pages, amount of memory usage
d. Central purchasing	Number of requisitions, number of purchase orders
e. Legal	Number of hours
f. Telecommunications	Number of lines, number of long-distance minutes

Ex. 22–5

a.	8	e.	2
b.	3	f.	6
c.	4	g.	7
d.	5	h.	1

Ex. 22–6

a. Help desk: $\dfrac{\$156{,}000}{6{,}500 \text{ calls}}$ = $24 per call

Network center: $\dfrac{\$547{,}560}{10{,}800 \text{ devices}}$ = $50.70 per device monitored

Electronic mail: $\dfrac{\$180{,}000}{30{,}000 \text{ accounts}}$ = $6.00 per e-mail account

Local voice support: $\dfrac{\$416{,}560}{25{,}400 \text{ accounts}}$ = $16.40 per phone extension

b. **March charges to the COMM sector:**

Help desk charge: (5,800 employees × 50% × 80% × 0.30) × $24/call = $16,704

Network center charge: [(5,800 employees × 50% × 80%) + 300] × $50.70/device = $132,834

Electronic mail: (5,800 employees × 50% × 80% × 90%) × $6.00/e-mail account = $12,528

Local voice support: (5,800 employees × 50%) × $16.40/phone extension = $47,560

Ex. 22–7

ACADIA ELECTRONICS COMPANY
Divisional Income Statements
For the Year Ended December 31, 2003

	Video Division		Audio Division	
Revenues.....................................		$3,500,000		$2,750,000
Cost of goods sold		2,800,000		1,500,000
Gross profit...............................		$ 700,000		$1,250,000
Operating expenses		250,000		400,000
Income from operations before service department charges		$ 450,000		$ 850,000
Less service department charges:				
Computer Support Department...........................	$234,000		$126,000	
Accounts Payable Department...........................	56,250	290,250	68,750	194,750
Income from operations............		$ 159,750		$ 655,250

Supporting calculations for controllable service department charges:

Computer Support Department: ($360,000 ÷ 500) × 325 = $234,000
($360,000 ÷ 500) × 175 = $126,000

Accounts Payable Department: ($125,000 ÷ 10,000) × 4,500 = $56,250
($125,000 ÷ 10,000) × 5,500 = $68,750

Ex. 22–8

a. The reported income from operations does not accurately measure perform-ance because the service department charges are based on revenues. Reve-nues are not associated with the profit center manager's use of the service department services. For example, the Reservations Department serves only the Passenger Division. Thus, by charging this cost on the basis of revenues, these costs are incorrectly charged to the Cargo Division. Additionally, the passenger division requires flight attendants. Since these flight attendants must be trained, the training costs assigned to the Passenger Division should be greater than the Cargo Division.

b.

ATLANTIC AIRLINES INC.
Divisional Income Statements
For the Year Ended October 31, 2003

	Passenger Division		Cargo Division	
Revenues.....................................		$ 6,500,000		$6,500,000
Operating expenses		5,500,000		5,000,000
Income from operations before service department charges		$ 1,000,000		$1,500,000
Less service department charges:				
Training (Note 1)...................	$240,000		$ 60,000	
Flight scheduling (Note 2) ...	144,000		256,000	
Reservations........................	600,000	984,000	—	316,000
Income from operations............		$ 16,000		$1,184,000

Note 1: Passenger Division, ($300,000 ÷ 200) × 160
         Cargo Division, ($300,000 ÷ 200) × 40

Note 2: Passenger Division, ($400,000 ÷ 500) × 180
         Cargo Division, ($400,000 ÷ 500) × 320

Ex. 22–9

TAHOE SPORTING GOODS CO.
Divisional Income Statements
For the Year Ended June 30, 2003

	Camping Equipment Division	Ski Equipment Division
Sales	$460,000	$745,000
Cost of goods sold	215,000	385,000
Gross profit	$245,000	$360,000
Divisional selling expenses	$ 80,000	$105,000
Divisional administrative expenses	45,400	66,800
	$125,400	$171,800
Income from operations before service department charges	$119,600	$188,200
Less service department charges:		
Advertising expense	$ 7,400	$ 12,500
Transportation expense	10,350	11,700
Accounts receivable collection expense	1,600	2,000
Warehouse expense	30,000	15,000
Total	$ 49,350	$ 41,200
Income from operations	$ 70,250	$147,000

Supporting Schedule:

Service Department Charges

	Camping Division	Ski Division	Total
Advertising expense	$ 7,400	$12,500	$19,900
Transportation rate per bill of lading	$ 4.50	$ 4.50	
Number of bills of lading	× 2,300	× 2,600	
Transportation expense	$10,350	$11,700	$22,050
Accounts receivable collection rate	$ 0.80	$ 0.80	
Number of sales invoices	× 2,000	× 2,500	
Accounts receivable collection expense.......	$ 1,600	$ 2,000	$ 3,600
Warehouse rate per sq. ft. ($45,000/15,000 sq. ft.)	$ 3.00	$ 3.00	
Number of square feet	×10,000	× 5,000	
Warehouse expense	$30,000	$15,000	$45,000

Ex. 22–10

a. Cheese Division: 14% ($133,000 ÷ $950,000)

Milk Division: 20% ($104,000 ÷ $520,000)

Butter Division: 16% ($182,400 ÷ $1,140,000)

b. Milk Division

Ex. 22–11

a.

	Cheese Division	Milk Division	Butter Division
Income from operations	$133,000	$104,000	$182,400
Minimum amount of income from operations:			
$950,000 × 12%	114,000		
$520,000 × 12%		62,400	
$1,140,000 × 12%			136,800
Residual income	$ 19,000	$ 41,600	$ 45,600

b. Butter Division

Ex. 22–12

a. Rate of Return on Investment = $\dfrac{\text{Income from operations}}{\text{Revenues}} \times \dfrac{\text{Revenues}}{\text{Invested assets}}$

Creative Content:
$$\dfrac{\$1,403}{\$10,302} \times \dfrac{\$10,302}{\$9,509}$$
$$= 13.62\% \times 1.08$$
$$= 14.71\%$$

Broadcasting:
$$\dfrac{\$1,325}{\$7,142} \times \dfrac{\$7,142}{\$20,099}$$
$$= 18.55\% \times 0.36$$
$$= 6.68\%$$

Theme Parks and Resorts:
$$\dfrac{\$1,287}{\$5,532} \times \dfrac{\$5,532}{\$9,214}$$
$$= 23.26\% \times 0.60$$
$$= 13.96\%$$

b. The three sectors are very different. The Theme Parks sector has the best profit margin of the three sectors at 23.26%, while the Creative Content sector has the smallest profit margin at 13.62%. The investment turnover is also different across the sectors. The Broadcasting sector has the smallest investment turnover. The Creative Content sector has the best investment turnover. Apparently, the Theme Parks and Broadcasting sectors are asset-intensive relative to the revenues generated. This seems reasonable. Movie production and the broadcasting network would require significant assets in studios and broadcasting assets. In contrast, the Creative Content division is able to generate licensing revenues with much smaller asset investments. Combining the profit margin and investment turnover together shows that the Creative Content sector generates the greatest rate of return on assets at 14.71%, with the Theme Parks sector not far behind at 13.96%. However, these two sectors earn their rate of return on assets from different directions. The Theme Parks sector has a very high profit margin, but a lower investment turnover, while the Creative Content sector has a lower profit margin combined with a high investment turnover. The Broadcasting sector lags behind with a rate of return on assets of 6.68%. The Broadcasting sector has a good profit margin, but the investment turnover is very low, causing the low rate of return on assets.

Ex. 22–13

a. 1.5 (27% ÷ 18%)

b. 24% (12% × 2.0)

c. 24% (18% ÷ 0.75)

d. 1.4 (21% ÷ 15%)

e. 14% (8% × 1.75)

Ex. 22–14

a.

$$\text{Rate of return on investment (ROI)} = \text{Profit margin} \times \text{Investment turnover}$$

$$\text{Rate of return on investment (ROI)} = \frac{\text{Income from operations}}{\text{Sales}} \times \frac{\text{Sales}}{\text{Invested assets}}$$

$$\text{ROI} = \frac{\$115,000}{\$500,000} \times \frac{\$500,000}{\$625,000}$$

$$\text{ROI} = 23\% \times 0.80$$

$$\text{ROI} = 18.4\%$$

b. The profit margin would increase from 23% to 27%, the investment turnover would remain unchanged, and the rate of return on investment would increase from 18.4% to 21.6%, as shown below.

$$\text{Rate of return on investment (ROI)} = \text{Profit margin} \times \text{Investment turnover}$$

$$\text{Rate of return on investment (ROI)} = \frac{\text{Income from operations}}{\text{Sales}} \times \frac{\text{Sales}}{\text{Invested assets}}$$

$$\text{ROI} = \frac{\$135,000}{\$500,000} \times \frac{\$500,000}{\$625,000}$$

$$\text{ROI} = 27\% \times 0.80$$

$$\text{ROI} = 21.6\%$$

Ex. 22–15

a. 12% ($54,000 ÷ $450,000)
b. $45,000 ($450,000 × 10%)
c. $9,000 ($54,000 – $45,000)
d. $30,800 ($220,000 × 14%)
e. 16% ($35,200 ÷ $220,000)
f. $67,000 ($50,250 + $16,750)

g. 20% ($67,000 ÷ $335,000)
h. 15% ($50,250 ÷ $335,000)
i. 15% ($77,250 ÷ $515,000)
j. $61,800 ($515,000 × 12%)
k. $15,450 ($77,250 – $61,800)

Ex. 22–16

a. (a) 17.5% ($119,000 ÷ $680,000)
   (b) 14% ($119,000 ÷ $850,000)
   (c) 1.25 ($850,000 ÷ $680,000)
   (d) $48,900 ($407,500 × 12%)
   (e) 15% ($48,900 ÷ $326,000)
   (f) 0.80 ($326,000 ÷ $407,500)
   (g) $480,000 ($60,000 ÷ 12.5%)
   (h) $750,000 ($480,000 ÷ 0.64)
   (i) 8% (12.5% × 0.64)
   (j) $58,400 ($365,000 × 16%)
   (k) $292,000 ($58,400 ÷ 20%)
   (l) 1.25 (20% ÷ 16%)

b. North Division: $51,000 [$119,000 – ($680,000 × 10%)]
   East Division: $8,150 [$48,900 – ($407,500 × 10%)]
   South Division: $(15,000) [$60,000 – ($750,000 × 10%)]
   West Division: $29,200 [$58,400 – ($292,000 × 10%)]

c. (a) The West Division has the highest return on investment (20%).
   (b) The North Division has the largest residual income. Even though the North Division's rate of return is slightly lower than the West Division's (17.5% vs. 20%), the residual income is larger because the investment is large, relative to the West Division.

Ex. 22–17

Although there is some judgment in classifying each of these measures, the following represents our assessment with explanations.

Average cardmember spending	Customer—demonstrates the usefulness of the card to the customer.
Cards in force	Customer—if customers did not value the card, they would not have one.
Earnings growth	Financial
Hours of credit consultant training	Internal process—advisors will do their job better if they are trained.
Investment in information technology	Internal process (or innovation)—shows the investment in improving processes.
Number of Internet features	Internal process (or innovation)—shows new process investments in a new channel.
Number of merchant signings	Customer—the larger the number of merchants that honor the card, the more valuable it is to cardholders.
Number of card choices	Customer—more choices are more valuable to customers.
Number of new card launches	Innovation—measures the new cards (affinity, regional, etc.) being developed and marketed.
Return on equity	Financial
Revenue growth	Financial

Ex. 22–18

a. UPS wanted a performance measurement system that would focus more on the underlying drivers, or levers, of financial success. It believed that focusing on the financial numbers by themselves would not reveal *how* financial objectives were to be achieved, especially with new demands coming from customers in the Internet age. The balanced scorecard provides information on how the financial targets are to be achieved. Using common measures throughout the organization also aligns the organization, while simultaneously communicating priorities. Apparently, UPS determined that its future success as an organization depended upon "point of arrival" measures. These measures emphasized customer performance to a much higher degree than would straight financial numbers.

b. The employee sentiment number is common in service businesses. The employees are the face of the company to the customer. If employees feel poorly about the organization, or if they feel that they don't make a difference, then they are not likely to deliver premium service experiences to their customers. Just think of the variety of fast food experiences you may have had in the past month. Sometimes, the service is excellent with a smile; at other times, it's poor with a scowl. Measuring the improving employee morale is critical to organizations relying on front-line employees that deliver the customer experience.

Ex. 22–19

a. $2,800,000. Structure Motors' total income from operations would increase by the difference between the market price of $260 and the Component Division's variable costs per unit of $190, multiplied by 40,000 units.

b. $1,200,000. The Truck Division's income from operations would increase by the difference between the market price of $260 and the transfer price of $230, multiplied by 40,000 units.

c. $1,600,000. The Component Division's income from operations would increase by the difference between the transfer price of $230 and the Component Division's variable costs per unit of $190, multiplied by 40,000 units.

Ex. 22–20

a. $2,800,000. Structure Motors' total income from operations would increase by the difference between the market price of $260 and the Component Division's variable costs per unit of $190, multiplied by 40,000 units. This amount is the same amount by which Structure Motors' income from operations increased in Ex. 22–19, when a transfer price of $230 was used.

b. $400,000. The Truck Division's income from operations would increase by the difference between the market price of $260 and the transfer price of $250, multiplied by 40,000 units.

c. $2,400,000. The Component Division's income from operations would increase by the difference between the transfer price of $250 and the Component Division's variable costs per unit of $190, multiplied by 40,000 units.

d. Any transfer price will cause the total income of the company to increase, as long as the supplier division capacity is used toward making materials for products that are ultimately sold to the outside. This is because the transfer price affects only the profit allocated between the two divisions, not the total profit. However, transfer prices should be set between variable cost and selling price in order to give the division managers proper incentives. A transfer price set below variable cost would cause the supplier division to incur a loss, while a transfer price set above market price would cause the purchasing division to incur opportunity costs. Neither situation is an attractive alternative for an investment center manager. Thus, the general rule is to negotiate transfer prices between variable cost and selling price when the supplier division has excess capacity. The range of acceptable transfer prices for Structure Motors would be between $190 and $260.

PROBLEMS

Prob. 22–1A

1.

Budget Performance Report—Manager, Eastern District
For the Month Ended September 30, 2003

	Budget	Actual	Over Budget	Under Budget
Sales salaries...	$ 625,700	$ 623,700		$2,000
Network administration salaries	321,900	320,100		1,800
Customer service salaries....................	173,400	189,200	$15,800	
Billing salaries	61,300	60,800		500
Maintenance..	162,000	162,800	800	
Depreciation of plant and equipment .	58,000	58,000		
Insurance and property taxes	31,400	31,600	200	
Total..	$1,433,700	$1,446,200	$16,800	$4,300

2. The customer service salaries exceed the budget by approximately 9% of budget ($15,800/$173,400). The maintenance and insurance and property taxes are also over budget; however, the relative amount is insignificant. The other favorable variances are also small relative to the budget amount. The manager should request additional detailed information about the customer service department. There are several possible reasons for the budget variance. The manager should determine if the cause is related to an increase in salaries or an increase in people. If the latter, the manager may wish to determine if there has been an increase in customer service problems, hence a need to hire additional people. Such information could be used by the manager to solve customer service complaints and to reduce the number of future complaints.

Prob. 22–1A   Concluded

This solution is applicable only if the GENERAL LEDGER SOFTWARE that accompanies the text is used.

EASTERN DISTRICT
Budget Report
For the Period Ended September 30, 2003

	Budget	Actual	Difference from Budget	%
Operating revenue..........................	$ 2,150,000	$ 2,125,000	$ (25,000)	– 1.16%
Operating expenses:				
Sales salaries	$ 625,700	$ 623,700	$ (2,000)	– 0.32%
Network administration				
salaries	321,900	320,100	(1,800)	– 0.56%
Customer service salaries......	173,400	189,200	15,800	9.11%
Billing salaries..........................	61,300	60,800	(500)	– 0.82%
Maintenance	162,000	162,800	800	0.49%
Depreciation of plant				
and equipment	58,000	58,000	0	0.00%
Insurance and property taxes	31,400	31,600	200	0.64%
Total operating expenses..	$ 1,433,700	$ 1,446,200	$ 12,500	0.87%
Net income	$ 716,300	$ 678,800	$ (37,500)	– 5.24%

Prob. 22–2A

1.

CONTINENTAL RAILROAD COMPANY
Divisional Income Statements
For the Quarter Ended December 31, 2004

	Northwest	Western	Northern
Revenues...	$1,850,000	$2,830,000	$2,180,000
Operating expenses	900,000	1,750,000	1,430,000
Income from operations before service department charges..................................	$ 950,000	$1,080,000	$ 750,000
Less service department charges:			
Dispatching ($210 × scheduled trains).....	$ 115,500	$ 178,500	$ 126,000
Equipment management ($30 × railroad cars).............................	150,000	180,000	180,000
	$ 265,500	$ 358,500	$ 306,000
Income from operations..................................	$ 684,500	$ 721,500	$ 444,000

Supporting schedules:

Service department charge rates for the two service departments, Dispatching and Equipment, are determined as follows:

	Northwest	Western	Northern	Total
Number of scheduled trains......	550	850	600	2,000
Number of railroad cars.............	5,000	6,000	6,000	17,000

	Service Cost	÷	Output	=	Rate
Dispatching rate	$420,000	÷	2,000	=	$210 per train
Equipment management rate	510,000	÷	17,000	=	30 per railroad car

Note: The Internal Auditing Department and general corporate officers' salaries are not controllable by division management and thus are not included in determining division income from operations.

Prob. 22–2A   Concluded

2. The CEO evaluates the three divisions using income from operations as a percent of revenues. This measure is calculated for the three divisions as follows:

Northwest Division: 37.00% ($684,500 ÷ $1,850,000)

Western Division: 25.49% ($721,500 ÷ $2,830,000)

Northern Division: 20.37% ($444,000 ÷ $2,180,000)

Thus, according to the CEO's measure, the Northwest Division has the highest performance.

3. To: CEO

The method used to evaluate the performance of the divisions should be re-evaluated. The present method identifies the amount of income from operations per dollar of earned revenue. However, this railroad requires a significant investment in fixed assets, such as track, engines, and railcars. In addition, the amount of assets may not be related to the revenue earned. For example, some regions may be able to concentrate assets in a densely populated regional area and run a high amount of traffic over those assets. Other regions, however, may have widely distributed assets over sparsely populated areas that run a small amount of traffic over those assets. The present measure fails to incorporate these differences in asset utilization into the measure. Naturally, the amount of assets used by a division in earning a return is a very important consideration in evaluating divisional performance. Therefore, a better divisional performance measure would be either (a) rate of return on investment (income from operations divided by divisional assets) or (b) residual income (income from operations less a minimal return on divisional assets). Both measures incorporate the assets used by the divisions.

Prob. 22–3A

1.

UNION TRUST INC.
Divisional Income Statements
For the Year Ended December 31, 2003

	Retail Broker Division	E-trade Division	Mutual Fund Division
Fee revenue...	$625,000	$250,000	$860,000
Operating expenses	350,000	225,000	705,200
Income from operations	$275,000	$ 25,000	$154,800

2.

$$\text{Rate of return on investment (ROI)} = \text{Profit margin} \times \text{Investment turnover}$$

$$\text{Rate of return on investment (ROI)} = \frac{\text{Income from operations}}{\text{Sales}} \times \frac{\text{Sales}}{\text{Invested assets}}$$

Retail Broker Division:
$$\text{ROI} = \frac{\$275,000}{\$625,000} \times \frac{\$625,000}{\$3,125,000}$$
$$\text{ROI} = 44\% \times 0.20$$
$$\text{ROI} = 8.8\%$$

E-trade Division:
$$\text{ROI} = \frac{\$25,000}{\$250,000} \times \frac{\$250,000}{\$125,000}$$
$$\text{ROI} = 10\% \times 2$$
$$\text{ROI} = 20\%$$

Mutual Fund Division:
$$\text{ROI} = \frac{\$154,800}{\$860,000} \times \frac{\$860,000}{\$1,000,000}$$
$$\text{ROI} = 18\% \times 0.86$$
$$\text{ROI} = 15.48\%$$

3. Per dollar of invested assets, the E-trade Division is the most profitable of the three divisions. Assuming that the rates of return on investments do not change in the future, an expansion of the E-trade Division will return 20 cents (20%) on each dollar of invested assets, while the Retail Broker and Mutual Fund Divisions will return only 8.8 cents (8.8%) and 15.48 cents (15.48%), respectively. Thus, when faced with limited funds for expansion, management should consider an expansion of the E-trade Division first.

Note to Instructors: The Retail Broker Division has excellent profit margins, but the investment turnover is very low. The investment in the "bricks and mortar" of the Retail Division offices causes the rate of return on assets to be unimpressive. However, the E-trade Division has very thin margins because the fees earned per trade are very small. However, the assets required to execute trades are much less than the Retail Broker Division because there is no need for offices (trades are executed over the Internet). As a result of the high investment turnover in the E-trade Division, the rate of return on assets is much better.

Prob. 22–4A

1.

$$\text{Rate of return on investment (ROI)} = \text{Profit margin} \times \text{Investment turnover}$$

$$\text{Rate of return on investment (ROI)} = \frac{\text{Income from operations}}{\text{Sales}} \times \frac{\text{Sales}}{\text{Invested assets}}$$

$$\text{Golf Equipment Division: ROI} = \frac{\$696,000}{\$4,800,000} \times \frac{\$4,800,000}{\$4,000,000}$$

$$\text{ROI} = 14.5\% \times 1.20$$

$$\text{ROI} = 17.40\%$$

2.

ST. ANDREWS INC.—GOLF EQUIPMENT DIVISION
Estimated Income Statements
For the Year Ended January 31, 2003

	Proposal 1	Proposal 2	Proposal 3
Sales..	$ 4,300,000	$ 4,800,000	$ 4,800,000
Cost of goods sold..........................	2,327,000	2,722,000	2,482,000
Gross profit.....................................	$ 1,973,000	$ 2,078,000	$ 2,318,000
Operating expenses........................	1,414,000	1,454,000	1,454,000
Income from operations	$ 559,000	$ 624,000	$ 864,000
Invested assets	$ 3,440,000	$ 3,000,000	$ 4,800,000

Prob. 22–4A   Concluded

3. Rate of return on investment (ROI) = Profit margin × Investment turnover

Rate of return on investment (ROI) = $\dfrac{\text{Income from operations}}{\text{Sales}} \times \dfrac{\text{Sales}}{\text{Invested assets}}$

Proposal 1: ROI = $\dfrac{\$559{,}000}{\$4{,}300{,}000} \times \dfrac{\$4{,}300{,}000}{\$3{,}440{,}000}$

ROI = 13% × 1.25

ROI = 16.25%

Proposal 2: ROI = $\dfrac{\$624{,}000}{\$4{,}800{,}000} \times \dfrac{\$4{,}800{,}000}{\$3{,}000{,}000}$

ROI = 13% × 1.60

ROI = 20.8%

Proposal 3: ROI = $\dfrac{\$864{,}000}{\$4{,}800{,}000} \times \dfrac{\$4{,}800{,}000}{\$4{,}800{,}000}$

ROI = 18% × 1.0

ROI = 18%

4. Proposal 2 would yield a rate of return on investment of 20.8%.

5. Rate of return on investment (ROI) = Profit margin × Required investment turnover

20% = 14.5% × Required investment turnover

Required investment turnover = 1.38   (20% ÷ 14.5%)

Current investment turnover = 1.20

Increase in investment turnover = 0.18

or

15% Increase (0.18 ÷ 1.20)

Prob. 22–5A

1.

VAN HORNE COMMERCIAL FURNITURE COMPANY
Divisional Income Statements
For the Year Ended July 31, 2003

	Office Division	Hotel Division
Sales	$6,500,000	$5,000,000
Cost of goods sold	3,200,000	2,200,000
Gross profit	$3,300,000	$2,800,000
Operating expenses	1,350,000	1,300,000
Income from operations	$1,950,000	$1,500,000

2.

Rate of return on investment (ROI) = Profit margin × Investment turnover

$$\text{Rate of return on investment (ROI)} = \frac{\text{Income from operations}}{\text{Sales}} \times \frac{\text{Sales}}{\text{Invested assets}}$$

Office Division:
$$\text{ROI} = \frac{\$1,950,000}{\$6,500,000} \times \frac{\$6,500,000}{\$16,250,000}$$

$$\text{ROI} = 30\% \times 0.40$$

$$\text{ROI} = 12\%$$

Hotel Division:
$$\text{ROI} = \frac{\$1,500,000}{\$5,000,000} \times \frac{\$5,000,000}{\$6,250,000}$$

$$\text{ROI} = 30\% \times 0.80$$

$$\text{ROI} = 24\%$$

3. Office Division: $325,000 [$1,950,000 − ($16,250,000 × 10%)]
Hotel Division: $875,000 [$1,500,000 − ($6,250,000 × 10%)]

Prob. 22–5A   Concluded

4. On the basis of income from operations, the Office Division generated $450,000 more income from operations than did the Hotel Division. However, income from operations does not consider the amount of invested assets in each division. On the basis of the rate of return on investment, the Hotel Division earned 24 cents (24%) on each dollar of invested assets, while the Office Division earned only 12 cents (12%) on each dollar of invested assets. Although the Office Division has the same profit margin as the Hotel Division (30%), the Hotel Division has a higher investment turnover (0.80 vs. 0.40), which generated its higher rate of return on investment. Residual income can be viewed as a combination of the preceding two performance measures. Residual income considers the absolute dollar amount of income from operations generated by each division and also considers a minimum rate of return to be earned by each division. On the basis of residual income, the Hotel Division is the more profitable of the two divisions.

Prob. 22–6A

1. No. When unused capacity exists in the supplying division (the Electronics Division), the use of the market price approach may not lead to the maximization of total company income.

2. The Electronics Division's income from operations would increase by $86,000 (the amount by which the transfer price of $2,000 exceeds the Electronics Division's variable expenses per unit of $1,570, multiplied by 200 units). By selling to the Instruments Division, the Electronics Division earns $430 per unit on these sales.

    The Instruments Division's income from operations would increase by $100,000 (the difference between the market price of $2,500 and the transfer price of $2,000, multiplied by 200 units). By purchasing from the Electronics Division, the Instruments Division saves $500 per unit on its purchases.

    Fisher Instrument Company's total income from operations would increase by $186,000 (the difference between the market price of $2,500, which the Instruments Division had been paying to outside suppliers, and the Electronics Division's variable expenses per unit of $1,570, multiplied by 200 units). The increase in total company income from operations is also equal to the sum of the increases in the division incomes from operations.

3.

FISHER INSTRUMENT COMPANY
Divisional Income Statements
For the Year Ended December 31, 2003

	Electronics	Instruments	Total
Sales:			
700 units × $2,500 per unit............	$1,750,000		$1,750,000
200 units × $2,000 per unit............	400,000		400,000
1,200 units × $5,500 per unit.........		$6,600,000	6,600,000
	$2,150,000	$6,600,000	$8,750,000
Expenses:			
Variable:			
900 units × $1,570 per unit........	$1,413,000		$1,413,000
200 units × $3,700* per unit.......		$ 740,000	740,000
1,000 units × $4,200** per unit..		4,200,000	4,200,000
Fixed	430,000	735,000	1,165,000
Total expenses..........................	$1,843,000	$5,675,000	$7,518,000
Income from operations......................	$ 307,000	$ 925,000	$1,232,000

* The 200 units are transferred in at $2,000 per unit plus $1,700 operating expenses in the division.

** The remaining 1,000 units are purchased on the outside at a price of $2,500 per unit plus $1,700 operating expenses in the division.

Prob. 22–6A   Concluded

4. The Electronics Division's income from operations would increase by $46,000 (the amount by which the transfer price of $1,800 exceeds the Electronics Division's variable expenses per unit of $1,570, multiplied by 200 units). By selling to the Instruments Division, the Electronics Division earns $230 per unit on these sales.

    The Instruments Division's income from operations would increase by $140,000 (the difference between the market price of $2,500 and the transfer price of $1,800, multiplied by 200 units). By purchasing from the Electronics Division, the Instruments Division saves $700 per unit on its purchases.

    Fisher Instrument Company's total income from operations would increase by the same amount as in (2), $186,000 (the difference between the market price of $2,500, which the Instruments Division had been paying to outside suppliers, and the Electronics Division's variable expenses per unit of $1,570, multiplied by 200 units). The increase in total company income from operations is also equal to the sum of the increases in the division incomes from operations.

5. a. Any transfer price greater than the Electronics Division's variable expenses per unit of $1,570 but less than the market price of $2,500 would be acceptable.

    b. If the division managers cannot agree on a transfer price, a price of $2,035 would be the best compromise. In this way, each division's income from operations would increase by $93,000.

Prob. 22–1B

1.

Budget Performance Report—Director, International Division
For the Month Ended April 30, 2003

	Budget	Actual	Over Budget	Under Budget
Software engineer salaries	$185,000	$183,400		$1,600
Customer service salaries	95,800	124,700	$28,900	
Logistics salaries......................	165,000	163,700		1,300
Marketing salaries	225,000	248,000	23,000	
Warehouse wages	115,500	115,000		500
Equipment depreciation...........	35,000	36,000	1,000	
Insurance and property taxes..	28,000	27,800		200
Total	$849,300	$898,600	$52,900	$3,600

2. The customer service and marketing salaries are significantly over budget. The director should investigate the cause of these results. One possibility is that the company is having an increase in sales, requiring greater marketing effort and customer service. However, the warehouse and logistics costs have not shown similar increases. Thus it's also possible that marketing and customer service salaries are increasing because of service problems and unplanned efforts to market the company's service.

Prob. 22–1B   Concluded

This solution is applicable only if the GENERAL LEDGER SOFTWARE that accompanies the text is used.

INTERNATIONAL DIVISION
Budget Report
For the Month Ended April 30, 2003

	Budget	Actual	Difference from Budget	%
Operating revenue............................	$1,000,000	$1,223,600	$ 223,600	22.36%
Operating expenses:				
Software engineer salaries........	$ 185,000	$ 183,400	$ (1,600)	– 0.86%
Customer service salaries.........	95,800	124,700	28,900	30.17%
Logistics salaries........................	165,000	163,700	(1,300)	– 0.79%
Marketing salaries.......................	225,000	248,000	23,000	10.22%
Warehouse wages.......................	115,500	115,000	(500)	– 0.43%
Equipment depreciation	35,000	36,000	1,000	2.86%
Insurance and property taxes ...	28,000	27,800	(200)	– 0.71%
Total operating expenses.....	$ 849,300	$ 898,600	$ 49,300	5.80%
Net income	$ 150,700	$ 325,000	$ 174,300	115.66%

Prob. 22–2B

1.

APPALACHIAN GAS COMPANY
Divisional Income Statements
For the Quarter Ended December 31, 2003

	Central	Coastal	Metro
Revenue...	$485,000	$732,000	$940,000
Operating expenses	282,400	432,500	575,000
Income from operations before service department charges......................................	$202,600	$299,500	$365,000
Less service department charges:			
Customer support ($7.80 × customer calls)	$ 15,600	$ 19,500	$ 42,900
Central accounting ($3.65 × number of accounting reports).....	30,660	38,325	25,915
	$ 46,260	$ 57,825	$ 68,815
Income from operations.....................................	$156,340	$241,675	$296,185

Supporting schedules:

Service department charge rates for the two service departments, Customer Support and Central Accounting, are determined as follows:

	Central	Coastal	Metro	Total
Number of customer calls.............	2,000	2,500	5,500	10,000
Number of accounting reports	8,400	10,500	7,100	26,000

	Service Cost	÷	Output	=	Rate
Customer call rate	$78,000	÷	10,000	=	$7.80 per call
Accounting report rate	94,900	÷	26,000	=	3.65 per report

Note: The Shareholder Relations Department and general corporate officers' salaries are not controllable by division management and thus are not included in determining division income from operations.

Prob. 22–2B   Concluded

2.   Central Division: 32.24% ($156,340 ÷ $485,000)

Coastal Division: 33.02% ($241,675 ÷ $732,000)

Metro Division: 31.51% ($296,185 ÷ $940,000)

According to the CEO's measure, the Coastal Division has the highest performance.

3.   To: CEO

The method used to evaluate the performance of the divisions should be re-evaluated. The present method identifies the amount of income from operations per dollar of earned revenue. However, this gas company requires a significant investment in fixed assets, such as pipelines and compressors. In addition, the amount of assets may not be related to the revenue earned. For example, some regions are able to concentrate assets in a densely populated regional area and use a high amount of gas over those assets (e.g., Metro Division). Other regions, however, have widely distributed assets over sparsely populated areas that use a smaller amount of gas over those assets. The present measure fails to incorporate these differences in asset utilization into the measure. Naturally, the amount of assets used by a division in earning a return is a very important consideration in evaluating divisional performance. Therefore, a better divisional performance measure would be either (a) rate of return on investment (income from operations divided by divisional assets) or (b) residual income (income from operations less a minimal return on divisional assets). Both measures incorporate the assets used by the divisions.

Prob. 22–3B

1.

RISE 'N SHINE FOOD COMPANY
Divisional Income Statements
For the Year Ended June 30, 2003

	Cereal Division	Fruit Juice Division	Bread Division
Sales	$1,000,000	$1,500,000	$625,000
Cost of goods sold	630,000	950,000	350,000
Gross profit	$ 370,000	$ 550,000	$275,000
Operating expenses	120,000	400,000	120,000
Income from operations.....................	$ 250,000	$ 150,000	$155,000

2.

$$\text{Rate of return on investment (ROI)} = \text{Profit margin} \times \text{Investment turnover}$$

$$\text{Rate of return on investment (ROI)} = \frac{\text{Income from operations}}{\text{Sales}} \times \frac{\text{Sales}}{\text{Invested assets}}$$

Cereal Division: $\text{ROI} = \dfrac{\$250,000}{\$1,000,000} \times \dfrac{\$1,000,000}{\$1,250,000}$

$\text{ROI} = 25\% \times 0.80$

$\text{ROI} = 20\%$

Fruit Juice Division: $\text{ROI} = \dfrac{\$150,000}{\$1,500,000} \times \dfrac{\$1,500,000}{\$2,000,000}$

$\text{ROI} = 10\% \times 0.75$

$\text{ROI} = 7.5\%$

Bread Division: $\text{ROI} = \dfrac{\$155,000}{\$625,000} \times \dfrac{\$625,000}{\$500,000}$

$\text{ROI} = 24.8\% \times 1.25$

$\text{ROI} = 31\%$

3. Per dollar of invested assets, the Bread Division is the most profitable of the three divisions. Assuming that the rates of return on investments do not change in the future, an expansion of the Bread Division will return 31 cents (31%) on each dollar of invested assets, while the Cereal and Fruit Juice Divisions will return only 20 cents (20%) and 7.5 cents (7.5%), respectively. Thus, when faced with limited funds for expansion, management should consider an expansion of the Bread Division first.

Prob. 22–4B

1. $\text{Rate of return on investment (ROI)} = \text{Profit margin} \times \text{Investment turnover}$

$$\text{Rate of return on investment (ROI)} = \frac{\text{Income from operations}}{\text{Sales}} \times \frac{\text{Sales}}{\text{Invested assets}}$$

Music Division: $\text{ROI} = \dfrac{\$90,200}{\$820,000} \times \dfrac{\$820,000}{\$512,500}$

$\text{ROI} = 11\% \times 1.60$

$\text{ROI} = 17.60\%$

2.

HOLLYWOOD ENTERTAINMENT INC.—MUSIC DIVISION
Estimated Income Statements
For the Year Ended December 31, 2003

	Proposal 1	Proposal 2	Proposal 3
Sales	$ 680,000	$ 820,000	$ 820,000
Cost of goods sold	285,000	379,600	248,400
Gross profit	$ 395,000	$ 440,400	$ 571,600
Operating expenses	299,800	374,800	374,800
Income from operations	$ 95,200	$ 65,600	$ 196,800
Invested assets	$ 425,000	$ 410,000	$ 1,025,000

Prob. 22–4B   Concluded

3. Rate of return on investment (ROI) = Profit margin × Investment turnover

$$\text{Rate of return on investment (ROI)} = \frac{\text{Income from operations}}{\text{Sales}} \times \frac{\text{Sales}}{\text{Invested assets}}$$

Proposal 1: $\text{ROI} = \dfrac{\$95,200}{\$680,000} \times \dfrac{\$680,000}{\$425,000}$

$\quad\quad\quad\quad\text{ROI} = 14\% \times 1.60$

$\quad\quad\quad\quad\text{ROI} = 22.4\%$

Proposal 2: $\text{ROI} = \dfrac{\$65,600}{\$820,000} \times \dfrac{\$820,000}{\$410,000}$

$\quad\quad\quad\quad\text{ROI} = 8\% \times 2.0$

$\quad\quad\quad\quad\text{ROI} = 16\%$

Proposal 3: $\text{ROI} = \dfrac{\$196,800}{\$820,000} \times \dfrac{\$820,000}{\$1,025,000}$

$\quad\quad\quad\quad\text{ROI} = 24\% \times 0.80$

$\quad\quad\quad\quad\text{ROI} = 19.2\%$

4. Proposal 1 would yield a rate of return on investment of 22.4%.

5. Rate of return on investment (ROI) = Profit margin × Required investment turnover

$\quad\quad\quad\quad\quad\quad\quad\quad\quad 20\% = 11\% \times$ Required investment turnover

$\quad\quad$ Required Investment Turnover $= 1.82\ (20\% \div 11\%)$

$\quad\quad$ Current Investment Turnover $= \underline{1.60}$

$\quad\quad$ Increase in Investment Turnover $= \underline{0.22}$

or

13.75% Increase (0.22 ÷ 1.60)

Prob. 22–5B

1.

FLEET SHOE COMPANY
Divisional Income Statements
For the Year Ended December 31, 2003

	Men's Division	Women's Division
Sales..	$3,000,000	$2,400,000
Cost of goods sold.....................................	1,800,000	1,250,000
Gross profit..	$1,200,000	$1,150,000
Operating expenses...................................	450,000	718,000
Income from operations.............................	$ 750,000	$ 432,000

2.

$$\text{Rate of return on investment (ROI)} = \text{Profit margin} \times \text{Investment turnover}$$

$$\text{Rate of return on investment (ROI)} = \frac{\text{Income from operations}}{\text{Sales}} \times \frac{\text{Sales}}{\text{Invested assets}}$$

$$\text{Men's Division: ROI} = \frac{\$750,000}{\$3,000,000} \times \frac{\$3,000,000}{\$4,000,000}$$

$$\text{ROI} = 25\% \times 0.75$$

$$\text{ROI} = 18.75\%$$

$$\text{Women's Division: ROI} = \frac{\$432,000}{\$2,400,000} \times \frac{\$2,400,000}{\$1,920,000}$$

$$\text{ROI} = 18\% \times 1.25$$

$$\text{ROI} = 22.5\%$$

3. Men's Division: $110,000 [$750,000 – ($4,000,000 × 16%)]

Women's Division: $124,800 [$432,000 – ($1,920,000 × 16%)]

Prob. 22–5B   Concluded

4. On the basis of income from operations, the Men's Division generated $318,000 more income from operations than did the Women's Division. However, income from operations does not consider the amount of invested assets in each division. On the basis of the rate of return on investment, the Women's Division earned 22.5 cents (22.5%) on each dollar of invested assets, while the Men's Division earned only 18.75 cents (18.75%) on each dollar. Although the profit margin of the Men's Division exceeds the Women's Division (25% vs. 18%), the investment turnover in the Men's Division is much less than the Women's Division (0.75 vs. 1.25). The combination of these factors caused the Women's Division to have a higher return on investment than did the Men's Division. Residual income can be viewed as a combination of the preceding two performance measures. Residual income considers the absolute dollar amount of income from operations generated by each division and also considers a minimum rate of return to be earned by each division. On the basis of residual income, the Women's Division is the more profitable of the two divisions.

Prob. 22–6B

1. No. When unused capacity exists in the supplying division (the Cardboard Division), the use of the market price approach may not lead to the maximization of total company income.

2. The Cardboard Division's income from operations would increase by $20,000 (the amount by which the transfer price of $70 exceeds the Cardboard Division's variable expenses per unit of $60 multiplied by 2,000 units). By selling to the Box Division, the Cardboard Division earns $10 per unit on these sales.

   The Box Division's income from operations would increase by $32,000 (the difference between the market price of $86 and the transfer price of $70, multiplied by 2,000 units). By purchasing from the Cardboard Division, the Box Division saves $16 per unit on its purchases.

   Oxford Container Company's total income from operations would increase by $52,000 (the difference between the market price of $86, which the Box Division had been paying to outside suppliers, and the Cardboard Division's variable expenses per unit of $60, multiplied by 2,000 units). The increase in total company income from operations is also equal to the sum of the increases in the division incomes from operations.

3.

OXFORD CONTAINER COMPANY
Divisional Income Statements
For the Year Ended December 31, 2003

	Cardboard	Box	Total
Sales:			
10,000 units × $86 per unit............	$ 860,000		$ 860,000
2,000 units × $70 per unit..............	140,000		140,000
15,000 units × $164 per unit..........		$ 2,460,000	2,460,000
	$ 1,000,000	$ 2,460,000	$ 3,460,000
Expenses:			
Variable:			
12,000 units × $60 per unit........	$ 720,000		$ 720,000
2,000 units × $112* per unit		$ 224,000	224,000
13,000 units × $128** per unit...		1,664,000	1,664,000
Fixed..	155,000	360,000	515,000
Total expenses	$ 875,000	$ 2,248,000	$ 3,123,000
Income from operations.....................	$ 125,000	$ 212,000	$ 337,000

* The 2,000 units are transferred in at $70 per unit plus $42 operating expense in the division.

** The remaining 13,000 units are purchased on the outside at a market price of $86 per unit plus $42 operating expense in the division.

Prob. 22–6B   Concluded

4. The Cardboard Division's income from operations would increase by $10,000 (the amount by which the transfer price of $65 exceeds the Cardboard Division's variable expenses per unit of $60, multiplied by 2,000 units). By selling to the Box Division, the Cardboard Division earns $5 per unit on these sales.

    The Box Division's income from operations would increase by $42,000 (the difference between the market price of $86 and the transfer price of $65, multiplied by 2,000 units). By purchasing from the Cardboard Division, the Box Division saves $21 per unit on its purchases.

    Oxford Container Company's total income from operations would increase by the same amount as in (2), $52,000 (the difference between the market price of $86, which the Box Division had been paying to outside suppliers, and the Cardboard Division's variable expenses per unit of $60, multiplied by 2,000 units). The increase in total company income from operations is also equal to the sum of the increases in the division incomes from operations.

5. a. Any transfer price greater than the Cardboard Division's variable expenses per unit of $60 but less than the market price of $86 would be acceptable.

    b. If the division managers cannot agree on a transfer price, a price of $73 would be the best compromise. In this way, each division's income from operations would increase by $26,000.

SPECIAL ACTIVITIES

Activity 22–1

This scenario is a negotiation between two divisions. Lee is not behaving unethically by attempting to get a good price from the Can Division. He is not behaving unethically because he refuses market price. This may not seem "fair," but price negotiation is a very typical business activity and is part of Lee's job. It would be unethical only if the Food Division refused to deal with the Can Division to purposefully hurt the Can Division's performance, so that Food could look good in comparison. This claim could only be supported if the Food Division's refusal to purchase from the Can Division was economically unsound. For example, maybe there are no transportation costs because the Can Division plant is on site. In this case, the total cost to the Food Division would be less by purchasing from the Can Division. Refusing to do so could be the basis for claiming an ethical breach.

The Food Division has overall profit responsibility and authority. This means that the Food Division has the choice of purchasing from the inside or the outside. The Food Division should have incentives to purchase from the inside in order to maximize overall corporate income. This means that the transfer price should be set below market price in order to give Lee an incentive to purchase from the Can Division. Tracy's refusal to budge on market price will likely hurt the Can Division and the company as a whole. If there are no alternative buyers, the Can Division should negotiate with the Food Division and accept a price lower than market price. This produces a win-win for both divisions. Thus, although neither party appears to be behaving unethically, Tracy's price position appears to be the weakest.

Activity 22–2

The department head is responsible for the quantity of service, but not the source of the service (i.e., not the price). Most accountants would hold the department head responsible for the cost by transferring the cost of the brochures to the Accounting Department, even though the price is 20% higher than could be obtained from the outside. This may not seem fair, but it does control the use of internal services to some degree. If there were no internal transfer price, departments would view the Publications Department as a "free good." This would likely result in an overdemand for the service, since there would be no pricing discipline on the user groups. This does not mean that all is well. On the contrary, the Publications Department is free to pass on its inefficiencies, since it has a captive client. A possible change in policy would be to allow internal users to go to outside vendors for printing services. This would have the effect of bringing the pressures of competition to the internal service group. It would have to offer the service competitively, or watch its demand disappear. In this way, the internal publications group would have an incentive to be as cost effective as outside printers. Another possible change in policy would be to charge Publications Department services at standard cost. In this way, inefficiencies in the Publications Department would not be transferred to user departments.

Activity 22–3

1. The rate of return on invested assets is computed as follows:

	Broadcasting	Music	Publications
Income from operations.....	$ 210,000	$ 360,000	$ 120,000
Invested assets	÷ $1,500,000	÷ $3,000,000	÷ $800,000
ROI	14%	12%	15%

The Publications Division appears to be making the best use of invested assets, since its ROI is the highest.

2. Not all projects that have greater than a 10% rate of return would be accepted. This is because all three divisions have an ROI that is greater than 10%. Thus, any project that is accepted between the 10% minimum and their existing ROI would cause their ROI to drop. This is true because of averaging. There would be little incentive to accept such projects if the divisions know they are competing against each other on the basis of ROI.

3. There are two approaches to improving ROI: (1) improving the profit margin or (2) improving the investment turnover. For all three divisions, the profit margin is excellent:

Broadcasting	35% ($210,000 ÷ $600,000)
Music	25.7% rounded ($360,000 ÷ $1,400,000)
Publications	24% ($120,000 ÷ $500,000)

However, the investment turnover is slow in all three divisions. The company doesn't return many sales dollars per dollar invested in assets, as shown below.

Broadcasting	0.40 ($600,000 ÷ $1,500,000)
Music	0.467 ($1,400,000 ÷ $3,000,000)
Publications	0.625 ($500,000 ÷ $800,000)

The divisions need to work on increasing revenues or reducing invested assets in order to improve ROI.

Activity 22–4

1.

	2002	2003	2004
Profit margin (Income from operations/Sales)..	15%	21%	25%

2.

	2002	2003	2004
Investment turnover (Sales/Invested assets)	2.000	1.000	0.650

3.

	2002	2003	2004
Rate of return on investment (Profit margin × Investment turnover)	30.00%	21.00%	16.25%

4. Janice is concerned about the Snack Foods Division because the return on investment appears to be deteriorating over the 2002—2004 operating periods. This is happening even though the profit margin is increasing over this time period. In order for this to occur, the investment turnover must be dropping, which is the case in (2).

The investment turnover is dropping faster than the profit margin is increasing. Thus, the rate of return on investment is dropping. It appears as though the Snack Foods Division is making very large investments in the business, but it is not able to reap the returns required to support the investment. Specifically, it appears as if the revenues are not growing fast enough to support the underlying asset investment. The invested asset base grew by approximately five times, while the revenues less than doubled over the same time period. The improving profit margins for each revenue dollar were not enough to make up for the revenue shortfall. In addition, the division is not able to maintain the minimum threshold rate of return on investment of 20%. Janice is concerned because if the trend continues, the division will be earning in the future a rate of return less than the minimum return on investment.

Activity 22–5

1. $$\text{Rate of return on investment (ROI)} = \frac{\text{Income from operations}}{\text{Invested assets}}$$

$$\text{ROI} = \frac{\$4,000,000}{\$20,000,000}$$

$$\text{ROI} = 20\%$$

or

$$\text{Rate of return on investment (ROI)} = \frac{\text{Income from operations}}{\text{Sales}} \times \frac{\text{Sales}}{\text{Invested assets}}$$

$$\text{ROI} = \frac{\$4,000,000}{\$16,000,000} \times \frac{\$16,000,000}{\$20,000,000}$$

$$\text{ROI} = 25\% \times 0.80$$

$$\text{ROI} = 20\%$$

2. $60,000 (12 × $5,000 = $60,000, where 12 = 20% − 8%)

3. $$\text{Rate of return on investment (ROI)} = \frac{\text{Income from operations}}{\text{Invested assets}}$$

$$\text{ROI} = \frac{\$1,200,000}{\$12,000,000}$$

$$\text{ROI} = 10\%$$

or

$$\text{Rate of return on investment (ROI)} = \frac{\text{Income from operations}}{\text{Sales}} \times \frac{\text{Sales}}{\text{Invested assets}}$$

$$\text{ROI} = \frac{\$1,200,000}{\$7,500,000} \times \frac{\$7,500,000}{\$12,000,000}$$

$$\text{ROI} = 16\% \times 0.625$$

$$\text{ROI} = 10\%$$

4. Even though the addition of the new product line would increase the overall company rate of return on investment, its addition would decrease the Sporting Goods Division's rate of return on investment from 20% to 16.25% ($5,200,000 ÷ $32,000,000). This decrease could negatively influence management's evaluation of the division manager. In addition, this decrease in the division's rate of return on investment would also decrease the division manager's bonus by approximately $20,000 (4 × $5,000, where 4 = 20% − 16%).

Activity 22–5   Concluded

5. Use of residual income as a performance measure and as the basis for granting bonuses would motivate division managers to accept investment opportunities that exceed a minimum rate of return. If the minimum rate of return was set at 8%, the overall company average rate of return, any investment opportunity whose rate exceeded 8% would be viewed as acceptable. If this performance measure had been used, the Sporting Goods Division manager would have increased the division's residual income by $240,000 through the addition of the new product line, as shown below.

Projected income from operations of new product line............	$1,200,000
Minimum amount of desired income from operations ($12,000,000 × 8%)...	960,000
Residual income from new product line.....................................	$ 240,000

In addition, nonfinancial performance indicators about product quality and customer satisfaction can be used to supplement the financial numbers.

Activity 22–6

This activity is designed to introduce students to two very popular divisional performance measurement approaches, the "balanced scorecard" and "economic value added" (EVA). Both methods are getting very strong support in corporate America. The two consulting firms' home pages provided in this activity have links to brief descriptions of the two methods. Thus, the student groups should not have trouble completing the first part of the assignment. Hopefully, the students will see that the two methods are different in one very important respect. The balanced scorecard uses multiple financial and nonfinancial measures within the customer, financial, innovation, and internal process dimensions to provide a "balanced" perspective of performance. One could argue that the balanced scorecard is probably better able to use the measurement system in communicating strategy through the organization. EVA, in contrast, is a single financial measure that is strongly oriented to maximizing wealth to the shareholder. Hopefully, the students will recognize EVA as a specific application of the residual income concept. EVA's strength is in its simplicity and its apparent association with wealth maximization (share values). It is interesting to note that the two methods flow from two different philosophies. The balanced scorecard takes a multiple stakeholder perspective, while EVA is taking a stockholder wealth maximization perspective. Both approaches have their supporters. For example, Sears, ExxonMobil Corporation, and FMC Corporation have had success with the balanced scorecard, while The Coca-Cola Company is a notable success story using EVA. This activity should provide some rich classroom discussion comparing the advantages of "balance" versus "stockholder wealth maximization."

CHAPTER 23
DIFFERENTIAL ANALYSIS AND PRODUCT PRICING

CLASS DISCUSSION QUESTIONS

1. a. Differential revenue is the amount of increase or decrease in revenue expected from a particular course of action compared with an alternative.

    b. Differential cost is the amount of increase or decrease in cost expected from a particular course of action compared with an alternative.

    c. Differential income is the difference between differential revenue and differential cost.

2. This decision is an example of a make vs. buy decision. Exabyte is focusing on its comparative advantages, which include marketing and distribution, while building partnerships with others to actually manufacture key elements of the product.

3. In the long run, the normal selling price must be set high enough to cover all costs (both fixed and variable) and provide a reasonable amount for profit.

4. The two primary methods for setting prices are the market methods and the cost-plus methods.

5. Total cost, product cost, and variable cost

6. Desired profit and total selling and administrative expenses

7. The variable cost concept includes only variable costs in the cost amount to which the markup is added to determine product price.

8. Total manufacturing costs

9. The use of ideal standards might not allow for such factors as normal spoilage or normal periods of idle time, with the result that these costs might not be covered by the product price. In such cases, the product price could be too low to earn a desired profit.

10. In setting prices, managers should also consider such factors as the prices of competing products and the general economic conditions of the marketplace.

11. Activity-based costing can be used to determine the product cost in a complex manufacturing setting.

12. The target cost concept begins with a price that can be sustained in the marketplace, then subtracts a target profit, thus determining the target cost. The cost is made to conform to the price required in the market. In contrast, under cost plus, a markup is added to the cost. The resulting price is assumed to be acceptable in the market.

13. A production bottleneck is a point in the production process where demand exceeds the ability to produce (i.e., the segment is operating at full capacity). As a result, the complete production system output is limited by the output of the bottleneck.

14. The proper measure of product value in a bottlenecked process is the contribution margin per bottleneck hour.

EXERCISES

Ex. 23–1

a.

Proposal to Lease or Sell Machinery
January 3, 2003

Differential revenue from alternatives:		
Revenue from lease..	$234,000	
Proceeds from sale..	220,000	
Differential revenue from lease		$14,000
Differential cost of alternatives:		
Repair, insurance, and property tax expenses	$ 23,000	
Commission on sale...	11,000	
Differential cost of lease		12,000
Net differential income from lease alternative............		$ 2,000

b. Lease the machinery. The net gain from leasing is $2,000.

Ex. 23–2

a.

Proposal to Discontinue Diet Kola
January 3, 2003

Differential revenue from annual sales of Diet Kola:		
Revenue from sales..		$ 350,000
Differential cost of annual sales of Diet Kola:		
Variable cost of goods sold...	$180,000*	
Variable operating expenses	105,000**	285,000
Annual differential income from sales of Diet Kola.......		$ 65,000

     * 225,000 × 80%   ** 140,000 × 75%

b. Diet Kola should be retained. As indicated by the differential analysis in (a), the income would decrease by $65,000 (excess of differential revenue over differential cost) if the product is discontinued.

a.

BOLD CERAMICS COMPANY
Differential Product Analysis Report
For the Year Ended December 31, 2003

	Bowls	Plates	Cups
Differential revenue from annual sales:			
Revenue from sales.................................	$150,000	$ 160,000	$ 125,000
Differential costs of annual sales:			
Variable cost of goods sold..................	$ 78,720	$ 68,880	$ 69,700
Variable selling and administrative			
expenses	22,400	36,400	33,600
	$101,120	$ 105,280	$ 103,300
Annual differential income from sales......	$ 48,880	$ 54,720	$ 21,700

b. The Cups line should be retained. As indicated by the differential analysis in (a), the income would decrease by $21,700 (excess of differential revenue over differential cost) if the Cups line is discontinued.

Ex. 23–4

Note to Instructors: Many students may be unfamiliar with the financial services industry. This exercise provides an opportunity to introduce students to some basic terms and concepts used within the industry.

a. The "Individual Investor" segment serves the retail customer, you and me. These are the brokerage, Internet, and mutual fund services used by individual investors. The "Institutional Investor" segment includes the same services provided for financial institutions, such as banks, mutual fund managers, insurance companies, and pension plan administrators. Although not required by the question, the "Capital Markets" segment provides wholesale trade execution services on the major exchanges and broker/dealer networks.

b. Variable costs in the "Individual Investor" segment:
   1. Commissions to brokers
   2. Fees paid to exchanges for executing trades
   3. Transaction fees incurred by Schwab mutual funds to purchase and sell shares
   4. Advertising

   Fixed costs in the "Individual Investor" segment:
   1. Depreciation on brokerage offices
   2. Depreciation on brokerage office equipment, such as computers and computer networks
   3. Property taxes on brokerage offices

c.

	Individual Investor	Institutional Investor	Capital Markets
Income from operations	$402,150	$ 92,842	$81,552
Plus: Depreciation	102,903	21,115	14,459
Estimated contribution margin	$505,053	$113,957	$96,011

d. If one assumes that the fixed costs that serve institutional investors (computers, servers, and facilities) would not be sold but would be used by the other two sectors, then the contribution margin of $113,957 would be an estimate of the reduced profitability. If the fixed assets were sold, then the operating income decline would approach $92,842. Since the institutional and retail investors use nearly the same assets, the $113,957 answer is probably the better estimate.

Ex. 23–5

The flaw in the decision was the failure to focus on the differential revenues and costs, which indicate that operating income would be reduced by $7,000 if Children's Shoes is discontinued. This differential income from sales of Children's Shoes can be determined as follows:

Differential revenue from annual sales of Children's Shoes:		
Revenue from sales...		$105,000
Differential cost of annual sales of Children's Shoes:		
Variable cost of goods sold...	$70,000	
Variable operating expenses.......................................	28,000	98,000
Annual differential income from sales of Children's		
Shoes...		$ 7,000

Ex. 23–6

a.

Proposal to Manufacture Carrying Case
June 5, 2003

Purchase price of carrying case		$35.00
Differential cost to manufacture carrying case:		
Direct materials..	$18.00	
Direct labor..	10.00	
Variable factory overhead...	4.50	32.50
Cost savings from manufacturing carrying case		$ 2.50

b. It would be advisable to manufacture the carrying cases because the cost savings would be $2.50 per unit. Fixed factory overhead is irrelevant, since it will continue whether the carrying cases are purchased or manufactured.

Ex. 23–7

a.

Annual variable costs—present equipment................	$ 150,000	
Annual variable costs—new equipment......................	90,000	
Annual differential decrease in cost...........................	$ 60,000	
Number of years applicable..	× 6	
Total differential decrease in cost	$ 360,000	
Proceeds from sale of present equipment..................	120,000	$ 480,000
Cost of new equipment...		450,000
Net differential income, 6-year total............................		$ 30,000
Annual differential income from new equipment ($30,000 ÷ 6)		$ 5,000

b. The sunk cost is the $200,000 book value ($500,000 cost less $300,000 accumulated depreciation) of the present equipment. The original cost and accumulated depreciation were incurred in the past and are irrelevant to the decision to replace the machine.

Ex. 23–8

a.

Proposal to Replace Machine
January 20, 2003

Annual costs and expenses—present machine	$244,800
Annual costs and expenses—new machine	212,800
Annual differential decrease in costs and expenses	$ 32,000*
Number of years applicable...	× 10
Total differential decrease in costs and expenses..........................	$320,000
Cost of new equipment...	350,000
Net differential increase in costs and expenses, 10-year total	$ 30,000
Annual differential increase in costs and expenses—new machine	$ 3,000

*The annual differential decrease in costs and expenses could be computed
 alternatively as follows:

Decrease in direct labor costs		$ 59,800
Less: Increase in power and maintenance	$25,300	
Increase in taxes, insurance, etc.......................	2,500	27,800
Annual differential decrease in costs and expenses .		$ 32,000

b. The proposal should not be accepted.

c. In addition to the factors given, consideration should be given to such factors as: Do both present and proposed operations provide the same capacity? What are the opportunity costs associated with alternative uses of the $350,000 outlay required to purchase the automatic machine? Is the product improved by using automatic machinery? Does the federal income tax have an effect on the decision?

Ex. 23–9

a.

Proposal to Sell to Barker Company
January 18, 2003

Differential revenue from accepting the offer:
　Revenue from sale of 12,000 additional units at $32................... $384,000
Differential cost of accepting the offer:
　Variable costs from sale of 12,000 additional units at $29 .... 　348,000
Differential income from accepting the offer..................................... $ 36,000

b.　The additional units can be sold for $32 each, and since unused capacity is available, the only costs that would be added if this additional production were accepted are the variable costs of $29 per unit. The differential revenue is therefore $32 per unit, and the differential cost is $29 per unit. Thus, the net gain is $3 per unit × 12,000 units, or $36,000.

c.　$29.01. Any selling price above $29 (variable costs per unit) will produce a positive contribution margin.

Ex. 23–10

a.　Differential revenue: $830 – $610 = $220

b.　Differential cost: $550 – $425 = $125

c.　Differential income: $220 – $125 = $95

Ex. 23–11

a.

Proposal to Process Columbian Coffee Further		
Differential revenue from further processing per batch:		
Revenue from sale of Decaf Columbian		
[(8,000 pounds – 400 pounds evaporation) × $9.60..........	$72,960	
Revenue from sale of Columbian Coffee		
(8,000 pounds × $8.40)..	67,200	
Differential revenue		$ 5,760
Differential cost per batch:		
Additional cost of producing Decaf Columbian................		8,420
Differential loss from further processing:		
Decaf Columbian per batch		$(2,660)

b. The differential revenue from processing further to Decaf Columbian is less than the differential cost of processing further. Thus, Star Coffee Company should sell Columbian Coffee and not process further to Decaf Columbian.

c. The price of Decaf Columbian would need to increase to $9.95 per pound in order for the differential analysis to yield neither an advantage or disadvantage (indifference). This is determined as follows:

$$\frac{\text{Net disadvantage of further processing}}{\text{Volume of Decaf Columbian}} = \frac{\$2,660}{7,600 \text{ pounds}} = 0.35$$

The price of Decaf Columbian would need to be $0.35 higher, or $9.95, to yield no net differential income or loss. This is verified by the following differential analysis:

Differential revenue from further processing per batch:		
Revenue from sale of Decaf Columbian [(8,000		
pounds – 400 pounds evaporation) × $9.95]......................	$75,620	
Revenue from sale of Columbian Coffee		
(8,000 pounds × $8.40)	67,200	
Differential revenue...		$8,420
Differential cost per batch:		
Additional cost of producing Decaf Columbian................		8,420
Differential income from further processing:		
Decaf Columbian per batch		$ 0

Ex. 23–12

$12 [($300,000 – $60,000) ÷ 20,000 batteries]. The lowest bid should cover all variable costs.

Ex. 23–13

a. $100,000 ($400,000 × 25%)

b. Total costs:

Variable ($250 × 4,000 units)	$1,000,00
Fixed ($200,000 + $100,000)	300,00
Total	$1,300,00

Cost amount per unit: $1,300,000 ÷ 4,000 units = $325

c. $$\text{Markup percentage} = \frac{\text{Desired profit}}{\text{Total costs}}$$

$$\text{Markup percentage} = \frac{\$100,000}{\$1,300,000}$$

Markup percentage = 7.7% (rounded)

d.

Cost amount per unit	$32
Markup ($325 × 7.7%)	2
Selling price	$35

Ex. 23–14

a. Total manufacturing costs:

Variable ($220 × 4,000 units)	$ 880,000
Fixed factory overhead	200,000
Total..	$1,080,000

Cost amount per unit: $1,080,000 ÷ 4,000 units = $270

b. $$\text{Markup percentage} = \frac{\text{Desired profit + Total selling and administrative expenses}}{\text{Total manufacturing costs}}$$

$$\text{Markup percentage} = \frac{\$100,000 + \$100,000 + (\$30 \times 4,000\,\text{units})}{\$1,080,000}$$

$$\text{Markup percentage} = \frac{\$100,000 + \$100,000 + \$120,000}{\$1,080,000}$$

$$\text{Markup percentage} = \frac{\$320,000}{\$1,080,000}$$

Markup percentage = 29.6% (rounded)

c.

Cost amount per unit...	$270.00
Markup ($270 × 29.6%)	80.00
Selling price	$350.00

Ex. 23–15

a. Total variable costs: $250 × 4,000 units... $1,000,000

Cost amount per unit: $1,000,000 ÷ 4,000 units = $250

b. Markup percentage = $\dfrac{\text{Desired profit} + \text{Total fixed costs}}{\text{Total variable costs}}$

Markup percentage = $\dfrac{\$100,000 + \$200,000 + \$100,000}{\$1,000,000}$

Markup percentage = $\dfrac{\$400,000}{\$1,000,000}$

Markup percentage = 40%

c. Cost amount per unit... $250.00

Markup ($250 × 40%) 100.00

Selling price $350.00

Ex. 23–16

a. The price will be set at the estimated market price required to remain competitive, or $32,000. Under the target cost concept, the market dictates the price, not the markup on cost.

b. The required profit margin of 20% of the estimated $32,000 price implies a $25,600 target product cost as follows:

Target Product Cost = $32,000 – ($32,000 × 20%)

Target Product Cost = $32,000 – $6,400

Target Product Cost = $25,600

Since the estimated manufacturing cost of $26,000 exceeds the target cost of $25,600, Toyota will try to remove $400 from its manufacturing costs in order to maintain competitive pricing within its profit objectives.

Note to Instructors: The target cost concept provides pressure to keep costs competitive. The method assumes that the company may not be able to successfully add a markup to its costs because the resulting price may be too high in the marketplace. For example, merely adding the 25% markup on the $26,000 product cost would result in an uncompetitive price of $32,500. The target cost concept moves backwards by taking the price as given and then determines the cost that is required for a given profit objective.

Ex. 23–17

a.

	Large	Medium	Small	Total
Units produced........................	2,000	2,000	2,000	
Revenues	$460,000	$380,000	$240,000	$1,080,000
Less: Variable costs	244,000	170,000	110,000	524,000
Contribution margin................	$216,000	$210,000	$130,000	$ 556,000
Less: Fixed costs				450,000
Income from operations				$ 106,000

b. The Large glass product is the most profitable, demonstrated as follows:

	Large	Medium	Small
Contribution margin per unit...........................	$ 108	$ 105	$ 65
Autoclave hours per unit.................................	÷ 12	÷ 15	÷ 10
Contribution margin per bottleneck hour	$9.00	$7.00	$6.50

Ex. 23–18

Large is the highest profit item, since it produces more contribution margin per autoclave hour. The prices of Medium and Small would need to be increased in order to match Large's profitability. The two calculations are as follows:

Revised price of Medium:

$$\text{Contribution margin per bottleneck hour of Large} = \frac{\text{Revised price of Medium} - \text{Variable cost per unit of Medium}}{\text{Bottleneck hours per unit of Medium}}$$

$$\$9 = \frac{\text{Revised price of Medium} - \$85}{15 \text{ hours}}$$

$$\$135 = \text{Revised price of Medium} - \$85$$

$$\$220 = \text{Revised price of Medium}$$

Revised price of Small:

$$\text{Contribution margin per bottleneck hour of Large} = \frac{\text{Revised price of Small} - \text{Variable cost per unit of Small}}{\text{Bottleneck hours per unit of Small}}$$

$$\$9 = \frac{\text{Revised price of Small} - \$55}{10 \text{ hours}}$$

$$\$90 = \text{Revised price of Small} - \$55$$

$$\$145 = \text{Revised price of Small}$$

Thus, prices of $220 for Medium and $145 for Small both produce a contribution margin per hour of bottleneck operation of $9. The price of Large would remain unchanged. At these prices, the company should be indifferent about the product mix.

Appendix Ex. 23–19

	Activity Base Usage	×	Activity Rate	=	Activity Cost
Stationary Bicycle					
Fabrication	1,795 machine hours	×	$28 per mach. hr.		$50,260
Assembly	448 direct labor hours	×	$10 per dlh.		4,480
Setup	45 setups	×	$60 per setup		2,700
Inspecting	700 inspections	×	$22 per inspection		15,400
Production scheduling	70 production orders	×	$18 per prod. order		1,260
Purchasing	180 purchase orders	×	$5 per purch. order		900
Total..					$75,000
Number of units					÷ 800
Activity costs per unit...					$ 93.75
Rowing Machine					
Fabrication	988 machine hours	×	$28 per mach. hr.		$27,664
Assembly	176 direct labor hours	×	$10 per dlh.		1,760
Setup	16 setups	×	$60 per setup		960
Inspecting	400 inspections	×	$22 per inspection		8,800
Production scheduling	12 production orders	×	$18 per prod. order		216
Purchasing	120 purchase orders	×	$5 per purch. order		600
Total..					$40,000
Number of units					÷ 800
Activity costs per unit...					$ 50.00

Appendix Ex. 23–20

a.

Activity Rates	Production Setup	Procurement	Quality Control	Materials Management
Overhead cost..	$ 43,200	$ 156,000	$ 175,000	$ 150,000
Activity base..... ÷	480	÷ 1,200	÷ 2,500	÷ 400
Activity rate	$ 90/Setup	$ 130/P.O.	$70/Inspection	$375/Component

b.

	Custom		Standard	
Number of setups	400		80	
Rate per setup..........................	× $90		× $90	
		$ 36,000		$ 7,20(
Number of purchase orders	1,000		200	
Rate per purchase order..........	× $130		× $130	
		130,000		26,00(
Number of inspections.............	2,000		500	
Rate per inspection	× $70		× $70	
		140,000		35,00(
Number of components	300		100	
Rate per component.................	× $375		× $375	
		112,500		37,50(
Total product cost		$418,500		$105,70(
Unit volume.............................		÷ 5,000		÷ 5,00(
Unit cost..............................		$ 83.70		$ 21.1(

c. The factory overhead allocated to each product on the basis of direct labo hours would be 50%, since each product has the same 5,000 direct labo hours. The factory overhead per direct labor hour for each product is

$$\frac{\$524,200}{10,000 \text{ hours}} = \$52.42 \text{ per hour}$$

Since each product requires one direct labor hour, the cost per unit is als $52.42 for each product.

d. The factory overhead allocated to the custom power unit is much higher un der the activity-based approach, compared to the direct labor method. Th reason is that the setup, procurement, and quality control activities are no directly related to the number of direct labor hours but are instead related t the number of setups, purchase orders, and inspections. In addition, the cus tom product had a more complex design (more components) than does th standard product. As a result, the custom product will consume more materi als management activities than will the standard product.

PROBLEMS

Prob. 23–1A

1.

Proposal to Operate Retail Store
July 1, 2003

Differential revenue from alternatives:		
Revenue from operating store	$ 3,420,000[1]	
Revenue from investment bonds...........................	1,296,000[2]	
Differential revenue from operating store.........		$ 2,124,000
Differential cost of alternatives:		
Costs to operate store	$ 1,620,000[3]	
Cost of store equipment less residual value	650,000	
Differential cost of operating store....................		2,270,000
Differential loss from operating store		$ (146,000)

[1] (9 yrs. × $260,000) + (9 yrs. × $120,000)

[2] 9% × $800,000 × 18

[3] $90,000 × 18

2. The proposal should be rejected.

3.

Total estimated revenue from operating store............		$ 3,420,000
Total estimated expenses to operate store:		
Costs to operate store, excluding depreciation	$ 1,620,000	
Cost of store equipment less residual value	650,000	2,270,000
Total estimated income from operating store		$ 1,150,000*

*The $1,150,000 income could also be determined by subtracting the $146,000 loss from operating the store as derived in (1) from the $1,296,000 of investment income forgone by electing to operate the store.

Prob. 23–2A

1.

Proposal to Replace Machine
August 11, 2003

Annual manufacturing costs associated with present machine	$	420,000
Annual manufacturing costs associated with proposed new machine		300,000
Annual reduction in manufacturing costs	$	120,000
Number of years applicable	×	8
Cost reduction attributable to difference in manufacturing costs .	$	960,000
Proceeds from sale of present machine		220,000
		$ 1,180,000
Cost of new machine		780,000
Differential income anticipated from replacement, 8-year total......	$	400,000

2. Other factors to be considered include:

a. Are there any improvements in the quality of work turned out by the new machine?

b. What effect does the federal income tax have on the decision?

c. What opportunities are available for the use of the $560,000 of funds ($780,000 less $220,000 sales price of old machine) that are required to purchase the new machine?

After considering such factors as those listed above, the net cost reduction anticipated over the 8-year period may not be sufficient to justify the replacement. For example, if there is an opportunity to invest the $560,000 ($780,000 – $220,000) of additional funds required for the replacement in a project that earns a return of 10%, the amount of the return over the 8-year period would be $448,000 ($560,000 × 10% × 8), which is more advantageous than the replacement, other factors being equal.

Prob. 23–3A

1.

Proposals for Sales Promotion Campaign
April 5, 2003

	Cologne	Perfume
Differential revenue from proposals............................	$450,000[1]	$577,500[2]
Differential cost of proposals:		
Direct materials...	$ 90,000	$147,000
Direct labor..	60,000	84,000
Variable factory overhead...	40,000	42,000
Variable selling expenses	100,000	168,000
Sales promotion expenses	50,000	50,000
Differential cost of proposals	$340,000	$491,000
Differential income from proposed sales		
promotion campaign	$110,000	$ 86,500

[1] 10,000 units × $45

[2] 10,500 units × $55

2. The sales manager's tentative decision should be opposed. The sales manager erroneously considered the full unit costs instead of the differential (additional) revenue and differential (additional) costs. An analysis similar to that presented in (1) would lead to the selection of cologne for the promotional campaign, since this alternative will contribute $23,500 more to operating income than would be contributed by promoting perfume.

Prob. 23–4A

1.

Proposal to Process Raw Sugar Further
May 30, 2003

Differential revenue from further processing per batch:		
Revenue from sale of refined sugar		
[(15,000 lbs. ÷ 1.25 lbs.) × $1.50]............................	$18,000	
Revenue from sale of raw sugar		
(15,000 lbs. × $0.90)..	13,500	
Differential revenue		$ 4,500
Differential cost per batch:		
Additional cost of processing refined sugar		
(15,000 lbs. × $0.25)..		3,750
Differential income from further processing raw sugar		
per batch..		$ 750

2. Sweet Sugar Company should decide to further process raw sugar to produce refined sugar, since profits would be increased by $750 per batch.

Prob. 23–5A

1. $400,000 ($2,500,000 × 16%)

2. a. Total costs:

Variable ($320 × 20,000 units)	$6,400,000
Fixed ($1,200,000 + $400,000)..	1,600,000
Total...	$8,000,000
Cost amount per unit: $8,000,000 ÷ 20,000 units	$ 400

b. $$\text{Markup percentage} = \frac{\text{Desired profit}}{\text{Total costs}}$$

$$\text{Markup percentage} = \frac{\$400,000}{\$8,000,000}$$

Markup percentage = 5%

c.

Cost amount per unit..	$400
Markup ($400 × 5%)	20
Selling price	$420

3. a. Total manufacturing costs:

Variable ($300 × 20,000 units)	$ 6,000,000
Fixed factory overhead	1,200,000
Total...	$ 7,200,000
Cost amount per unit: $7,200,000 ÷ 20,000 units	$ 360

b. $$\text{Markup percentage} = \frac{\text{Desired profit} + \text{Total selling and administrative expenses}}{\text{Total manufacturing costs}}$$

$$\text{Markup percentage} = \frac{\$400,000 + \$400,000 + (\$20 \times 20,000 \ \text{units})}{\$7,200,000}$$

$$\text{Markup percentage} = \frac{\$400,000 + \$400,000 + \$400,000}{\$7,200,000}$$

$$\text{Markup percentage} = \frac{\$1,200,000}{\$7,200,000}$$

Markup percentage = 16.67% (rounded)

c.

Cost amount per unit..	$360
Markup ($360 × 16.67%)	60
Selling price	$420

Prob. 23–5A   Concluded

4. a. Variable cost amount per unit: $320
       Total variable costs: $320 × 20,000 units = $6,400,000

   b. Markup percentage = $\dfrac{\text{Desired profit + Total fixed costs}}{\text{Total variable costs}}$

       Markup percentage = $\dfrac{\$400,000 + \$1,200,000 + \$400,000}{\$6,400,000}$

       Markup percentage = $\dfrac{\$2,000,000}{\$6,400,000}$

       Markup percentage = 31.25%

   c. Cost amount per unit.. $320
       Markup ($320 × 31.25%) 100
       Selling price $420

5. The cost-plus approach price of $420 should be viewed as a general guideline (or target) for establishing long-run normal prices. Other considerations, such as the price of competing products and general economic conditions of the marketplace, could lead management to establish a short-run price more or less than $420.

6. a.

Proposal to Sell to Kane Company
September 3, 2003

Differential revenue from accepting offer:	
Revenue from sale of 3,000 additional units at $280..................	$ 840,000
Differential cost of accepting offer:	
Variable costs of 3,000 additional units at $300*........................	900,000
Differential loss from accepting offer...	$ (60,000)

*Excluding variable selling and administrative expenses

   b. The proposal should be rejected.

Prob. 23–6A

1.

	High Grade	Good Grade	Regular Grade
Selling price	$400	$370	$346
Variable conversion cost per unit ($5 per process hour)	$ 75	$ 75	$ 60
Direct materials cost per unit	140	135	130
	$215	$210	$190
Contribution margin per unit	$185	$160	$156

2. The contribution margin per unit may give false signals when an organization has production bottlenecks. Instead, Indy Valley should use the contribution margin per bottleneck hour to determine relative product profitability, as follows:

	High Grade	Good Grade	Regular Grade
Contribution margin per unit	$ 185	$160	$156
Furnace (bottleneck) hours per unit..........	÷ 10	÷ 8	÷ 6
Contribution margin per furnace hour	$18.50	$ 20	$ 26

Unlike the analysis in (1), this analysis shows Regular Grade steel to be the most profitable product, while High Grade steel is the least profitable. The reason is that Regular Grade steel delivers more contribution margin per bottleneck hour than does High Grade steel ($26.00 vs. $18.50).

Prob. 23–6A   Concluded

3. One way to revise the pricing would be to increase the price to the point where all three products produce profitability equal to the highest profit product. This would be determined as follows:

Revised price of High Grade steel:

$$\text{Contribution margin per furnace hour for Regular Grade} = \frac{\text{Revised price of High Grade} - \text{Variable cost per unit of High Grade}}{\text{Furnace hours of High Grade per unit}}$$

$26 = (Revised price of High Grade – $215) ÷ 10 hrs.

$260 = (Revised price of High Grade – $215)

$475 = Revised price of High Grade

High Grade steel would require a revised price of $475 in order to deliver the same contribution margin per bottleneck hour as does Regular Grade steel.

Revised price of Good Grade steel:

$$\text{Contribution margin per furnace hour for Regular Grade} = \frac{\text{Revised price of Good Grade} - \text{Variable cost per unit of Good Grade}}{\text{Furnace hours of Good Grade per unit}}$$

$26 = (Revised price of Good Grade – $210) ÷ 8 hrs.

$208 = (Revised price of Good Grade – $210)

$418 = Revised price of Good Grade

Good Grade steel would require a revised price of $418 in order to deliver the same contribution margin per bottleneck hour as does Regular Grade steel.

Prob. 23–1B

1.

Proposal to Operate Warehouse
December 1, 2003

Differential revenue from alternatives:		
Revenue from operating warehouse.........................	$1,925,000[1]	
Revenue from investment in bonds	448,000[2]	
Differential revenue from operating warehouse .		$1,477,000
Differential cost of alternatives:		
Costs to operate warehouse....................................	$ 980,000[3]	
Cost of equipment less residual value	335,000	
Differential cost of operating warehouse		1,315,000
Differential income from operating warehouse		$ 162,000

[1] (7 yrs. × $150,000) + (7 yrs. × $125,000)

[2] 8% × $400,000 × 14 yrs.

[3] $70,000 × 14 yrs.

2. The proposal should be accepted.

3.

Total estimated revenue from operating warehouse		$1,925,000
Total estimated expenses to operate warehouse:		
Costs to operate warehouse, excluding depreciation	$980,000	
Cost of equipment less residual value	335,000	1,315,000
Total estimated income from operating warehouse		$ 610,000*

*The $610,000 income from operations could also be determined by adding the $162,000 gain from operating the warehouse as derived in (1) to the $448,000 of investment income forgone by electing to operate the warehouse.

Prob. 23–2B

1.

Proposal to Replace Machine
March 22, 2003

Annual manufacturing costs associated with present machine	$ 80,000
Annual manufacturing costs associated with proposed	
new machine...	42,000
Annual reduction in manufacturing costs	$ 38,000
Number of years applicable	× 6
Cost reduction attributable to difference in manufacturing costs .	$ 228,000
Proceeds from sale of present machine...	175,000
	$ 403,000
Cost of new machine...	360,000
Differential income anticipated from replacement, 6-year total......	$ 43,000

2. Other factors to be considered include:

    a. Are there any improvements in the quality of work turned out by the new machine?

    b. What effect does the federal income tax have on the decision?

    c. What opportunities are available for the use of the $185,000 of funds ($360,000 less $175,000 sales price of old machine) that are required to purchase the new machine?

After considering such factors as those listed above, the net cost reduction anticipated over the 6-year period may not be sufficient to justify the replacement. For example, if there is an opportunity to invest the $185,000 ($360,000 – $175,000) of additional funds required for the replacement in a project that earns a return of 8%, the amount of the return over the 6-year period would be $88,800 ($185,000 × 8% × 6), which is more advantageous than the replacement, other factors being equal.

Prob. 23–3B

1.

Proposals for Sales Promotion Campaign
March 3, 2003

	Tennis Shoes	Walking Shoes
Differential revenue from proposals.................	$ 408,000[1]	$ 595,000[2]
Differential cost of proposals:		
Direct materials...	$ 126,000	$ 196,000
Direct labor..	84,000	140,000
Variable factory overhead..............................	30,000	49,000
Variable selling expenses...............................	60,000	98,000
Sales promotion expenses	28,000	28,000
Differential cost of proposals	$ 328,000	$ 511,000
Differential income from proposed sales		
promotion campaign	$ 80,000	$ 84,000

[1] 6,000 shoes × $68
[2] 7,000 shoes × $85

2. The sales manager's tentative decision should be opposed. The sales manager erroneously considered the full unit costs instead of the differential (additional) revenue and differential (additional) costs. An analysis similar to that presented in (1) would lead to the selection of Walking Shoes for the promotional campaign, since this alternative will contribute $4,000 more to operating income than would be contributed by promoting Tennis Shoes.

Prob. 23–4B

1.

Proposal to Process Aluminum Ingot Further
February 20, 2003

Differential revenue from further processing per batch:		
Revenue from sale of rolled aluminum		
[(50 tons ÷ 1.125 tons) × $1,260]..............................	$56,000	
Revenue from sale of aluminum ingot		
(50 tons × $800)..	40,000	
Differential revenue		$16,000
Differential cost per batch:		
Additional cost of processing rolled aluminum		
(50 tons × $350)..		17,500
Differential loss from further processing aluminum		
ingot, per batch..		$ (1,500)

2. Aluminum Company of Tennessee should decide not to further process aluminum ingot to produce rolled aluminum, since profits would be decreased by $1,500 per batch.

Prob. 23–5B

1. $300,000 ($2,000,000 × 15%)

2. a. Total costs:

Variable ($50.00 × 25,000 units)	$ 1,250,000
Fixed ($150,000 + $100,000)	250,000
Total	$ 1,500,000
Cost amount per unit: $1,500,000 ÷ 25,000 units	$ 60.00

b. Markup percentage = $\dfrac{\text{Desired profit}}{\text{Total costs}}$

Markup percentage = $\dfrac{\$300,000}{\$1,500,000}$

Markup percentage = 20%

c.

Cost amount per unit	$60.00
Markup ($60 × 20%)	12.00
Selling price	$72.00

3. a. Total manufacturing costs:

Variable ($46 × 25,000 units)	$ 1,150,000
Fixed factory overhead	150,000
Total	$ 1,300,000
Cost amount per unit: $1,300,000 ÷ 25,000 units	$ 52.00

b. Markup percentage = $\dfrac{\text{Desired profit + Total selling and administrative expenses}}{\text{Total manufacturing costs}}$

Markup percentage = $\dfrac{\$300,000 + \$100,000 + (\$4 \times 25,000 \text{ units})}{\$1,300,000}$

Markup percentage = $\dfrac{\$300,000 + \$100,000 + \$100,000}{\$1,300,000}$

Markup percentage = $\dfrac{\$500,000}{\$1,300,000}$

Markup percentage = 38.46% (rounded)

c.

Cost amount per unit	$52.00
Markup ($52.00 × 38.46%)	20.00
Selling price	$72.00

Prob. 23–5B   Concluded

4. a. Variable cost amount per unit: $50.00
        Total variable costs: $50 × 25,000 units = $1,250,000

    b. Markup percentage = $\dfrac{\text{Desired profit + Total fixed costs}}{\text{Total variable costs}}$

        Markup percentage = $\dfrac{\$300,000 + \$150,000 + \$100,000}{\$1,250,000}$

        Markup percentage = $\dfrac{\$550,000}{\$1,250,000}$

        Markup percentage = 44%

    c. Cost amount per unit... $50.00
        Markup ($50.00 × 44%) 22.00
        Selling price $72.00

5. The cost-plus approach price of $72.00 should be viewed as a general guide-line (or target) for establishing long-run normal prices. Other considerations, such as the price of competing products and general economic conditions of the marketplace, could lead management to establish a short-run price more or less than $72.00.

6. a.

Proposal to Sell to Lights Inc.
May 5, 2003

Differential revenue from accepting offer:	
Revenue from sale of 2,000 additional units at $49.00..............	$98,000
Differential cost of accepting offer:	
Variable costs of 2,000 additional units at $46.00*....................	92,000
Differential income from accepting offer...................................	$ 6,000

   *Excluding variable selling and administrative expenses

    b. The proposal should be accepted.

Prob. 23–6B

1.

	Ethylene	Butane	Ester
Selling price	$202	$175	$164
Variable conversion cost per unit ($3 per process hour)	$ 30	$ 30	$ 24
Direct materials cost per unit	100	80	80
	$130	$110	$104
Contribution margin per unit	$ 72	$ 65	$ 60

2. The contribution margin per unit may give false signals when an organization has production bottlenecks. Instead, California Chemical Company should use the contribution margin per bottleneck hour to determine relative product profitability as follows:

	Ethylene	Butane	Ester
Contribution margin per unit	$72	$ 65	$60
Reactor (bottleneck) hours per unit	÷ 6	÷ 4	÷ 3
Contribution margin per reactor hour	$12	$16.25	$20

Unlike the analysis in (1), this analysis shows ester to be the most profitable product, while ethylene is the least profitable. The reason is that ester delivers more contribution margin per bottleneck hour than does ethylene ($20 vs. $12).

Prob. 23–6B   Concluded

3. One way to revise the pricing would be to increase the price to the point where all three products produce profitability equal to the highest profit product. This would be determined as follows:

<u>Revised price of Ethylene:</u>

$$\text{Contribution margin per reactor hour for Ester} = \frac{\text{Revised price of Ethylene} - \text{Variable cost per unit of Ethylene}}{\text{Reactor hours of Ethylene per unit}}$$

$20 = (\text{Revised price of Ethylene} - \$130) \div 6 \text{ hrs.}$

$120 = (\text{Revised price of Ethylene} - \$130)$

$250 = \text{Revised price of Ethylene}$

Ethylene would require a revised price of $250 in order to deliver the same contribution margin per bottleneck hour as does Ester.

<u>Revised price of Butane:</u>

$$\text{Contribution margin per reactor hour for Ester} = \frac{\text{Revised price of Butane} - \text{Variable cost per unit of Butane}}{\text{Reactor hours of Butane per unit}}$$

$20 = (\text{Revised price of Butane} - \$110) \div 4 \text{ hrs.}$

$80 = (\text{Revised price of Butane} - \$110)$

$190 = \text{Revised price of Butane}$

Butane would require a revised price of $190 in order to deliver the same contribution margin per bottleneck hour as does Ester.

SPECIAL ACTIVITIES

Activity 23–1

No, it would be unethical for Sanchez to attend the meeting. Such a meeting would be considered price fixing and would be a violation of federal law. Thus, Sanchez's attendance would be a criminal act, which would discredit the profession of accountancy.

Activity 23–2

The contribution margin is $2 per dozen on the special order. Thus, the Winner's manager can contribute to fixed costs by accepting the order. However, there are some additional considerations the manager must consider before accepting this order:

1. Have we ever done business overseas? Exports require additional administrative activities. Have these additional administrative costs been considered in the differential analysis?

2. Will the customer sell the golf balls overseas, or will they relabel the golf balls and have them imported back into the United States? Such a situation would cause Winner's to be competing against itself.

3. Is it likely that other customers will learn of the "special deal" the overseas company received and demand equal treatment? In other words, is there a risk that we'll spoil the pricing structure in the domestic market?

4. Is the overseas customer likely to want to do business in the future, or is this just a single case? If the overseas customer is expected to purchase more golf balls in the future, then it is likely that the customer will come to expect the $10 price in the future.

5. Is there a possibility that another customer will come along that will be willing to purchase the golf balls at the $18 price? If so, we may not want to commit capacity to the overseas customer. Once the capacity is committed, it will be difficult to sell to anyone else.

6. Will we help the overseas customer establish a presence in the overseas golf ball market where we may wish to compete in the future?

Activity 23–3

First, Marriott has excess capacity for this day. Thus, it should not be concerned about using its capacity to accept business from the priceline.com customer. The priceline.com customer is incremental revenue that will not crowd out other business. Given this, however, the price must at least cover variable cost, or else Marriott would lose money on the deal. The variable cost per room night is shown below.

Housekeeping labor cost	$ 25
Cost of room supplies (soap, paper, etc.)	5
Laundry labor and material cost	10
Utility cost (mostly air conditioning)	3
Total variable cost per day per room	$ 43

These costs are mostly avoidable, or variable to room nights. This answer assumes that the maid and laundry staff hours are highly flexible and can be staffed to demand. Likewise, the air conditioning and lights can be turned off if the room is not rented for the night, saving most of the utility cost. The desk staff and hotel depreciation are either sunk (depreciation) or mostly fixed to the number of room nights. Therefore, they are not variable to accepting this business. The total variable costs are $43 per night, so the $50 customer bid should be accepted.

Note to Instructors: There could be some discussion about the degree that some of these costs are fully variable. For example, it's likely that some utility cost must be incurred for the room, whether it is occupied or not. Likewise, the housekeeping and laundry staff hours may not be as flexible to demand as assumed here. There should be very little question about the room supplies (full variable) or the hotel depreciation (sunk). Regardless of the assumptions, the decision would remain the same.

Activity 23–4

The analysis should determine relative profitability by reviewing the contribution margin per bottleneck hour, as opposed to just the contribution margin per unit. This analysis is only appropriate if there are bottlenecks, as is evident in this case. The contribution margin per bottleneck hour is:

	Small Window	Medium Window	Large Window
Sales price	$14.00	$24.00	$32.00
Variable cost	6.00	14.00	18.00
Contribution margin	$ 8.00	$10.00	$14.00
Furnace hours	÷ 2	÷ 4	÷ 5
Contribution margin per furnace hour	$ 4.00	$ 2.50	$ 2.80

As can be seen, the small window is the most profitable use of resources. This leads to three possible recommendations or some combination of them:

1. Increase sales effort on the small window line.

2. Reprice the medium and large windows so that they provide the same contribution margin per furnace hour as does the small window. This would mean increasing the price of medium windows to $30* per unit and large windows to $38** per unit. At these prices, the management should be indifferent to product mix. One should take some care, in that pricing will also be determined by market conditions.

3. Improve operations so that the variable costs per unit in the medium and large window lines are reduced to the point that the contribution margin per furnace hour is equal across all products. This would require a variable cost per unit of $8*** for the medium window and $12**** for the large window.

4. Improve the furnace cycle times on the medium and large windows to at least 2.5 hours ($10/$4) and 3.5 hours ($14/$4), respectively.

*4 = (X – 14) ÷ 4	**4 = (X – 18) ÷ 5	***$4 × 4 = $16	****$4 × 5 = $20
X = 30	X = 38	$24 – $16 = $8	$32 – $20 = $12

Activity 23–5

a.

Proposal to Purchase Material TS-101
March 15, 2003

Purchase price of material TS-101..............................		$ 9.00
Administrative costs to import.....................................		0.80
Transportation cost..		0.40
Hazardous material handling costs		1.40
Total cost to purchase material TS-101.......................		$11.60
Differential cost to manufacture material TS-101:		
Direct materials...	$6.70	
Direct labor...	2.50	
Variable factory overhead...................................	1.20	
Hazardous material handling cost	1.40	11.80
Cost disadvantage per unit from manufacturing		
material TS-101		$ (0.20)

There is a $0.20 per unit cost savings from purchasing material TS-101 from the outside supplier.

b. The cost savings from purchasing on the outside is small. However, there may be a great deal of risk from purchasing from the outside. Since the supplier is overseas, it is possible that delivery dates will be missed due to storms at sea, delays at customs, and other transportation-related events. If material TS-101 is critical to further processing in the Roanoke facility, missed delivery dates could translate into shutting down the plant. Since the material is hazardous, it is possible that future regulatory import restrictions could eliminate Red Hawk's access to the material from the supplier. As a result, Red Hawk would need to put TS-101 back up to production—an expensive possibility. In addition, since the supplier can deliver only once per month, it is possible that this will result in a large average inventory. Additional costs that might be considered are inventory carrying costs associated with having to store large amounts of material from month to month. The supplier is not familiar with Red Hawk from past dealings. Thus, there is another risk associated with working with a new supplier. The new supplier may provide material with inferior quality or may miss delivery commitments. Red Hawk Company would probably need to incur some costs in order to determine if the supplier could reliably deliver the product at the required quality standards.

Activity 23–6

a. Adam believes that the fixed costs should be treated as a sunk cost and ignored in the pricing decision. In essence, Adam is suggesting that the new computer model be treated as an incremental decision. However, the new model is not a special incremental decision. It is a core product that must contribute to covering fixed costs. If the product price does not cover fixed costs and provide a profit, then Francois Computer Company will not be competitive in the long term. In the long term, the price must cover all costs, plus a profit markup. Thus, Adam's solution to the pricing decision is not a good one.

b. Target costing provides a different perspective to the pricing issue. Under target costing, Francois Computer Company should begin with the price the market is willing to pay, which is $2,500. This price should then be reduced by the required profit markup. This would yield a target cost of $2,000 ($2,500 ÷ 1.25), which is $400 lower than the present product cost. The new target cost should be established as a cost reduction target. The company should vigorously improve the product design and processes in order to achieve a $2,000 product cost. In this way, the company can compete profitably.

Target costing takes the market price as given and adjusts the cost in order to yield the required profitability. This approach is best used in highly competitive product markets where declining prices require cost reduction in order to compete.

Activity 23–7

a. This activity is designed to have students access a number of products and services on the Internet to see its commercial potential. Each of the listed sites will provide product descriptions and pricing.

The list of costs in the product will not be determined at the Internet site but must be assumed. Some examples include:

Delta Air Lines—Airline tickets	Fixed or Variable?
Fuel	V
Crew salaries..	F
Plane depreciation	F
Landing fees...	V
Travel agent commissions..	V
Lease costs (gates)..	F
Ground salaries..	F
Equipment depreciation	F

Assume that the activity base is the number of passenger miles for a flight for determining fixed and variable costs.

Amazon.com, Inc.—Books	Fixed or Variable?
Cost of books (purchased for resale)	V
Web page design and programming..............................	F
Advertising	F
Order handling and packing wages	V
Freight..	V

Assume that the activity base is the number of books sold for determining fixed and variable costs. One could argue that advertising might be variable.

Dell Computer Co.—Computers	Fixed or Variable?
Cost of computers (dl, dm, and foh)	V (mostly)
Web page design and programming..............................	F
Advertising	F
Order handling and packing wages	V
Freight..	V
Bundled software...	V (depends on contract terms with software vendor)

Assume that the activity base is the number of PCs sold for determining fixed and variable costs. One could argue that advertising might be variable.

Activity 23–7   Concluded

b. The product with the largest markup on variable cost is the airline ticket. The portion of variable cost to total cost for an airline flight will be much smaller (more fixed cost) than the other two products. Thus, the markup on variable cost will be a greater percent. As a result, the airline product has a larger contribution margin, but it also has a larger fixed cost to cover. This creates larger operating leverage (and risk) than the other two products.

CHAPTER 24
CAPITAL INVESTMENT ANALYSIS

CLASS DISCUSSION QUESTIONS

1. Average rate of return and cash payback methods.

2. Net present value and internal rate of return methods.

3. The average rate of return is computed by dividing the expected average annual earnings by the average investment.

4. The principal objections to the use of the average rate of return method are its failing to consider the expected cash flows from the proposals and the timing of these flows.

5. The principal limitations of the cash payback method are its failure to consider cash flows occurring after the payback period and its failure to use present value concepts.

6. Net present value method.

7. The $9,750 net present value indicates that the proposal is desirable because the proposal is expected to recover the investment and provide more than the minimum rate of return.

8. The present value index is determined as follows:

Total present value of net cash flows

Amount to be invested

9. The computations for the net present value method are more complex than those for the methods that ignore present value. Also, the method assumes that the cash received from the proposal during its useful life will be reinvested at the rate of return used to compute the present value of the proposal. This assumption may not always be reasonable.

10. The computations for the internal rate of return method are more complex than those for the methods that ignore present value. Also, the method assumes that the cash received from the proposal during its useful life will be reinvested at the internal rate of return.

11. Allowable deductions for depreciation.

12. The life of the proposal with the longer life can be adjusted to a time period that is equal to the life of the proposal with the shorter life.

13. The major advantages of leasing are that it avoids the need to use funds to purchase assets and reduces some of the risk of loss if the asset becomes obsolete. There may also be some income tax advantages to leasing.

14. The speed-up of delivery of products, higher production quality, and greater manufacturing flexibility are examples of qualitative factors that should be considered.

15. Monsanto indicated that it recognized that the market was demanding higher product quality that could be achieved only with a large investment in process control technology and automated laboratory equipment. The process control technology could reduce the variation in the size of fibers. More uniform fibers, in turn, improve the efficiency of the processes used by carpet manufacturers. The local area network (LAN) was not a stand-alone investment, but it linked the process control information to operators and management via computer linkages. Thus, the LAN was an integral part of the investment portfolio. Monsanto indicated the following considerations in making its investment:

   a. After-tax cash flows.

   b. Labor savings.

   c. Accepting projects that do not have a quantifiable payback, such as enablers that allow projects with more visible benefits to be put into place (such as LAN enabling the process control technology to communicate information).

   d. Allowing estimates of increased sales due to higher quality.

   e. Considering inventory reductions in the cost of savings.

f. Avoiding reactive investment but considering the organizational vision and long-term strategic direction in the investment decision.

Source: Raymond C. Cole and H. Lee Hales, "How Monsanto Justifies Automation," *Management Accounting*, January 1992, pp. 39–43.

Ex. 24–1

	Turning Machine	Milling Machine
Estimated average annual income:		
$9,000 ÷ 4	$2,250	
$12,000 ÷ 5		$2,400
Average investment:		
($36,000 + 0) ÷ 2	$18,000	
($48,000 + 0) ÷ 2		$24,000
Average rate of return:		
$2,250 ÷ $18,000	12.5%	
$2,400 ÷ $24,000		10%

Ex. 24–2

$$\text{Average rate of return} = \frac{\text{Average annual income}}{\text{Average investment}}$$

$$= \frac{\text{Average savings* } - \text{ Annual depreciation } - \text{ Additional operating costs}}{\left(\text{Beginning cost} + \text{Residual value}\right) \div 2}$$

$$= \frac{\$18,000 \ - \left(\$55,000 \div 11\right) - \$9,315}{\left(\$61,000 + \$6,000\right) \div 2}$$

$$= \frac{\$3,685}{\$33,500}$$

$$= 11\%$$

* The effect of the savings in wages expense is an increase in income.

Ex. 24–3

$$\text{Average rate of return} = \frac{\text{Average annual income}}{\text{Average investment}}$$

$$= \frac{\text{Annual revenues} - \text{Annual product costs}^*}{\left(\text{Beginning cost} + \text{Residual value}\right) \div 2}$$

$$= \frac{(\$75 \times 18{,}000\text{ units}) - (\$55 \times 18{,}000\text{ units})}{(\$870{,}000 + \$30{,}000) \div 2}$$

$$= \frac{\$360{,}000}{\$450{,}000}$$

$$= 80\%$$

* The depreciation of the equipment is included in the factory overhead cost per unit and should not be included in the numerator as a separate calculation.

Ex. 24–4

	Year 1	Years 2–14	Last Year
Initial investment	$ (206,000)		
Operating cash flows:			
Annual revenues (8,000 units × $24)	$ 192,000	$ 192,000	$ 192,000
Selling expenses (5% × $192,000)	(9,600)	(9,600)	(9,600)
Cost to manufacture			
(8,000 units × $14.75)*	(118,000)	(118,000)	(118,000)
Net operating cash flows	$ 64,400	$ 64,400	$ 64,400
Total for year 1..	$ (141,600)		
Total for years 2–14 (operating cash flow)....		$ 64,400	
Residual value...			10,000
Total for last year...			$ 74,400

*The fixed overhead relates to the depreciation on the equipment [($160,000 – $10,000) ÷ 15 years ÷ 8,000 units = $1.25]. Depreciation is not a cash flow and should not be considered in the analysis.

Proposal 1: $200,000 ÷ $40,000 = 5-year cash payback period.

Proposal 2: 4-year cash payback period, as indicated below.

	Net Cash Flow	Cumulative Net Cash Flows
Year 1...	$70,000	$ 70,000
Year 2...	50,000	120,000
Year 3...	40,000	160,000
Year 4...	40,000	200,000

Ex. 24–6

a. The Cosmetics product line is recommended, based on its shorter cash payback period. The cash payback period for both products can be determined using the following schedule:

Initial investment: $360,000

	Liquid Soap		Cosmetics	
	Net Cash Flow	Cumulative Net Cash Flows	Net Cash Flow	Cumulative Net Cash Flows
Year 1	$ 50,000	$ 50,000	$90,000	$ 90,000
Year 2	60,000	110,000	90,000	180,000
Year 3	70,000	180,000	90,000	270,000
Year 4	80,000	260,000	90,000	360,000
Year 5	100,000	360,000		

Liquid Soap has a 5-year cash payback, and Cosmetics has a 4-year cash payback period.

b. The cash payback periods are different between the two product lines because Cosmetics earns cash faster than does Liquid Soap. Even though both products earn the same total net cash flow over the 8-year planning horizon, Cosmetics returns cash faster in the earlier years. The cash payback method emphasizes the initial years' net cash flows in determining the cash payback period. Thus, the project with the greatest net cash flows in the early years of the project life will be favored over the one with less net cash flows in the initial years.

Ex. 24–7

a.

Year	Present Value of $1 at 12%	Net Cash Flow	Present Value of Net Cash Flow
1	0.893	$140,000	$ 125,020
2	0.797	100,000	79,700
3	0.712	80,000	56,960
4	0.636	80,000	50,880
Total		$400,000	$ 312,560
Amount to be invested			300,000
Net present value			$ 12,560

b. Yes. The $12,560 net present value indicates that the return on the proposal exceeds the minimum desired rate of return of 12%.

Ex. 24–8

a. Year 1 cash flow:

Revenues ($120,000,000 × 0.006)	$720,000
Expenses	670,000
Year 1 cash flow...	$ 50,000

Annual cash flows:

The annual cash flows are determined by multiplying the previous year's cash flow by 1.1 as follows:

Year 1: $50,000
Year 2: $50,000 × 1.1 = $55,000
Year 3: $55,000 × 1.1 = $60,500
Year 4: $60,500 × 1.1 = $66,550

Net present value:

Year	Present Value of $1 at 15%	Net Cash Flow	Present Value of Net Cash Flow
1	0.870	$ 50,000	$ 43,500
2	0.756	55,000	41,580
3	0.658	60,500	39,809
4	0.572	66,550	38,067
Total		$ 232,050	$ 162,956
Amount to be invested			100,000
Net present value...........................			$ 62,956

b. The Web site has a positive net present value of $62,956, which means that the project exceeds the minimum desired rate of return of 15%. Thus, the project is acceptable.

Ex. 24–9

a. <u>Cash inflows:</u>

Hours of operation....................................	1,500	
Revenue per hour	× $90.00	
Revenue per year....................................		$ 135,000

<u>Cash outflows:</u>

Hours of operation....................................		1,500	
Fuel cost per hour....................................	$25.00		
Labor cost per hour...............................	32.00		
Total fuel and labor costs per hour.......		× $57.00	
Fuel and labor costs per year....................			(85,500)
Maintenance costs per year........................			(8,000)
Annual net cash flow..................................			$ 41,500

b.

Annual net cash flow (at the end of each of five years)	$ 41,500
Present value of annuity of $1 at 10% for five periods.....................	× 3.791
Present value of annual net cash flows..	$ 157,327
Less: Amount to be invested..	160,000
Net present value..	$ (2,673)

c. No. Laidlow should not accept the investment because the bulldozer cost exceeds the present value of the cash flows at the minimum desired rate of return of 10%. The bulldozer might be an attractive investment if Laidlow could get a price reduction, increase the annual hours of use, or extend the useful life of the bulldozer.

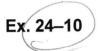

Ex. 24–10

Apartment Complex

Year	Present Value of $1 at 15%	Net Cash Flow	Present Value of Net Cash Flow
1	0.870	$160,000	$ 139,200
2	0.756	150,000	113,400
3	0.658	120,000	78,960
4	0.572	100,000	57,200
4	0.572	140,000	80,080
Total		$670,000	$ 468,840
Amount to be invested			(460,000)
Net present value			$ 8,840

Office Building

Year	Present Value of $1 at 15%	Net Cash Flow	Present Value of Net Cash Flow
1	0.870	$180,000	$ 156,600
2	0.756	180,000	136,080
3	0.658	150,000	98,700
4	0.572	150,000	85,800
Total		$660,000	$ 477,180
Amount to be invested			(460,000)
Net present value			$ 17,180

The net present value of both projects are positive; thus, both proposals are acceptable. However, the net present value of the office building exceeds that of the apartment complex. Thus, the office building should be preferred if there is enough investment money for only one of the projects.

Ex. 24–11

a.
Revenues (3,100 × 70% × 300 days × $245)		$ 159,495,000
Less: Variable expenses (3,100 × 70% × 300 days × $50)		32,550,000
Fixed expenses (other than depreciation)		21,000,000
Annual net cash flow		$ 105,945,000

b.
Present value of annual net cash flows ($105,945,000 × 5.65)	$ 598,589,250
Present value of salvage value ($50,000,000 × 0.322)	16,100,000
Total present value	$ 614,689,250
Initial investment	600,000,000
Net present value	$ 14,689,250

c. Annual cash flow assuming $260 revenue per day:

Revenues (3,100 × 70% × 300 days × $260)		$ 169,260,000
Less: Variable expenses (3,100 × 70% × 300 days × $50)		32,550,000
Fixed expenses (other than depreciation)		21,000,000
Annual net cash flow		$ 115,710,000

Net present value calculation at 15% minimum rate of return:

Present value of annual net cash flows ($115,710,000 × 5.019)	$ 580,748,490
Present value of salvage value ($50,000,000 × 0.247)	12,350,000
Total present value	$ 593,098,490
Initial investment	600,000,000
Net present value	$ (6,901,510)

The net present value is negative. Thus, the increase in price is not sufficient to earn a 15% rate of return.

Ex. 24–12

$$\text{Present value index} = \frac{\text{Total present value of net cash flow}}{\text{Amount to be invested}}$$

Present value index of Proposal A: $\dfrac{\$267,240}{\$262,000} = 1.02$

Present value index of Proposal B: $\dfrac{\$321,750}{\$325,000} = 0.99$

Ex. 24–13

a. Annual net cash flow—
      Sewing Machine: $56,000 = 2,000 hours × 40 baseballs × $0.70

  Annual net cash flow—
      Packing Machine: $33,600 = 1,600 × $21 labor cost saved per hour

Sewing Machine:

Annual net cash flow (at the end of each of eight years)	$ 56,000
Present value of an annuity of $1 at 15% for 8 years (Exhibit 2)	× 4.487
Present value of annual net cash flows	$251,272
Less amount to be invested	230,525
Net present value	$ 20,747

Packing Machine:

Annual net cash flow (at the end of each of eight years)	$ 33,600
Present value of an annuity of $1 at 15% for 8 years (Exhibit 2)	× 4.487
Present value of annual net cash flows	$150,763
Less amount to be invested	136,027
Net present value	$ 14,736

b.   Present value index = $\dfrac{\text{Total present value of net cash flow}}{\text{Amount to be invested}}$

  Present value index of the sewing machine: $\dfrac{\$251,272}{\$230,525} = 1.09$

  Present value index of the packing machine: $\dfrac{\$150,763}{\$136,027} = 1.11$

c.   The present value index indicates that the packing machine would be the preferred investment, assuming that all other qualitative considerations are equal. Note that the net present value of the sewing machine is greater than the packing machine's. However, the sewing machine requires a greater investment than the packing machine, for very little extra net present value. Thus, the present value index indicates the packing machine is favored.

Ex. 24–14

a. Average rate of return on investment: $\dfrac{\$56{,}250 \ ^*}{\$375{,}000 \div 2} = 30\%$

   * The annual earnings are equal to the cash flow less the annual depreciation expense, shown as follows:

   $\$93{,}750 - (\$375{,}000 \div 10 \text{ years}) = \$56{,}250$

b. Cash payback period: $\dfrac{\$375{,}000}{\$93{,}750} = 4 \text{ years}$

c. Present value of annual net cash flows ($\$93{,}750 \times 5.65^*$) $529,688
   Amount to be invested 375,000
   Net present value .... $\underline{\$154{,}688}$
   *Present value of an annuity of $1 at 12% for 10 periods from chapter table.

Ex. 24–15

a. $\begin{aligned}\text{Present value factor for an annuity of \$1 for 8 periods} &= \dfrac{\text{Amount to be invested}}{\text{Annual net cash flow}}\\[2mm] &= \dfrac{\$62{,}818}{\$14{,}000}\\[2mm] &= 4.487\end{aligned}$

b. 15%

Ex. 24–16

Equal annual savings per year: $\dfrac{\$250{,}000{,}000}{3} = \$83{,}333{,}333$

Present value of an annuity factor: $\dfrac{\$175{,}500{,}000}{\$83{,}333{,}333} = 2.106$

Go to row three in Exhibit 2. In row three, the column associated with the factor 2.106 is 20%. Thus, the internal rate of return under these assumptions is 20%.

Ex. 24–17

a. Delivery Truck

Cash received from additional delivery (35,000 bags × $0.30)	$10,500
Cash used for operating expenses (14,000 miles × $0.25)..............	3,500
Net cash flow for delivery truck..	$ 7,000

$$\text{Present value factor for an annuity of \$1 for 6 periods} = \frac{\text{Amount to be invested}}{\text{Annual net cash flow}}$$

$$= \frac{\$28,777}{\$7,000}$$

$$= 4.111$$

Internal Rate of Return = 12% (from text Exhibit 2)

Bagging Machine

Direct labor savings (2.0 hrs./day × $12/hr. × 250 days/yr.)	$6,000

$$\text{Present value factor for an annuity of \$1 for 6 periods} = \frac{\text{Amount to be invested}}{\text{Annual net cash flow}}$$

$$= \frac{\$22,710}{\$6,000}$$

$$= 3.785$$

Internal Rate of Return = 15% (from text Exhibit 2)

Ex. 24–17   **Concluded**

b. **To: Management**

Re: Investment Recommendation

An internal rate of return analysis was performed for the delivery truck and bagging machine investments. The internal rate of return for the bagging machine is 15%, while the delivery truck is 12% (detailed analysis available). In addition, there do not appear to be any qualitative considerations that would favor the delivery truck. Therefore, the recommendation is to invest in the bagging machine. If additional funds become available, however, the delivery truck would be an acceptable investment because the internal rate of return of 12% exceeds the company's minimum rate of return of 11%.

Ex. 24–18

a. Present value of annual net cash flows ($20,000 × 4.16*)............... $83,200
Amount to be invested 91,280
Net present value.. $ (8,080)

*Present value of an annuity of $1 at 15% for 7 periods from text Exhibit 2.

b. The rate of return is less than 15% because there is a negative net present value.

c. Present value factor for an annuity of $1 $=\dfrac{\text{Amount to be invested}}{\text{Annual net cash flow}}$

$$= \dfrac{\$91,280}{\$20,000}$$

$= 4.564$

Internal rate of return $=$ 12% (from text Exhibit 2)

Ex. 24–19

With an expected useful life of 4 years, the cash payback period could not be greater than 4 years. This would indicate that the cost of the initial investment would not be recovered during the useful life of the asset. However, there would be no average rate of return in such a case because a net loss would result. If the 25% average rate of return and useful life are correct, the cash payback period must be less than 4 years. Alternatively, if both the 25% average rate of return and 4.5 years for the cash payback period are correct, the machinery must have a useful life of more than 4 years.

Ex. 24–20

a. Since all the cash flows are incurred in the local economy under this assumption, it is likely that the internal rate of return of the new plant will decline. This is because the cash profits earned on the plant will be less in U.S. dollars as a result of the devaluation. For example, if the product sold for a profit of 10 units of local currency, it would need to double to 20 units of local currency in order to generate the same U.S. dollars of profit. This could only be done with a large price increase. However, such a price increase would probably significantly reduce demand. If the price stayed the same, then the number of U.S. dollars earned in profit would be halved.

b. If the plant produced for export only, then the expenses would be incurred in local currency, while the revenues would be earned in U.S. dollars. This could work in favor of the project because the expenses in U.S. dollar terms would decline. For example, if the local wages were 16 units of local currency per hour, then after the devaluation, these 16 units would cost half as much in U.S. dollar terms (from $4 to $2). Since the product is sold in the United States, the currency exchange rate would have no impact on revenues. The net result is that the cash flows in U.S. dollar terms would potentially increase, increasing the internal rate of return.

PROBLEMS

Prob. 24–1A

1. a. Average annual rate of return for both projects:

$$\frac{\$25,000 \div 5}{(\$50,000 + \$0) \div 2} = \frac{\$5,000}{\$25,000} = 20\%$$

b. Net present value analysis:

Year	Present Value of $1 at 10%	Net Cash Flow Greenhouse	Net Cash Flow Skid Loader	Present Value of Net Cash Flow Greenhouse	Present Value of Net Cash Flow Skid Loader
1	0.909	$15,000	$25,000	$13,635	$22,725
2	0.826	15,000	20,000	12,390	16,520
3	0.751	15,000	15,000	11,265	11,265
4	0.683	15,000	10,000	10,245	6,830
5	0.621	15,000	5,000	9,315	3,105
Total............................		$75,000	$75,000	$56,850	$60,445
Amount to be invested...				50,000	50,000
Net present value...				$ 6,850	$10,445

2. The report to the capital investment committee can take many forms. The report should, as a minimum, present the following points:

   a. Both projects offer the same average annual rate of return.

   b. Although both projects exceed the selected rate established for discounted cash flows, the skid loader offers a larger net present value. The skid loader has a larger net present value because larger cash flows occur earlier in time for the skid loader compared to the greenhouse. Thus, if only one of the two projects can be accepted, the skid loader would be the more attractive.

Prob. 24–2A

1. a. Cash payback period for both projects: 3 years (the year in which accumulated net cash flows equal $380,000).

    b. Net present value analysis:

Year	Present Value of $1 at 20%	Net Cash Flow Plant Expansion	Net Cash Flow Retail Store Expansion	Present Value of Net Cash Flow Plant Expansion	Present Value of Net Cash Flow Retail Store Expansion
1	0.833	$100,000	$150,000	$ 83,300	$124,950
2	0.694	130,000	120,000	90,220	83,280
3	0.579	150,000	110,000	86,850	63,690
4	0.482	130,000	110,000	62,660	53,020
5	0.402	170,000	190,000	68,340	76,380
Total.................................		$680,000	$680,000	$391,370	$401,320
Amount to be invested...				380,000	380,000
Net present value..				$ 11,370	$ 21,320

2. The report can take many forms and should include, as a minimum, the following points:

    a. Both projects offer the same total net cash flow.

    b. Both projects offer the same cash payback period.

    c. Because of the timing of the receipt of the net cash flows, the retail store expansion offers a higher net present value.

    d. Both projects provide a positive net present value. This means both projects would be acceptable, since they exceed the minimum rate of return.

Prob. 24–3A

1.

Route Expansion

Year	Present Value of $1 at 15%	Net Cash Flow	Present Value of Net Cash Flow
1	0.870	$200,000	$174,000
2	0.756	250,000	189,000
3	0.658	350,000	230,300
Total...		$800,000	$593,300
Amount to be invested..			560,000
Net present value..			$ 33,300

Acquire Railcars

Year	Present Value of $1 at 15%	Net Cash Flow	Present Value of Net Cash Flow
1	0.870	$140,000	$121,800
2	0.756	130,000	98,280
3	0.658	125,000	82,250
Total...		$395,000	$302,330
Amount to be invested..			280,000
Net present value..			$ 22,330

New Maintenance Yard

Year	Present Value of $1 at 15%	Net Cash Flow	Present Value of Net Cash Flow
1	0.870	$175,000	$152,250
2	0.756	175,000	132,300
3	0.658	200,000	131,600
Total...		$550,000	$416,150
Amount to be invested..			425,000
Net present value..			$ (8,850)

Prob. 24–3A   Concluded

2. Present value index = $\dfrac{\text{Total present value of net cash flow}}{\text{Amount to be invested}}$

Present value index of route expansion: $\dfrac{\$593{,}300}{\$560{,}000} = 1.06^*$

Present value index of railcars: $\dfrac{\$302{,}330}{\$280{,}000} = 1.08^*$

Present value index of maintenance yard: $\dfrac{\$416{,}150}{\$425{,}000} = 0.98^*$

*Rounded.

3. Railcars. Although route expansion has the largest net present value, it returns less present value per dollar invested than do the railcars, as revealed by the present value indexes (1.08 to 1.06). (The present value index for the maintenance yard is less than 1, indicating that it does not meet the minimum rate of return standard.)

Prob. 24–4A

1. **a.** <u>Generating Unit:</u>

Annual net cash flow (at the end of each of four years)	$260,000
Present value of an annuity of $1 at 10% for 4 years (Exhibit 2)....	× 3.17
Present value of annual net cash flows..	$824,200
Less amount to be invested..	789,620
Net present value...	$ 34,580

<u>Distribution Network Expansion:</u>

Annual net cash flow (at the end of each of four years)	$ 90,000
Present value of an annuity of $1 at 10% for 4 years (Exhibit 2)....	× 3.17
Present value of annual net cash flows..	$285,300
Less amount to be invested..	256,950
Net present value...	$ 28,350

b. Present value index = $\dfrac{\text{Total present value of net cash flow}}{\text{Amount to be invested}}$

Present value index of the generating unit: $\dfrac{\$824,200}{\$789,620} = 1.04*$

Present value index of the distribution network expansion:

$\dfrac{\$285,300}{\$256,950} = 1.11*$

*Rounded.

2. **a.** Present value factor for an annuity of $1 = $\dfrac{\text{Amount to be invested}}{\text{Annual net cash flow}}$

Generating unit: $\dfrac{\$789,620}{\$260,000} = 3.037$

Distribution network expansion: $\dfrac{\$256,950}{\$90,000} = 2.855$

b. Internal rate of return: (determined from Exhibit 2 in text)
Generating unit: 12%
Distribution network expansion: 15%

Prob. 24–4A   Concluded

3. By using the internal rate of return method, all projects are automatically placed on a common basis. For example, the net present value analyses in (1a) indicated that the net present value was greater for the generating unit. However, it was necessary to use the present value index to determine that the distribution network expansion had a greater present value per dollar of investment (greater rate of return). By using the internal rate of return method, it can be easily seen that the distribution network expansion's rate of return of 15% is greater than the generating unit's rate of 12%.

Prob. 24–5A

1. Net present value analysis:

Project I:

Annual net cash flow (at the end of each of six years)	$ 40,000
Present value of an annuity of $1 at 15% for 6 years (Exhibit 2)	× 3.785
Present value of annual net cash flows	$151,400
Less amount to be invested...	145,000
Net present value...	$ 6,400

Project II:

Annual net cash flow (at the end of each of four years)..................	$ 55,000
Present value of an annuity of $1 at 15% for 4 years (Exhibit 2)	× 2.855
Present value of annual net cash flows	$157,025
Less amount to be invested...	145,000
Net present value...	$ 12,025

2. Net present value analysis:

Year	Present Value of $1 at 15%	Net Cash Flow Project I	Net Cash Flow Project II	Present Value of Net Cash Flow Project I	Present Value of Net Cash Flow Project II
1	0.870	$ 40,000	$ 55,000	$ 34,800	$ 47,850
2	0.756	40,000	55,000	30,240	41,580
3	0.658	40,000	55,000	26,320	36,190
4	0.572	40,000	55,000	22,880	31,460
Residual value.....	0.572	60,000	0	34,320	0
Total		$220,000	$220,000	$148,560	$157,080
Amount to be invested				145,000	145,000
Net present value..				$ 3,560	$ 12,080*

* This amount differs from the net present value calculation in (1) due to rounding error.

3. To: Investment Committee

Both Projects I and II have a positive net present value. This means that both projects meet our minimum expected return of 15% and would be acceptable investments. However, if funds are limited and only one of the two projects can be funded, then the two projects must be compared over equal lives. Thus, the residual value of Project I at the end of period 4 is used to equalize the two lives. The net present value of the two projects over equal lives indicates that Project II has a higher net present value and would be a superior investment.

Prob. 24–6A

1. Proposal A: 4-year cash payback period, as follows:

Year	Net Cash Flow	Cumulative Net Cash Flows
1	$160,000	$160,000
2	160,000	320,000
3	160,000	480,000
4	120,000	600,000

Proposal B: 3-year cash payback period, as follows:

Year	Net Cash Flow	Cumulative Net Cash Flows
1	$200,000	$200,000
2	160,000	360,000
3	160,000	520,000

Proposal C: 2-year, 8-month cash payback period, as follows:

Year	Net Cash Flow	Cumulative Net Cash Flows
1	$80,000	$ 80,000
2	60,000	140,000
8 months*	40,000	180,000

*The cash flow required for investment payback in Year 3 is $40,000, which is two-thirds ($40,000 ÷ $60,000) of Year 3's cash flow. Thus, 8 months (two-thirds of 12 months) are needed to accumulate an additional $40,000.

Proposal D: 3-year, 3-month cash payback period, as follows:

Year	Net Cash Flow	Cumulative Net Cash Flows
1	$100,000	$100,000
2	100,000	200,000
3	40,000	240,000
3 months*	10,000	250,000

*The cash flow required for investment payback in Year 4 is $10,000, which is 25% ($10,000 ÷ $40,000) of Year 4's cash flow. Thus, 3 months (25% of 12 months) are needed to accumulate an additional $10,000.

Prob. 24–6A   Continued

2. Proposal A: 8% average rate of return, determined as follows:

$$\frac{\$120,000 \div 5}{(\$600,000 + \$0) \div 2} = \frac{\$24,000}{\$300,000} = 8\%$$

Proposal B: 24% average rate of return, determined as follows:

$$\frac{\$312,000 \div 5}{(\$520,000 + \$0) \div 2} = \frac{\$62,400}{\$260,000} = 24\%$$

Proposal C: 30.8% average rate of return, determined as follows:

$$\frac{\$138,500 \div 5}{(\$180,000 + \$0) \div 2} = \frac{\$27,700}{\$90,000} = 30.8\%$$

Proposal D: 11.2% average rate of return, determined as follows:

$$\frac{\$70,000 \div 5}{(\$250,000 + \$0) \div 2} = \frac{\$14,000}{\$125,000} = 11.2\%$$

Prob. 24–6A   Continued

3. Of the four proposed investments, only Proposals B and C meet the company's requirements, as the following table indicates:

Proposal	Cash Payback Period	Average Rate of Return	Accept for Further Analysis	Reject
A	4 yrs.	8 %		X
B	3 yrs.	24	X	
C	2 yrs., 8 mos.	30.8	X	
D	3 yrs., 3 mos.	11.2		X

4.

Proposal B:

Year	Present Value of $1 at 10%	Net Cash Flow	Present Value of Net Cash Flow
1	0.909	$200,000	$181,800
2	0.826	160,000	132,160
3	0.751	160,000	120,160
4	0.683	160,000	109,280
5	0.621	152,000	94,392
Total		$832,000	$637,792
Amount to be invested			520,000
Net present value			$117,792

Proposal C:

Year	Present Value of $1 at 10%	Net Cash Flow	Present Value of Net Cash Flow
1	0.909	$ 80,000	$ 72,720
2	0.826	60,000	49,560
3	0.751	60,000	45,060
4	0.683	60,000	40,980
5	0.621	58,500	36,329
Total		$318,500	$244,649
Amount to be invested			180,000
Net present value			$ 64,649

Prob. 24–6A   Concluded

5. Present value index = $\dfrac{\text{Total present value of net cash flow}}{\text{Amount to be invested}}$

Present value index of Proposal B: $\dfrac{\$637,792}{\$520,000} = 1.23^*$

Present value index of Proposal C: $\dfrac{\$244,649}{\$180,000} = 1.36^*$

*Rounded.

6. Based upon the net present value, the proposals should be ranked as follows:

Proposal B: $117,792

Proposal C: $64,649

7. Based upon the present value index (the amount of present value per dollar invested), the proposals should be ranked as follows:

Proposal C: 1.36

Proposal B: 1.23

8. The present value indexes indicate that although Proposal B has the larger net present value, it is not as attractive as Proposal C in terms of the amount of present value per dollar invested. Proposal B requires the larger investment. Thus, management should use investment resources for Proposal C before investing in Proposal B.

Prob. 24–1B

1. a. Average annual rate of return for both projects:

$$\frac{\$270,000 \div 5}{(\$480,000 + \$0) \div 2} = \frac{\$54,000}{\$240,000} = 22.5\%$$

b. Net present value analysis:

Year	Present Value of $1 at 12%	Net Cash Flow Warehouse	Net Cash Flow Tracking Technology	Present Value of Net Cash Flow Warehouse	Present Value of Net Cash Flow Tracking Technology
1	0.893	$150,000	$130,000	$133,950	$116,090
2	0.797	150,000	140,000	119,550	111,580
3	0.712	150,000	150,000	106,800	106,800
4	0.636	150,000	160,000	95,400	101,760
5	0.567	150,000	170,000	85,050	96,390
Total................................		$750,000	$750,000	$540,750	$532,620
Amount to be invested...				480,000	480,000
Net present value...				$ 60,750	$ 52,620

2. The report to the capital investment committee can take many forms. The report should, as a minimum, present the following points:

a. Both projects offer the same average annual rate of return.

b. Although both projects exceed the selected rate established for discounted cash flows, the warehouse offers a larger net present value. The warehouse has a larger net present value because larger cash flows occur earlier in time for the warehouse compared to the tracking technology. Thus, if only one of the two projects can be accepted, the warehouse would be the more attractive.

Prob. 24–2B

1. a. Cash payback period for both products: 2 years (the year in which accumulated net cash flows equal $700,000).

   b. Net present value analysis:

Year	Present Value of $1 at 15%	Net Cash Flow DVD Player	Net Cash Flow Digital TV	Present Value of Net Cash Flow DVD Player	Present Value of Net Cash Flow Digital TV
1	0.870	$ 350,000	$ 200,000	$304,500	$ 174,000
2	0.756	350,000	500,000	264,600	378,000
3	0.658	200,000	400,000	131,600	263,200
4	0.572	200,000	50,000	114,400	28,600
5	0.497	100,000	50,000	49,700	24,850
Total............................		$ 1,200,000	$ 1,200,000	$864,800	$ 868,650
Amount to be invested...				700,000	700,000
Net present value...				$164,800	$ 168,650

2. The report can take many forms and should include, as a minimum, the following points:

   a. Both products offer the same total net cash flow.

   b. Both products offer the same cash payback period.

   c. Because of the timing of the receipt of the net cash flows, the digital TV offers a higher net present value.

   d. Both products provide a positive net present value. This means both products would be acceptable, since they exceed the minimum rate of return.

Prob. 24–3B

1.

Branch Office Expansion

Year	Present Value of $1 at 20%	Net Cash Flow	Present Value of Net Cash Flow
1	0.833	$250,000	$208,250
2	0.694	220,000	152,680
3	0.579	200,000	115,800
Total		$670,000	$476,730
Amount to be invested			450,000
Net present value			$ 26,730

Computer System Upgrade

Year	Present Value of $1 at 20%	Net Cash Flow	Present Value of Net Cash Flow
1	0.833	$150,000	$ 124,950
2	0.694	125,000	86,750
3	0.579	125,000	72,375
Total		$400,000	$ 284,075
Amount to be invested			300,000
Net present value			$ (15,925)

Install ATM Network

Year	Present Value of $1 at 20%	Net Cash Flow	Present Value of Net Cash Flow
1	0.833	$150,000	$ 124,950
2	0.694	130,000	90,220
3	0.579	100,000	57,900
Total		$380,000	$ 273,070
Amount to be invested			250,000
Net present value			$ 23,070

Prob. 24–3B   Concluded

2. Present value index = $\dfrac{\text{Total present value of net cash flow}}{\text{Amount to be invested}}$

Present value index of branch office: $\dfrac{\$476,730}{\$450,000}$ = 1.06*

Present value index of computer system: $\dfrac{\$284,075}{\$300,000}$ = 0.95*

Present value index of ATM network: $\dfrac{\$273,070}{\$250,000}$ = 1.09*

*Rounded.

3. The ATM network. Although the branch office has the largest net present value, it returns less present value per dollar invested than does the ATM network, as revealed by the present value indexes (1.09 to 1.06). (The present value index for the computer system is less than 1, indicating that it does not meet the minimum rate of return standard.)

Prob. 24–4B

1. a. <u>Radio Station:</u>

Annual net cash flow (at the end of each of four years)	$	150,000
Present value of an annuity of $1 at 12% for 4 years (Exhibit 2)	×	3.037
Present value of annual net cash flows..	$	455,550
Less amount to be invested		388,350
Net present value...	$	67,200

<u>TV Station:</u>

Annual net cash flow (at the end of each of four years)	$	400,000
Present value of an annuity of $1 at 12% for 4 years (Exhibit 2)	×	3.037
Present value of annual net cash flows..	$	1,214,800
Less amount to be invested		1,142,000
Net present value...	$	72,800

   b. Present value index = $\dfrac{\text{Total present value of net cash flow}}{\text{Amount to be invested}}$

   Present value index of the radio station: $\dfrac{\$455,550}{\$388,350} = 1.17^*$

   Present value index of the TV station: $\dfrac{\$1,214,800}{\$1,142,000} = 1.06^*$

   *Rounded.

2. a. Present value factor for an annuity of $1 = $\dfrac{\text{Amount to be invested}}{\text{Annual net cash flow}}$

   Radio Station: $\dfrac{\$388,350}{\$150,000} = 2.589$

   TV Station: $\dfrac{\$1,142,000}{\$400,000} = 2.855$

   b. Internal rate of return: (determined from Exhibit 2 in text)
   Radio Station: 20%
   TV Station: 15%

3. By using the internal rate of return method, all proposals are automatically placed on a common basis. For example, the net present value analyses in (1a) indicated that the net present value was greater for the TV station. However, it was necessary to use the present value index to determine that the radio station had a greater present value per dollar of investment (greater rate of return). By using the internal rate of return method, it can be easily seen that the radio station's rate of 20% is greater than the TV station's rate of 15%.

Prob. 24–5B

1. Net present value analysis:

Site A:

Annual net cash flow (at the end of each of six years)	$100,000
Present value of an annuity of $1 at 15% for 6 years (Exhibit 2)	× 3.785
Present value of annual net cash flows	$378,500
Less amount to be invested...	340,000
Net present value	$ 38,500

Site B:

Annual net cash flow (at the end of each of four years)...................	$130,000
Present value of an annuity of $1 at 15% for 4 years (Exhibit 2)	× 2.855
Present value of annual net cash flows	$371,150
Less amount to be invested...	340,000
Net present value	$ 31,150

2. Net present value analysis:

Year	Present Value of $1 at 15%	Net Cash Flow Site A	Net Cash Flow Site B	Present Value of Net Cash Flow Site A	Present Value of Net Cash Flow Site B
1	0.870	$100,000	$130,000	$ 87,000	$113,100
2	0.756	100,000	130,000	75,600	98,280
3	0.658	100,000	130,000	65,800	85,540
4	0.572	100,000	130,000	57,200	74,360
Residual value........	0.572	160,000	0	91,520	0
Total		$560,000	$520,000	$377,120	$371,280
Amount to be invested				340,000	340,000
Net present value..				$ 37,120	$ 31,280*

*This amount differs from the net present value calculation in (1) due to rounding error.

3. To: Investment Committee

Both Sites A and B have a positive net present value. This means that both projects meet our minimum expected return of 15% and would be acceptable investments. However, if funds are limited and only one of the two projects can be funded, then the two projects must be compared over equal lives. Thus, the residual value of Site A at the end of period 4 is used to equalize the two lives. The net present value of the two projects over equal lives indicates that Site A has a higher net present value and would be a superior investment.

Prob. 24–6B

1. Proposal A: 3-year and 4 months cash payback period, as follows:

Year	Net Cash Flow	Cumulative Net Cash Flows
1	$240,000	$240,000
2	240,000	480,000
3	240,000	720,000
4 months*	80,000	800,000

* The net cash flow per year is $240,000. Hence, the net cash flow per month is $20,000 ($240,000 ÷ 12). Thus, 4 months are needed to accumulate an additional $80,000.

Proposal B: 2-year cash payback period, as follows:

Year	Net Cash Flow	Cumulative Net Cash Flows
1	$40,000	$40,000
2	56,000	96,000

Proposal C: 4-year cash payback period, as follows:

Year	Net Cash Flow	Cumulative Net Cash Flows
1	$60,000	$ 60,000
2	60,000	120,000
3	60,000	180,000
4	60,000	240,000

Proposal D: 3-year cash payback period, as follows:

Year	Net Cash Flow	Cumulative Net Cash Flows
1	$56,000	$ 56,000
2	56,000	112,000
3	56,000	168,000

Prob. 24–6B   **Continued**

2.   Proposal A: 18% average rate of return, determined as follows:

$$\frac{\$360{,}000 \div 5}{(\$800{,}000 + \$0) \div 2} = \frac{\$72{,}000}{\$400{,}000} = 18\%$$

Proposal B: 25% average rate of return, determined as follows:

$$\frac{\$60{,}000 \div 5}{(\$96{,}000 + \$0) \div 2} = \frac{\$12{,}000}{\$48{,}000} = 25\%$$

Proposal C: 5% average rate of return, determined as follows:

$$\frac{\$30{,}000 \div 5}{(\$240{,}000 + \$0) \div 2} = \frac{\$6{,}000}{\$120{,}000} = 5\%$$

Proposal D: 23% average rate of return, determined as follows:

$$\frac{\$96{,}600 \div 5}{(\$168{,}000 + \$0) \div 2} = \frac{\$19{,}320}{\$84{,}000} = 23\%$$

Prob. 24–6B   Continued

3. Of the four proposed investments, only Proposals A and C meet the company's requirements, as the following table indicates:

Proposal	Cash Payback Period	Average Rate of Return	Accept for Further Analysis	Reject
A	3 yrs., 4 mos.	18%		X*
B	2 yrs.	25	X	
C	4 yrs.	5		X
D	3 yrs.	23	X	

* Proposal A is rejected because it fails to meet the maximum payback period requirement, even though it meets the minimum accounting rate of return requirement.

4.

Proposal B:

Year	Present Value of $1 at 10%	Net Cash Flow	Present Value of Net Cash Flow
1	0.909	$ 40,000	$ 36,360
2	0.826	56,000	46,256
3	0.751	20,000	15,020
4	0.683	20,000	13,660
5	0.621	20,000	12,420
Total		$156,000	$123,716
Amount to be invested			96,000
Net present value			$ 27,716

Proposal D:

Year	Present Value of $1 at 10%	Net Cash Flow	Present Value of Net Cash Flow
1	0.909	$ 56,000	$ 50,904
2	0.826	56,000	46,256
3	0.751	56,000	42,056
4	0.683	50,600	34,560
5	0.621	46,000	28,566
Total		$264,600	$202,342
Amount to be invested			168,000
Net present value			$ 34,342

Prob. 24–6B   Concluded

5. Present value index = $\dfrac{\text{Total present value of net cash flow}}{\text{Amount to be invested}}$

Present value index of Proposal B: $\dfrac{\$123,716}{\$96,000} = 1.29^*$

Present value index of Proposal D: $\dfrac{\$202,342}{\$168,000} = 1.20^*$

*Rounded.

6. Based upon the net present value, the proposals should be ranked as follows:

Proposal D: $34,342

Proposal B: $27,716

7. Based upon the present value index (the amount of present value per dollar invested), the proposals should be ranked as follows:

Proposal B: 1.29

Proposal D: 1.20

8. The present value indexes indicate that although Proposal D has the larger net present value, it is not as attractive as Proposal B in terms of the amount of present value per dollar invested. Proposal D requires the larger investment. Thus, management should use investment resources for Proposal B before investing in Proposal D.

SPECIAL ACTIVITIES

Activity 24–1

Sherry's manager wants a project to become accepted and places pressure on the analyst to come up with the "right numbers." I. M. is right when he states that the net present value analysis has many assumptions and room for interpretation. Many use this room for interpretation to work the numbers until they satisfy the hurdle rate. In fact, some analysts state that they start with the hurdle rate and back into the numbers. Clearly, this is not what should be expected of Sherry.

Sherry made an honest effort to discuss the assumptions. Sherry's last statement was an open attempt to begin a conversation around assumptions. This is legitimate. Notice that I. M. jumped on that opening and dictated a course of action. Instead of discussing assumptions, I. M. stated what the assumptions are to be and how they are to be reflected in the analysis. This is no more than "cooking" the analysis. Sherry needs to respond strongly to this attempt by I. M. to circumvent the process by countering his argument. For example, Sherry might point out that it is by no means clear that more storage space translates into more sales. In fact, it is probably just the opposite. More storage space means that more product waits a long time before being shipped to the customer. This means that the customer is guaranteed to receive dated product that may be inferior to product that has been recently produced. More warehouse space is counter to a just-in-time orientation. Sherry is really trying to prevent the plant manager from going down the wrong path. I. M. needs to work on his systems so that he doesn't need the warehouse space.

This very difficult issue revolves around the nature of ethical dilemmas. Sherry has brief tenure with the organization. She has very little organizational clout and could easily find her career short-circuited by crossing I. M. It might be tempting for Sherry to slide on this one—after all, who would know? If the project is eventually a failure, it's unlikely that the decision would come back to haunt Sherry. Much time will have passed, and Sherry will likely be in another job in the company. The decision to confront I. M. has immediate repercussions. This is the heart of real world ethical dilemmas. The dilemma occurs when the ethical decision has grave short-term consequences (I. M. short-circuits the career) and few seemingly long-term rewards (no one sees the ethical decision), while the unethical decision looks appealing in the short term (I. M. is my friend) and potentially safe in the long term (who's going to find out?). The ethical management accountant will recognize these pressures and make the short-term decisions in order to build a strong reputation that can be a very powerful asset later in one's career. The key is to recognize that trading off short-term gain for one's long-term reputation can be very harmful. Thus, enlightened self-interest indicates that the ethical course of action to rebuff I. M. is rational and correct.

Activity 24–2

More and more companies are discovering that mere automation is not the answer to their competitiveness problems. Instead, automation must be coupled with an organizational strategy and improvement and learning culture in order to be effective. For example, Federal Mogul automated itself out of being flexible. This is an example of not coupling automation with strategy. Instead of large, high-speed, inflexible machines, companies need automation that provides a high degree of changeover flexibility. Changeover flexibility is the ability to change over from one product to another without incurring much downtime or expense. In addition, automation should support enhancing quality rather than merely replacing direct labor. Indeed, automation will likely require extensive indirect labor support in the form of engineering and maintenance. Operators will require extensive retraining.

As an example of coupling automation with a learning culture, Corning Glass employs just enough automated sensors on a ceramic extrusion process to help workers improve the process. It lets the workers adjust and learn about the process, rather than placing the process under the automated direction of a computer. In the words of one of its managers, "The human mind is such a wondrous thing that we want to tap that. Even for boring and repetitive jobs, we have moved away from automation because humans adapt and robots don't."

Activity 24–3

1. Payback period: $\dfrac{\$1,250,000}{\$250,000} = 5$ years

2. Net present value:

    Present value factor for an annuity of $1, 10 periods at 10%: 6.145

    Net present value = (6.145 × $250,000) – $1,250,000 = $286,250

3. Some critical elements that are missing from this analysis are:

    a. The manager is viewing the acquisition of robots as a labor-saving device. This is probably a limited way to view the investment. Instead, the robots should allow the company to produce the product with higher quality and higher flexibility. This should translate into greater sales volume, better pricing, and lower inventories. All of these could be brought into the analysis.

    b. The cost of the robots does not stop with the initial purchase price and installation costs. The robots will require the company to hire engineers and support personnel to keep the machines running, to program the software, and to debug new programs. The operators will require new training. Thus, extensive training costs will likely be incurred. It would not be surprising to see a large portion of the direct labor savings lost by hiring expensive indirect labor support for the technology.

    c. There will likely be a start-up or learning curve with this new technology that will cause the benefits to be delayed.

    d. The analysis fails to account for taxes.

Activity 24–4

In all three companies, the executives indicate that financial investment analysis plays a minor role in the selection of projects. The reason is that all three companies deal with products that have highly uncertain future cash flows. Thus, any attempt at a financial investment analysis could be highly suspect. Instead, these managers rely on strategic considerations. These considerations include responding to competitors, developing new markets and products for customers, and improving quality. The executives indicate that business judgment is more important for these strategic, longer-term decisions than is financial investment analysis. This suggests that financial investment analysis is better suited for investments that have more predictable cash flows with possible short duration.